LANDRECIES TO CAMBRAI

CASE STUDIES OF GERMAN OFFENSIVE AND DEFENSIVE OPERATIONS ON THE WESTERN FRONT 1914-17

Captain G.C. Wynne

Edited with an Introduction and Bibliography by Duncan Rogers

Helion Studies in Military History Number 3

Helion & Company Ltd

Helion & Company Limited
26 Willow Road
Solihull
West Midlands B91 1UE
England
Tel. 0121 705 3393
Fax 0121 711 4075
Email: info@helion.co.uk
Website: www.helion.co.uk
Twitter: @helionbooks
Visit our blog http://blog.helion.co.uk/

Published by Helion & Company 2011. This hardback edition 2013.

Designed and typeset by Farr out Publications, Wokingham, Berkshire
Cover designed by Farr out Publications, Wokingham, Berkshire
Printed by Lightning Source, Milton Keynes, Buckinghamshire

Text and Maps © Estate of G.C. Wynne
Introduction & Bibliography © Duncan Rogers 2010

ISBN 978-1-909384-03-3

British Library Cataloguing-in-Publication Data.

A catalogue record for this book is available from the British Library.
All rights reserved. No part of this publication may be reproduced, stored in a retrieval system, or transmitted, in any form, or by any means, electronic, mechanical, photocopying, recording or otherwise, without the express written consent of Helion & Company Limited.

For details of other military history titles published by Helion & Company Limited contact the above address, or visit our website: http://www.helion.co.uk.

We always welcome receiving book proposals from prospective authors.

Contents

List of maps		iv
Introduction		5
1	The Night Attack at Landrecies	9
2	Neuve Chapelle	15
3	Aubers Ridge	28
4	The Fight for Hill 70	34
5	The German Attack at Vimy Ridge	44
6	The German Defence during the Battle of the Somme, July 1916	54
7	The German Defence of Bernafay and Trônes Woods 2–14 July 1916	76
8	Mametz Wood and Contalmaison	93
9	Delville Wood	105
10	The Somme	115
11	The Capture of Thiepval	124
12	In Front of Beaumont-Hamel	132
13	Battle of Arras	140
14	The Battle of Vimy Ridge	156
15	The Fight for Inverness Copse	162
16	The Fight for Zonnebeke	168
17	Cambrai	176
Annotated Bibliography		181

List of Maps

1.	Landrecies, 25 August 1914	10
2.	Neuve Chapelle, mid-day, 10 March 1915	16
3.	Aubers Ridge, Rue du Bois, 9 May 1915	29
4.	Loos, 25 September 1915	35
5.	Vimy Ridge, May 1916	45
6.	German Front Line, 1 July 1916	55
7.	Somme, 1 July 1916 – Position of German 26th Reserve Division	67
8.	Trônes Wood	77
9.	Contalmaison, 10 July 1916	94
10.	Delville Wood, July 1916	106
11.	The Somme, 15 September 1916	116
12.	Thiepval, 26 September 1916	125
13.	Beaumont Hamel, 13 November 1916	133
14.	German position in the Arras Battle, 9 April 1917	141
20.	Diagram showing normal defensive dispositions of a German Regiment at Arras, April 1917	148
16.	Vimy Ridge	157
17.	Inverness Copse and surrounding area	163
18.	Zonnebeke, 26 September 1917	169
19.	Cambrai, 1917	177

Introduction

*L*andrecies to Cambrai represents a series of articles that ran in the *Army Quarterly* between January 1924 and April 1939. The author, Captain G.C. Wynne, was a Great War veteran, and thus had a working knowledge of the British Army during the conflict, as well as a thorough knowledge of the subsequent historiography of the conflict that was imparted from his work with the Historical Section of the Committee for Imperial Defence. With a fluency in German, he seems to have kept very much up-to-date with the latest publications in that language; the interwar output of German unit histories and other materials was prodigious. Indeed, Wynne appears to have contributed numerous book reviews and notices of the latest Great War German literature to the *Army Quarterly*.

The original running order of the series was as follows:

'The German defence during the Battle of the Somme July 1916 part 1'
January 1924, pp 245-259

'The German defence during the Battle of the Somme July 1916 part 2'
April 1924, pp 72-85

'The fight for Hill 70, 25-26 September 1915'
July 1924, pp 261-273

'Mametz Wood and Contalmaison, 9-10 July 1916'
January 1925, pp 245-259

'Delville Wood, 14-19 July 1916'
October 1925, pp 58-69

'The German defence of Bernafay and Trônes Woods, 2-14 July 1916 part 1'
October 1926, pp 19-32

'The German defence of Bernafay and Trônes Woods, 2-14 July 1916 part 2'
January 1927, pp 252-260

'The German attack at Vimy Ridge, May 1916'
October 1928, pp 66-77

'Cambrai – the action of the German 107th Division'
July 1930, pp 286-291

'The Somme, 15 September 1916'
July 1933, pp 300-308

'The capture of Thiepval, 26 September 1916'
January 1934, pp 215-224

'In front of Beaumont-Hamel, 13 November 1916'
April 1934, pp 27-36

'The night attack at Landrecies, 25 August 1914'
July 1934, pp 247-254

'The fight for Zonnebeke, 26 September 1917'
October 1934, pp 54-62

'The fight for Inverness Copse, 22-24 August 1917'
January 1935, pp 297-303

'The Battle of Vimy Ridge, 9 April 1917'
October 1936, pp 51-57

'Aubers Ridge, 9 May 1915'
July 1938, pp 242-248

'Neuve Chapelle, 10-12 March 1915'
October 1938, pp 30-46

'Battle of Arras, 9 April 1917'
April 1939, pp 29-47

The tenet of the articles is to compare and contrast British and German practices on the one hand, and perhaps more particularly to shed light on 'The Other Side of the Hill', which was the name for the series as it appeared in the *Army Quarterly*. As Wynne wrote in a footnote to his first article:

> Mr. Croker, in his *Correspondence and Diaries*, relates that once when he and the Duke of Wellington were travelling on the north road they amused themselves by guessing what sort of country they would find on the other side of the hills they drove up, "and, when I expressed surprise at some extraordinary good guesses he had made, he (the Duke) said, 'Why, I have spent all my life in trying to guess what was at the other side of the hill.'" We propose in a series of articles, of which this is the first to appear, to give our readers a description, from the enemy's point of view, of what was happening on "the other side of the hill" during some of the principal battles during the late war.[1]

Wynne's comments about British tactics and training are frequently critical, particularly when discussing wider issues, such as the insistence of the use of what the Germans

---

1 'The German defence during the Battle of the Somme July 1916 Part 1', *Army Quarterly* January 1924, p.245.

termed the *Materialschlacht*, with its use of massed bombardment. But, it is in the series' extensive use (and quotation) from German regimental histories wherein its chief use lies. Even now, this huge literature is frequently ignored. Yet with a high proportion of the original records destroyed during the Second World War, these books stand as a vital testament of the Imperial German Army's activities. This collection seeks to rescue some of this information from obscurity.

Drawing upon his articles for the *Army Quarterly* and further research Wynne wrote the classic, if controversial, *If Germany Attacks* in the late 1930s. It was prepared for publication in 1939, and a first printing was completed by Faber and Faber, only for this to fall foul of wartime sensitivities. The publishers declared "…that it would be inappropriate to issue the volume during the hostilities as the text was highly critical of the British command and would lead to discouragement and lack of confidence in the army authorities."[2] Instead, a considerably watered-down edition was published, with offending passages in which Wynne criticised members of the British High Command excised or altered. The interested reader is urged to consult the unexpurgated edition published in 2008 by Tom Donovan Editions, including an important new introduction by Dr Robert T. Foley.[3] Despite the excisions, the tenet of Wynne's arguments – that the British had failed to learn lessons whilst the Germans were tactical innovators *par excellence* – remained, even in the excised version. Thus, in a sense, the book is a clear successor to the articles presented herein.

Since these articles and *If Germany Attacks* were written military historians have produced a number of paradigms to explain how the stalemate of the Western Front came to be – and how it was ended, along with the virtues and defects of the contending armies and commanders. In a sense, Wynne's ability to mine German materials and to seek a greater understanding of how Britain's enemy operated at a tactical level on the battlefield remains undimmed, even if his scathing criticism of British fighting methods and praise of German ones may seem a little less supported by the arguments today. Such paradigms are beyond the scope of this introduction, and this study, but the reader is recommended to the following:

For the British Expeditionary Force:
Badsey, Stephen, *The British Army in Battle and its Image 1914-18* (London: Continuum, 2009)
Beckett, Ian F.W. & Keith Simpson (eds.), *A Nation in Arms: A Social History of the British Army in the First World War* (Manchester: Manchester University Press, 1985)
Green, Andrew, *Writing the Great War. Sir James Edmonds and the Official Histories 1915-1948* (London: Cass, 2003)
Griffith, Paddy, *Battle Tactics of the Western Front. The British Army's Art of Attack 1916-18* (London: Yale University Press, 1994)
Griffith, Paddy (ed.), *British Fighting Methods in the Great War* (London: Cass, 1996)

---

2   Quoted on p.vii of the unexpurgated edition of *If Germany Attacks* (Brighton: Tom Donovan Editions, 2008).
3   Captain G.C. Wynne, *If Germany Attacks: The Battle in Depth in the West. Development of the German Defence in Depth on the Western Front in the First World War*. With new introduction by Dr Robert T. Foley (Brighton: Tom Donovan Editions, 2008. Published in a limited edition of 300 copies).

Howard, Michael & Stephen Badsey (eds.), *A Part of History: Aspects of the British Experience of the First World War* (London: Continuum, 2008)

Sheffield, Gary & Dan Todman (eds.), *Command and Control on the Western Front: the British Army's Experience 1914-1918* (Staplehurst: Spellmount, 2004)

Travers, Tim, *The Killing Ground: The British Army, the Western Front and the Emergence of Modern Warfare 1900-1918* (London: Allen & Unwin, 1987)

For the German Army[4]:

Gudmundsson, Bruce, *Stormtroop Tactics. Innovation in the German Army 1914-18* (Westport CT: Greenwood Press, 1989)

Junger, Ernst, *Storm of Steel* (Harmondsworth: Penguin, 2004 – new translation with annotations by Michael Hofmann)

Lupfer, Timothy T., *The Dynamics of Doctrine: The Changes in German Tactical Doctrine during the First World War* (Fort Leavenworth KS: Leavenworth Papers No. 4, 1981)

Passingham, Ian, *All the Kaiser's Men: The Life and Death of the German Army on the Western Front 1914-1918* (Stroud: Sutton, 2003)

Wynne, Capt. G.C., *If Germany Attacks: The Battle in Depth in the West. Development of the German Defence in Depth on the Western Front in the First World War* (Brighton: Turner Donovan, 2008, unexpurgated edition)

Zabecki, David T., *Steel Wind: Colonel Georg Bruchmüller and the Birth of Modern Artillery* (Westport CT: Greenwood Press, 1994)

Zabecki, David T., *The German 1918 Offensives: A Case Study of the Operational Level of War* (London: Routledge, 2006)

The events of 1918 are obviously missing from the studies in this collection, although Wynne dealt with some of these in *If Germany Attacks*. Certainly, as of 1939, the official histories of both the British and German armies were incomplete for that vital final year of the war, and would have hindered Wynne somewhat in his task. The British series covering France and Belgium was completed in 1949, the German coverage remained unpublished until the late 1950s. However, even allowing for that shortfall, this collection of studies recounting German actions at the regimental and battalion level in a number of key actions has much to commend it.

A bibliography has been added, setting out the correct data for all of the titles quoted briefly by the series' author in his footnotes. In addition, a few later works of reference that are germane have been listed.

---

4 There are fewer studies and collections of articles for the German Army compared to the B.E.F. The titles listed here are a selection for flavour, including Junger's memoir. A large amount of valuable material remains untranslated and virtually unknown to English readers –memoirs as well as tactical and strategic studies.

1

The Night Attack at Landrecies

25 August 1914

The publication a few weeks ago of the history of the Prussian 27th Infantry Regiment[1] is of especial interest as this Regiment was the chief participant on the German side in the fight at Landrecies, and its account amplifies considerably the rather scanty information available when the revised edition of Volume 1 of the British Official History was published last autumn.

By the close of the second day of the retreat of the British Expeditionary Force from Mons, after a march that had begun in the early hours and continued throughout a blazing hot morning and afternoon, the I Corps had reached the Landrecies area and the II Corps was about Le Cateau. The Germans were hot in pursuit, filling every road leading southward on Paris. To gain time and give the British troops a breathing space, Sir John French decided to stand and fight on the open uplands at and east of Le Cateau. A rough line of trench had been hastily dug by French civilian labour and here it was hoped to force the Germans to deploy and so check them if only for twenty-four hours. The I Corps was to move from the Landrecies area to that part of the line immediately south of Le Cateau as early as possible on the 26th, the II Corps taking up position on its left, the main Paris road to be the boundary between them.

Such was the intention when at 4.30 p.m. the I Corps arrived in its billeting area after a most exhausting march. The 4th Guards Brigade occupied Landrecies itself and detailed the 3rd Coldstream Guards to be responsible for the security of the entrances to the village during the night. Nos. 2 and 4 Companies were to guard the eastern and western entrances and Nos. 1 and 3 the northern and most important. The road here, on leaving the main street of the village, crosses the Sambre bridge and 50 yards farther on the railway, by a level crossing. For some two hundred yards it is then flanked by a row of cottages on either side, named the Faubourg Soyeres. Shortly after emerging from these the road forks, one bearing right handed to Englefontaine and the other striking due north through half a mile of cultivation with thick hedgerows and thence into the depths of that forest of wonderful beeches, the Forêt de Mormal.

The outpost company of the Coldstream halted at the end of the Faubourg Soyeres. The picquet was posted and a sentry group with a machine gun placed in position in the ditch by the roadside further on near the fork. Meanwhile the intense heat of the afternoon was followed by a violent thunderstorm that now passed over the district, followed by a deluge of rain. The heavy clouds brought on the dusk early. At 7 p.m. in the first gathering darkness, civilians fleeing in terror from their homes reported that German cavalry was approaching with about 1,000 infantry and some guns behind them. Shortly afterwards a

---

1 *Das Königlich Preuss. Inf. Regt. No. 27 im Weltkriege, 1914–1918*. Verlag Bernard and Graefe, Berlin, 1933.

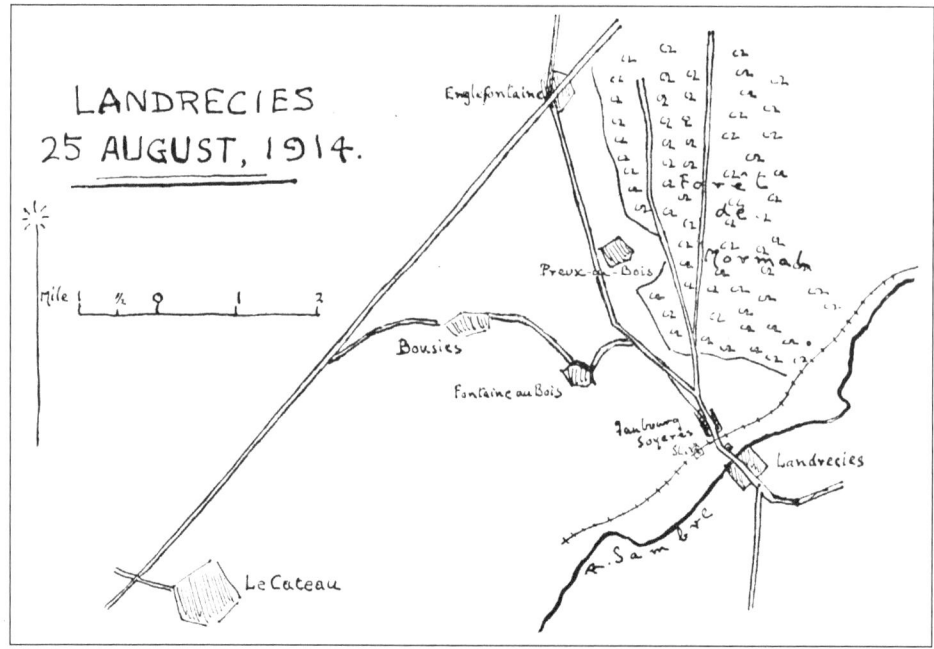

1. Landrecies, 25 August 1914

German cavalry patrol trotted up to the forked roads. It was fired at by the machine gun. Two of the patrol dropped to the ground and the remainder galloped back taking the forest road, and were unable to return to the column in time to give warning. As the forest road could not be seen from the sentry post, the, sentries and the machine gun were now moved forward to the road junction so as to be able to sweep both roads with their fire. It was dark when about 7.30 p.m. the rumble of wheels and the tramp of infantry singing songs was heard in the distance in the direction of Englefontaine. The picquet stood to arms and Captain Monck, the company commander, went forward to the sentry post.

The German IV Corps which had taken part in the fight against the British at Mons had followed close on their heels. By the late afternoon of the 25th the head of its 7th Division had reached Englefontaine where it was to halt for the night. Its advanced guard was to cover the front: the 27th Regiment, with three batteries 4th Field Artillery Regiment and a squadron 10th Hussars, with outposts south of Preux-au-Bois and the 165th Regiment, with the remaining three batteries of the 4th F.A. Regiment, about Fontaine-au-Bois and Bousies.

The German advanced guard had scarcely reached these places when at 7 p.m. an order was received by the 27th Regiment to push on a mile farther and occupy the Sambre crossing at Landrecies as the English were still in full retreat. It was this alteration of orders at the last moment, apparently unimportant in itself, that was to be the cause of all the trouble that followed.

On receipt of this order from 14th Brigade headquarters, Colonel von Below, commanding the 27th Regiment, ordered the march to be continued, the 1st Battalion to cross the Sambre and place outposts south of Landrecies, the 2nd and 3rd Battalions to halt in that village and be billeted there for the night. The point of the vanguard, half a company of infantry with Lieutenant John at its head, moved off followed closely by the vanguard itself, the rest of the 1st Battalion and a battery of artillery: 300 yards in rear followed the main guard, that is, the two remaining battalions and batteries. The road was wide and the infantry and artillery moved side by side. With no word of any enemy from the cavalry patrol and with dinner and bed so near at hand after a most trying day, the column took this last lap almost recklessly, throwing caution to the winds. When within a few hundred yards of the forked roads Colonel von Below with other staff officers began to ride forward through the vanguard for the purpose of allocating the billets in Landrecies. The baggage column trotted forward level with the main guard, and the two batteries pressed on to join up with the battery of the vanguard.

At this moment Lieutenant John marching at the head of the point reached the fork roads. He was challenged by Captain Monck, only a few yards away, and replied in French that they were friends. A light was flashed on Captain Monck's face. Simultaneously one of the sentry post flashed a light up the road and revealed a group of German soldiers just in front. Captain Monck at once gave the order to fire. The Germans rushed in. Captain Monck was fired at with a revolver, but succeeded in getting back unhurt with the sentry post to the picquet. Private Robson at the machine gun was able to send a hail of bullets down the road before the Germans reached and bayoneted him. The Coldstream picquet ran forward and the Germans withdrew leaving behind them the machine gun they had attempted to take away, but now so battered as to be useless. The picquet at once spread out and fired a succession of volleys at the shouting and confused uproar they could hear a few hundred yards in front.

The burst of machine-gun fire, which had cost Private Robson his life, had in fact been more effective than he could have anticipated. The bullets whistled down the road into the mass of men and horses, to him unseen in the darkness, that filled it. The infantry rushed to cover leaving a number of dead and wounded on the road. Most of the horses of the leading gun-team collapsed burying their riders under them, the battery commander fell, severely wounded, and the second-in-command was crushed under his horse. Some unwounded horses, panic-stricken, reared up, broke free of their harness and galloped back through the astonished throng behind, a number of guns and ammunition-limbers were overturned and for a time there was a state of utter chaos such as can well be imagined in the circumstances.

As soon as the first confusion of surprise was over Colonel von Below ordered the companies of the leading battalion to extend on both sides of the road and work forward to the village. Their only way was across country as the fire from the Coldstream picquet made any advance along the road impossible. The Coldstream throughout the attack fired almost entirely by volleys. The fire-commander whistled and then gave the word of command on which the men emptied their magazines into the darkness ahead. The Germans quickly got into the way of this. At the sound of the whistle they rushed to cover and as soon as the burst of fire was over they began to work forward again. A donkey tethered in a field near the picquet acted as a loud-speaker of the warning for, by some freak of fancy, it took to braying loud and long each time the word of command was given and caused much jest and merriment in the German ranks. In the intervals of the firing the Germans were able to unhook two of the guns of the second battery, and by levelling the ditch and making a passage through the hedge got them into the field on the right of the road. In the same way two guns of the third battery were moved to the left of the road. The guns of the leading battery were left entangled in a maze of dead horses and overturned limbers.[2]

The attack now began. On the right the ground was so overgrown with trees and undergrowth that the two guns could not be brought into action and the infantry was checked by dense thorn hedges. On the left, however, was an open field and the two guns were manhandled over this to the hedge bordering the forest road. Here with infantry supporting them on either flank they opened on the Coldstream at point-blank range. The German infantry did not fire owing to a lesson expensively learnt a few days previously when two of the battalions had fired on each other during a night attack near Liége. They therefore were told on no account to load their rifles, but to rely on the bayonet when within storming distance of the enemy. The password for recognizing friend from foe was "*Parole Potsdam*," and it constantly echoed through the night as the Germans gradually worked their way forward. But the Coldstream soon caught on to this and as frequently shouted it back, so that it confused the Germans more than it helped them.

None the less, the situation of the picquet at about 10 o'clock was becoming very unpleasant. The support company of the Coldstream was sent forward and extended the line to the left of the forked roads, and the 2nd Battalion Grenadier Guards with one section of a howitzer battery and one section R.F.A. were sent up in readiness to the railway level-crossing. Soon after the support company was in position the Germans, who had by now worked forward with great difficulty on the right of the road, charged, shouting "Hurrahs." They were assisted by men from the machine-gun company who had left their machine guns and advanced with hand-grenades. They came within bombing distance of the Coldstream, but a succession of well-controlled volleys checked the attack and caused heavy casualties, including two officers. Several efforts to get forward were also made by the Germans on the left, lining the forest road. Here in the course of the fighting a haystack was twice set alight and lit up the Coldstream position. Both times it was rapidly extinguished by Lance-Corporal Wyatt, but not before the Germans had been given a good glimpse of their opponents line. This they tried to rush after firing point-blank into it with high-explosive and shrapnel from the two field guns and throwing a shower of hand-grenades. The Coldstream, in spite of considerable losses and their faces covered with a yellow powder from the shell bursts, held their ground and here too repulsed the attack with a succession of controlled volleys.

The German losses were mounting up rapidly and Colonel von Below now realized that the enemy was not to be easily dislodged. He had no idea of the strength of the force opposed to him, and not only did he consider the chances of his Regiment sleeping in Landrecies that night to be most remote but, from various reports, believed, the English to be working round his flanks by tracks to right and left, and his situation precarious. He therefore sent his adjutant back to Brigade headquarters to ask for reinforcements.

The action of the brigade commander, General von Oven, was definitely unorthodox and would not have gained many marks in an examination paper. He ordered the 165th Regiment to leave two companies to guard the three batteries of the 4th Field Artillery

---

2 *Das Feldartillerie Regiment Nr. 4*. Verlag Faber, Magdeburg, 1928.

Regiment in Bousies and the rest of the Regiment to march to the assistance of the 27th Regiment held up in front of Landrecies. During the midnight hours the small force in Bousies was thus the only defence of the four miles of country between the Landrecies and Le Cateau roads. The move was however justified by the circumstances and by the fact that a counter-attack by night across the Sambre was, to say the least, highly improbable. The order was not received with much joy by the Regiment concerned, judging by the account of Lieutenant Lohrisch.[3] He had been allotted a sitting room and bedroom in Bousies in a house of luxury and had spent the evening hours revelling in the anticipation of a night of bliss. He was about to get between a pair of spotlessly clean sheets on a perfectly sprung bed when the alarm sounded through the village. "*Ach herrje*! The gaze of the owner of the burnt-out castle in Schiller's 'Glocke' as he looked upon the charred ruins of all his worldly goods could not have been more pathetic, more despairing than was mine as I gave a last glance around that most delectable room whose charms were thus snatched from me just as I was on the point of tasting them."

Shortly after midnight the sound of drums and fifes was heard coming along the Englefontaine road. It was the band of the 165th Regiment making a brave effort with doubtful success, to cheer up the two and a half battalions before joining the fight for Landrecies. Half a mile from the forked roads the battalions were ordered to deploy out into the fields, the 1st and 3rd to the left, the 2nd to the right. The leading companies were to leading extend only to arm's breadth so as not to lose touch, and as the whereabouts of the various units of the 27th Regiment were not known, rifles were to be kept unloaded and only the bayonet used.[4] They had not advanced very far before they came up against what appeared to be a high-wall, but which, on closer inspection, proved to be a massive hedge strung through with wire and stretching for some hundreds of yards on both sides of the road. Half an hour passed before holes could be hacked through this obstacle and the men, creeping through, had formed up on the further side. After a short advance another almost impenetrable hedge loomed up in front of them, and they were still some distance from the front line of the 27th. Patrols were sent to discover a way round but they found none, and the main road itself was impassable owing to the constant bursts of fire that swept down it from the Coldstream picquet. Colonel von Dassel, commanding the 165th Regiment, therefore rode back to divisional headquarters and represented the hopelessness of continuing the attack by night in such conditions. He gained his point and by 1.30 a.m. had returned and ordered the withdrawal of his 1st and 3rd Battalions, which were marched back to their night positions. His 2nd Battalion he left behind at the disposal of Colonel von Below.

In the meantime isolated attacks had been continued against the Coldstream position, but the latter made no attempt to counter-attack nor did they show any intention of giving way. Soon after 1 a.m. Colonel Feilding, commanding the 3rd Coldstream Battalion, had sent up a howitzer from the railway level-crossing that fired point-blank at the flashes of the German field guns and had the effect of silencing them.

On hearing Colonel von Dassel's decision, Colonel von Below decided that it was useless to press the attack any farther that night. The guns were manhandled back and the infantry withdrawn as best they could across the fields to an assembly position a thousand yards in rear, where they were reorganized, the 27th Regiment to the right of

---

3   *Im Siegessturm von Lüttich an die Marne*. Leipzig, 1917.
4   *Das Hannover. Inf. Regt. Nr. 165 im Weltkriege*. Otto Fliess, Oldenburg, 1927.

the road and the 2nd Battalion 165th Regiment to the left. It was already getting light before this was accomplished. Sentry posts were put out in front while the remainder lay down in the wet fields and got what short rest they could. At 4.30 a.m. the soup kitchens arrived and all had a warm meal.

In the meantime, at 3 a.m., the 4th Guards Brigade began to march away out of Landrecies. The 3rd Battalion Coldstream Guards, which had so stubbornly held the entrance to the village during the night, packed up and followed. Their losses had been 12 killed, 105 wounded, and 7 missing, including 2 officers killed and 3 wounded. The Germans, before moving on, collected their wounded, and Colonel von Below and the officers attended a funeral service over the dead. The Regiment had lost 1 officer and 33 men killed, 5 officers and 77 men wounded, and 39 missing: the casualties of the 4th Field Artillery Regiment were 3 officers and 16 men killed.

The fight at Landrecies may be regarded as a minor outpost affair caused by British and German troops wishing to spend the same night in a village far too small to be comfortable for both. Nevertheless it will be seen from these German accounts that at one time the fight had every prospect of developing into an important action. Had the advance of the 165th Regiment not been held up by the unusual height and thickness of the hedges, the 3rd Battalion Coldstream Guards would have been faced by an attack of five and a half battalions of infantry. The attack would have developed about 1 a.m. and with daylight approaching it is impossible to say how the 4th Guards Brigade would have met it or what the results might have been.

The fact remains that General Haig's requests for support to Sir John French during the night were even more reasonable than he thought, as also was his decision to retire due south instead of south-west. Owing to the reports of the further retirement of the French troops on his right Sir John French had, the previous evening, decided to abandon his idea of giving battle on the Le Cateau line, but in any case the German show of strength at Landrecies had the effect of preventing the junction of the Expeditionary Force. The II Corps retired south-west on Busigny, the I Corps southward on Guise, and they did not regain direct touch until the 1st of September south of the Aisne.

2

Neuve Chapelle

10–12 March 1915

In many respects the battle of Neuve Chapelle is one the most instructive of the Great War. It is a complete representative miniature of twentieth-century position warfare. The principal tactical problems that arose in those three days of March 1915, were constantly to recur in the succession of British offensives during the three following years, and were never, nor yet have been effectively solved. In the attack there quickly became evident, for example, the small margin between success and failure in the first assault, the essential need and yet the great difficulty of maintaining the impetus of the advance after the breach was made, the difficulties of command, the problem of overcoming the series of machine-gun nests in a second line of defence, and the difficulty of preventing the attack being forced into a bottle-neck within the defender's position and then hammered from both flanks. So, too, in the defence this battle showed that the best means of holding and reinforcing the front defences had not been found, nor how, when or where to deliver either the immediate counter-attack with the local reserve or the methodical counter-attack with the general reserve.

In a modern battle between opponents fairly evenly matched in resources, whether in open or in position warfare, these same problems will recur. Aeroplanes and tanks have complicated but not solved them.

General Idea

The German advance into Northern France was finally checked in October and November, 1914, during the battles of Ypres, that epic of British stubbornness and endurance. As a result of the continued resistance offered by the Russian Army, the German Supreme Command (O.H.L.) decided, before again attempting to break up the Western Front, to carry out a great campaign against Russia in the spring of 1915 and crush its opposition. To that end every available man, gun and shell was transferred to the Eastern Front, and the Western was left extremely weakly held—at least in manpower—especially against the British sector of the line. Accordingly, there began a series of offensives by the French and British Armies to break through this apparently feeble resistance and, at the same time, to relieve the pressure about to be employed against Russia.

The first British offensive was to be delivered in the Neuve Chapelle area on the 10th of March, 1915. In this flat, low-lying district the water-level was only a couple of feet below the surface, so that breastworks had to be built up to supplement the shallow trenches. The village of Neuve Chapelle, a long, straggling collection of ruined cottages, lay immediately in front of the main British assault sector. Beyond the village was a thousand yards of open grassland intersected by water-logged ditches lined with occasional pollard willows which, being still leafless, did not materially affect the field of fire. Then

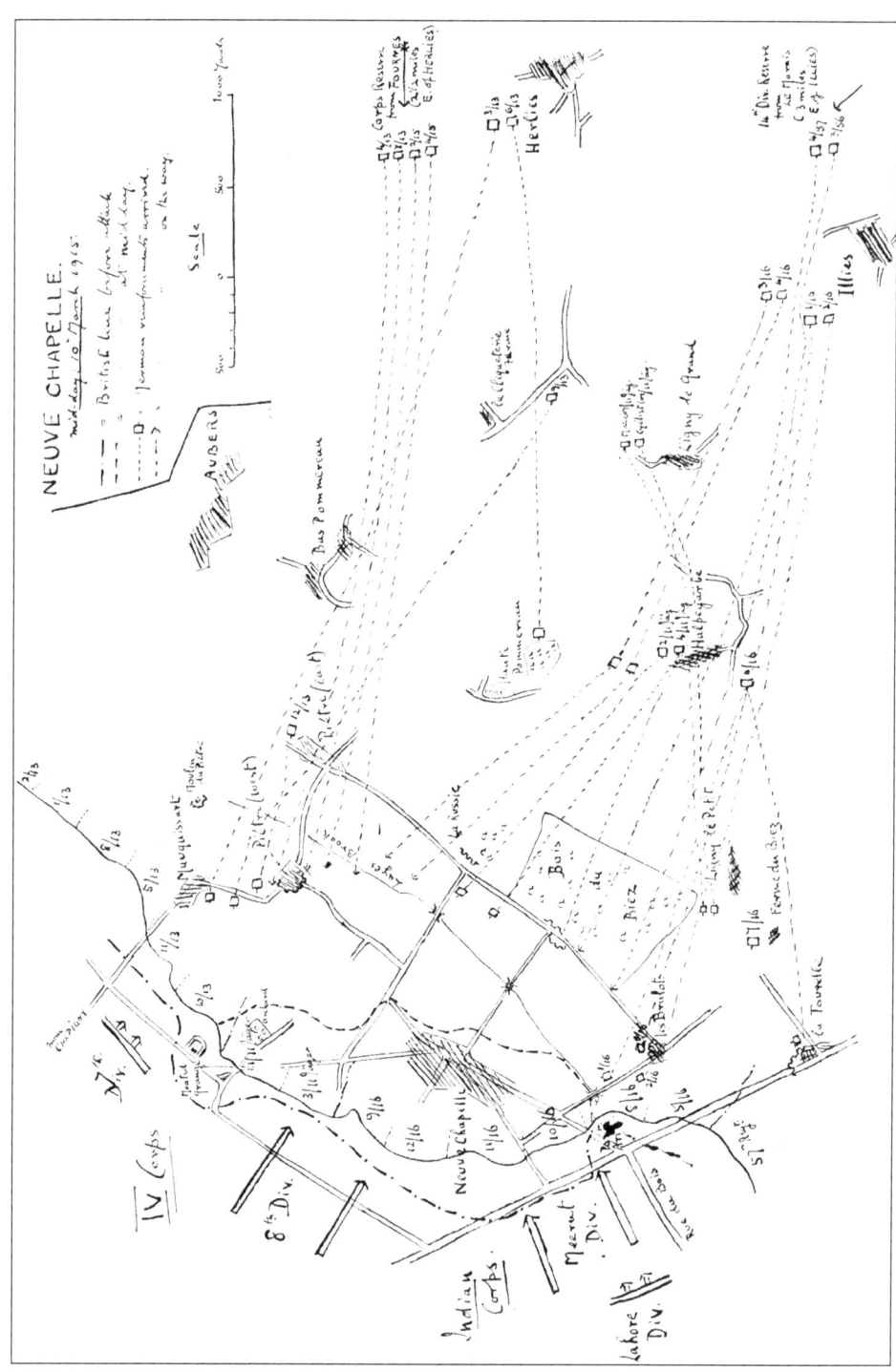

2. Neuve Chapelle, mid-day, 10 March 1915

came the Bois du Biez, a shell-torn wood about a thousand yards long and five hundred deep, which was the principle feature of the middle distance. Behind it the ground sloped gently upwards on to the low ridge that took its name from the nearby village of Aubers.

The First Army (General Sir Douglas Haig) was to break through in a sector where the German breastwork formed a salient around the village, between Port Arthur and the Moated Grange (*see* Map), a frontage of 2,000 yards. For this purpose the First Army massed facing it, and the sectors immediately adjoining, the four divisions of the Indian and IV Corps. A Special Order of the Day issued on the eve of the battle stated that 48 British battalions (about 30,000 men) were about to attack three German battalions (about 2,000 men). Further, the Intelligence Section of British G.H.Q. calculated that, allowing for the arrival of the additional reinforcements from reserve on both flanks, not more than 4,000 additional rifles need be expected within twelve hours of the first assault, although a further 16,000 might arrive from Sixth Army reserve near Lille within thirty-six hours.

It is no small wonder, if manpower was the only consideration, that First Army headquarters regarded success as a foregone conclusion. The entanglement and breastwork were to be shelled to pieces by 250 field guns and 40 4.5-inch howitzers. Then, while 82 siege and heavy artillery silenced the comparatively few German batteries, the forty-eight battalions of infantry were, in words of First Army Instructions "to carry the Germans off their legs and push forward at once across the mile of water-meadows, and then up the slope on to the Aubers Ridge, their objective."

The 8th and Meerut Divisions were to form the centre or spearhead of the battering-ram and, after overrunning the front breastwork of the Neuve Chapelle salient held by 6 German companies (about 800 rifles and 12 machine guns), they were to fan outwards behind it to right and left. This would be the signal for the advance of the 7th and Lahore Divisions astride the Chapigny-Piétre and Estaires—La Bassée roads respectively, and the divisions and corps on either flank were to be ready to "assume a vigorous offensive" and so achieve a general break-up of the German battle-line.

The actual objective for the infantry was a line Herlies–Illies, six miles distant on the Aubers Ridge, but so few and scattered were the enemy that, from the angle of view of First Army instructions there appeared to be no limit to the possible achievements of a battering-ram of forty-eight battalions once loosed behind the German lines. In the same way, disregarding the firepower of quick-firing artillery, of machine-guns spitting out five hundred bullets a minute and of magazine rifles, one can almost sympathize with the First Army order to the two Cavalry Corps, almost all the available British cavalry formations, to ride through, as soon as passage could be made, on to the Aubers ridge and make a right wheel behind the German line between Neuve Chapelle and La Bassée. In this manner they were to clear the ridge of any enemy, while the forty-eight infantry battalions consolidated their position along it.

The German Defence

Although the German defence seemed weak at first sight, it was weak only in manpower. In firepower it was strong, and skilfully organized.[1]

---

1   The books from which these details of the German defence have been taken, and which are recommended to any student requiring further information, are: *Mein Kriegstagebuch* (Kronprinz Rupprecht von Bayern), Vols. I and III; *Das Infanterie Regiment 13*. Groos, Oldenburg, 1927; *Das Infanterie Regiment 16*. Balderstein, Oldenburg, 1927; *Kriegstagebuch des Jaegerbattailons 11*, Otto, Schmalkalden, 1931; *Das*

The sandbag breastwork of the front line, 80 to 150 yards from the British front line, had had to be built up four feet above ground, as the water-level in this district was only a couple of feet below the surface. It was made of earth—sandbags and wood-fascines, and being only five feet thick a direct hit by a shell smashed a hole through it. It was protected in front by barbed wire on a single row of knife-rests. During the latter part of February the strength of the position was greatly increased by the construction of a line of well-concealed concrete machine-gun nests or strongpoints (*Stützpunkte*), 800–1,200 yards behind the front breastwork. Although about 800 yards apart they were sited so as to cover by fire most of the flat intervening ground. Five of these strongpoints were to play a part in the battle; one in a cottage-garden at the road-junction in Piétre (west), another in a ruined cottage near La Russie, a third in the ruins of a farm building at the Bois du Biez–Neuve Chapelle road-junction, a fourth at the Les Brulots road-junction, and a fifth near the group of houses, La Tourelle, on the Estaires—La Bassée road.[2] These strongpoints were normally unoccupied, but in the event of an attack were to be garrisoned by machine guns and men of the support company and to act as centres of resistance and pivots for a rallying line (*Anklammerungs-punkte*) in the event of the front line breaking.

The manner of distribution of the German manpower on the Western Front in the early days of 1915 gives the foundation on which the German defensive battles were to be fought throughout the War. Already they had evolved a system which, by force of circumstances and numerical weakness, was deeper and more widely extended than anything hitherto practised or imagined.

The 13th Regiment, facing the northern sector of the British assault, had its 3 battalions in the line each on a frontage of 800 yards, but with their companies distributed in depth back to 5,000 or 8,000 yards. Its left (3rd) battalion, which was to be engaged in the battle, held the front breastwork between the Piétre—Chapigny road and the Moated Grange with 2 companies (about 280 men, averaging one man to three yards of front);[3] another company was in support at Piétre (east), 1,800 yards in rear, and its fourth company in reserve 3,000 yards behind again at L'Aventure. As a further assistance 2 companies of the regiment, one each from the centre (2nd) and right (1st) battalions were resting six miles back at Fournes in Corps reserve, together with 2 companies of the neighbouring (15th) regiment to the north.

The Neuve Chapelle salient, the 2,400 yards of breast-work from the Moated Grange southward to the Estaires-La Bassée road, had been given up a few days previously, on the 5th of March, by the 53rd Regiment and its place taken by the 16th Regiment with its tactically attached 11th *Jäger* Battalion. The 53rd Regiment had been disposed on similar lines to the 13th; just mentioned, with 3 battalions in the line and support companies behind the Bois du Biez ready to occupy the machine-gun nests (*Stützpunkte*) in front of the wood and near Les Brulots, but the commander of the 16th Regiment altered this arrangement. The *Jäger* battalion held the right battalion sector with 2 companies, its 2 remaining companies being 3,000 yards back at Halpegarde, in support. The 3rd and

---

Infanterie Regiment 57. Castendyk, Oldenburg, 1936; *Das K. Bayerische Reserve Infanterie Regiment 21.* Braun, Munich, 1923.

2 The history of the 53rd Regiment, which handed over this sector on the 5th March, says (p. 34) that the first four mentioned, which were in its sector, were completed by the 3rd March.

3 This figure may be a slight exaggeration. The 57th Regiment in the sector south of the Estaires—La Bassée road states in its history (p. 63) that at this period "each company, allowing for sickness and men absent on other duties, averaged about 120 rifles in the position."

2nd Battalions of the 16th Regiment carried on the garrison of the front breastwork to the La Bassée road, the 3rd with all 4 companies in the front line and the 2nd with 2 in front, 1 in support at the Ferme du Biez and 1 in reserve at Halpegarde. The 1st Battalion was resting in 14th Divisional reserve at Le Marais, five miles away. The fact that the front line formed a salient round Neuve Chapelle village and that the flanks of a break-in could be satisfactorily blocked between Piétre and Les Brulots probably explains this new arrangement.

In the event of an assault the general idea of the defence was for the support companies either to reinforce the front-line companies; or to block at once the flanks of a break-in, according to circumstances. This flank defence was to pivot on any machine-gun nests (*Stützpunkte*) conveniently available, and the distance of the support companies, 1,500–2,000 yards, from the front line would give time for it to be organized. It was believed that this action, assisted by the front-line companies, would suffice to check by firepower further progress of an assault until the reserve companies arrived on the scene.[4] These were to counter-attack, and with the co-operation of the support companies on the flanks, recapture the original position. If not strong enough for the purpose, the Sixth Army reserve from Lille would be able to reach the battlefield within twenty-four hours and give further assistance.

The line of machine-gun nests (*Stützpunkte*) 800 to 1,000 yards behind the front line was recognized as the backbone of the defence. Some of the regimental commanders asked permission at this time to construct a continuous cover-trench (*Deckungsgraben*) connecting these machine-gun nests, or support points—a beginning, as they said, of a defence organized in depth (*Tiefengliederung*) but this request was refused by the corps commander "because the battle was to be fought in and for the front line, which was to be held at all costs."[5] This decision shows the determination of the Higher Command, confirmed by the statement of General von Falkenhayn,[6] then Chief of-the Staff, to lose no foot of ground, irrespective of its tactical value, an idea which was to govern the German defence to the end of the Somme battles in the autumn of 1916. It was the basis of the so-called rigid defence system.

The artillery support consisted of 6 four-gun batteries of the 7th Field Artillery Regiment, of which 1 was in a forward position hidden near cottages between La Russie and the Bois du Biez, and the others along a line Bas Pommereau—Ferme du Biez—Lorgies at the foot of the ridge, at an average range of 2,500 yards from the British front line. Their fire could be reinforced as soon as the battle opened by batteries of the 22nd, 43rd and 58th Field Artillery Regiments in the neighbouring sectors and by 2 heavy (foot artillery) regiments in rear.[7]

It is interesting as a sidelight on the German defensive arrangements at this period that, although a second-line position for the infantry was forbidden, a second line of battery positions for the artillery was already being constructed. For example, behind the Neuve Chapelle front extra field-battery positions were ready on the Aubers Ridge on a general line La Cliqueterie Farm—Bas Vailly—Le Willy—Gravelin about 2,500

4 *Das 57. Inf. Regt.*, p.67.
5 Ibid., p.65.
6 See *General Headquarters, 1914–1916, and its Critical Decisions* by General Erich von Falkenhayn.
7 The histories of the German 7th, 22nd, 43rd, 58th Field Artillery Regiments, all published since the British Official History was written, make a valuable addition to the history of the battle for any student requiring fuller details.

yards behind the occupied battery positions. The general idea was that the batteries, if the enemy should succeed in breaking through to any considerable depth, might have to retire temporarily, but, immediately sufficient infantry from the Sixth Army reserve at Lille arrived, the counter-attack would be delivered, supported by the batteries in the rear positions, and the original front line retaken. The Germans were confident that the superiority of their infantry in open warfare would enable them to do this.

The British Attack

The bombardment opened at 7 a.m. on the 10th of March. It was accurate and well planned. The three thousand shells fired in the next thirty-five minutes broke passages through the wire entanglement and shattered the narrow sandbag breastwork. At 8.5 a.m. 8 battalions of the 8th and Meerut Divisions, forming the head of the battering-ram, advanced. The morning was damp and misty, and the Germans, stunned by the sudden intensity of the bombardment, were unable to man the shattered remnants of the breastwork to check the assault. Within twenty minutes a great breach 1,600 yards wide had been made in the German line. On both flanks, for 200–300 yards, the assault had failed, nevertheless the mass of the assaulting battalions were able to press on into the German position. Unfortunately the plan of attack ordered the assault battalions to halt along a line 200 yards beyond the breastwork, and to wait there for fifteen minutes. The intention was to allow the village to be given a further shelling before the infantry entered it, but, on the other hand, it took away the whole of the advantage that had been gained by surprise.[8] Time was given for the few Germans who had escaped from the front breastwork to be rallied near the Bois du Biez, and time was given for the German battalions on either side to block the flanks of the break-in and make the necessary defensive arrangements.

The mist was clearing when the centre of attack, reinforced by two more battalions, pressed on through the village ruins, meeting little opposition. By 9 a.m. the men were in the open meadows beyond its eastern edge and except for a few small groups of the enemy retiring, many without rifles, no enemy was to be seen.[9] A message to this effect was sent back to brigade headquarters and the centre battalion commander (2/Rifle Brigade) at the same time asked if the advance should be continued. The critical moment of the offensive had arrived. The request was refused, and from then onwards a paralysis crept over the whole movement.

About this same time (9.30 a.m.) the lines of the left leading battalion (1/R. Irish Rifles) of the breakthrough, advancing through the cottage-gardens in the road-triangle north of the village into alignment along their objective, were suddenly enfiladed by machine-gun fire from their left flank and suffered heavy losses. For the first time the

---

8 The Germans were expecting an offensive. A week earlier, on the 3rd, fifteen Indians had deserted to the 13th Regiment, holding southward from Neuve Chapelle village, and told them that preparations were being made for an offensive 'within a few days' (*in den nachsten Tagen*). *Das 16th Inf. Regt.*, p. 73. Tactically, however, surprise was obtained, as witness the following extract from the history of the German 58th Field Artillery Regiment (p. 83): "On the morning of the 10th the battery commanders were going their usual rounds expecting a day of peaceful routine. The meadows were covered with a shroud of dense white mist. Suddenly a great burst of artillery fire came from the direction of Neuve Chapelle. It was the first real drum-fire (*Trommelfeur*) yet heard."

9 The diary of the German advanced battery at La Russie says that its guns did not fire at first, as they were not sure whether the troops coming out of the village, about 1,000 yards away, were friend or foe. They seemed to be wearing German helmets and were waving white flags, and it was not till the smoke of the bombardment had cleared away that the situation was appreciated and the battery opened fire.

German machine guns, which had occupied the concealed strongpoint at Piétre (west) as a precautionary measure during the bombardment, gave warning of the fate awaiting any further advance towards the Bois du Biez. But the British battering-ram had already been halted, not by German bullets, but by its own unwieldiness.

For about 300 yards on both flanks the assault, as already mentioned, had failed. Owing to a mistake of direction on the extreme right and to a failure of the bombardment on the extreme left, the assaulting battalions on the outer flanks had been checked. It is difficult to see why this should have prevented the fan-out of the mass of the assaulting troops from the centre, except the fact that the battle directors were the two corps commanders and this would not accord with the corps plan. Under the existing chain system of command that plan, once set in motion, was, like an Aldershot Tattoo, most difficult to alter. The corps had become a great battle-unit, with battalions corresponding to platoons and their commanders with no more responsibility in the scheme of things than non-commissioned officers. Such an organization, rigid under the corps commander, might work smoothly so long as no opposition was met, but, if anything went amiss, the situation had to be reported back through battalion, brigade, and divisional to corps headquarters. The corps commander had to make a decision in some room four or five miles from the battle on the flimsiest and often false information, and the necessary orders had then to travel back along the same chain, be considered and translated in greater detail at each stage, until, finally, they reached the front-line companies, which had to carry them out. This most cumbersome system of transmission took some hours under battle conditions and, meanwhile, from soon after 9 a.m. onwards, the leading battalions of the battering-ram were halted until the flanks could get forward according to plan, a check that caused a great block in the battalions moving up in rear.

As each brigade and battalion had its allotted task, the brigades facing the uncaptured sectors of breastwork on the flanks had to make their own arrangements, and for this reason each sent forward another battalion into the great breach, with orders to attack outwards and roll up the offending garrisons. In addition to these two, a third was ordered forward by the left (8th) divisional commander with orders to close the gap of 500 yards he saw must exist between the left of the leading battalions beyond the village and the right of the battalions checked in no-man's-land. It was a strange order, for a single machine gun could have effectively covered this gap of flat open ground against any attempt by the few enemy present to enter it in broad daylight, and it is a small example of that squandering of manpower, due to ignorance of the use of firepower, which was to continue to be characteristic of British tactics.

At about 10 a.m. with these 3 battalions squeezing forward into the breach there were 11 battalions, roughly 9,000 men, in that narrow space between Neuve Chapelle village and the original lines of breastwork. They lay, sat, or stood uselessly in the mud, waiting patiently to go forward. The strength of the battering-ram at this moment was limited to the firepower of its leading companies maximum of about 800 rifles and a few machine guns on the 1,600 yards frontage of the break-in; the remainder of the 48 battalions were useless cannon-fodder until they could fan out behind the German position, if such an operation was at any time possible. Had it not been for the fact of surprise and that many of the German batteries had therefore only a small store of ammunition ready for immediate use, the casualties from shellfire must have been considerably heavier.[10] Neither

---

10 *Das Inf. Regt. Nr. 13*, Groos, 1927, p. 77.

of these three battalions achieved its purpose and they soon became hopelessly enmeshed in the crowd. At 11.30 a.m., however, after another heavy shelling, the garrison of the northern breastwork, 1 officer and 63 men of the 11th *Jäger* Battalion, came out from it and, walking across the dead, estimated at about 1,000, lying literally in rows, that they had slain that morning, surrendered.

The IV Corps commander, on hearing of this, ordered a strip of orchard close behind, believed to contain a German strongpoint, to be captured before the general advance of his corps was resumed. There did not happen to be a strongpoint or any Germans there, and it was occupied almost at once, but this information did not reach the corps commander until an hour after the event. In fact, it was not till 2 p.m. that he, five miles from the battlefield, was able to obtain some clear outline of the situation and considered his tangled column sufficiently reorganized to justify the resumption of the general advance and fan-out towards the Aubers Ridge. Owing to this waste of time in the transmission of information and orders the 7th Division, on the left, had been kept inactive.

Meanwhile, the sector of German breastwork holding up the right of the battering-ram had been delayed in rather similar manner and the Indian Corps commander told the IV Corps commander that his troops would not be ready by 2 p.m. The movement was therefore postponed as it was considered that "the advance of the two corps to be effective should be simultaneous."

It is not surprising that Sir Douglas Haig, at Merville eight miles away, was by now getting impatient. At 2.45 p.m. he telephoned to the IV Corps commander, who said he was waiting for the Indian Corps, but, by that time, the Indian Corps commander realized that the situation was not so unfavourable as he had imagined. It was thereupon agreed, at 2.50 p.m., that the two corps should continue the advance at 3.30 p.m., and orders were issued accordingly. Seven hours had thus elapsed since their leading battalions had forced the great breach, killed or taken prisoners almost the entire German front-line garrison, and looked ahead confidently towards the Aubers Ridge, that Promised Land to be reached by a mile walk with only a few scattered German companies to oppose them.

Nearly three more hours elapsed, however, between the writing of these two corps orders for the attack and the time when the companies in the front line received them and could start to carry them out. It was between 5.30 and 6 p.m., and nearly dark, when the advance began, and by that time the new German line of defence was, as British G.H.Q. Intelligence had forecast, more strongly held, in rifle and machine-gun power per yard, than had been the front breastwork in the morning. In addition, there was no surprise and no adequate artillery preparation: the thin German firing line and its five pivot strongpoints (*Stützpunkte*) had not yet been definitely located. Moreover, the gathering strength of the opposition had been known to the front battalion commanders all the afternoon. At every move their companies were swept by machine-gun and rifle fire, with heavy losses. But so little were the facts of the situation appreciated at corps and First Army headquarters that the latter ordered forward a cavalry division, at 4 p.m., to be ready behind the attack to ride through on to the Aubers Ridge. The attack failed and the ride of the cavalry was of the stuff of dreams.

The German Movements

Four of the German companies (three of the 16th Regiment and one of the 11th *Jäger* Battalion) had been overrun in the first rush, and only a few escaped back. Meanwhile, before the bombardment had been completed, the support company (12th) of the 13th Regiment at Piétre (east) had occupied with machine guns the strongpoint at Piétre (west) and at the same time, on the southern flank, a support company (7th) of the 16th Regiment from the Ferme du Biez garrisoned the strongpoint at Les Brulots. If the British assaulting battalions had pressed on at once through Neuve Chapelle, a gap of 2,500 yards lay open in front of them between the strongpoints at Piétre (west) and Les Brulots, with only two guns of an advanced field battery (1st of the 7th F.A. Regiment) at La Russie, and a few stragglers from the front breastwork collected there, to defend it.[11]

The intervening ground was, however, to a great extent covered by those two strongpoints which could have made an advance on the Bois du Biez especially in the British lineal formation of attack, a very costly one.

By 9 a.m., when the British assault battalions were emerging from the ruins of Neuve Chapelle village, the support company (12/13) at Piétre (west) had also occupied for defence a disused trench that lay between the strongpoint and the front breastwork at the Piétre—Chapigny road. From this it was able to enfilade still more effectively any further British advance eastward from Neuve Chapelle and also to block any attempt to fan out northward behind the front breastwork. So, too, on the southern flank another support company (6th) of the 16th Regiment had been sent forward from Halpegarde to La Tourelle, where it, together with the 7th Company at Ferme du Biez and Les Brulots, could block by fire any further British advance eastward or southward from the southern part of Neuve Chapelle village. Already a bottle-neck had been formed into which any further British progress was to be confined, with a gap of 2,500 yards still open at its eastern end. The history of the 11th *Jäger* Battalion tells how this central gap was gradually filled.

From messages received by runner (all telephone cables had been broken) within half an hour of the end of the bombardment the *Jäger* Battalion commander at Halpegarde gathered that the British assault had broken through the front of his two *Jäger* companies and of the 16th Regiment south of them, but that the left of the 13th Regiment held firm at the Moated Grange, though the extent of the breakthrough to the south, in the 16th Regiment sector, was not known. His first intention, on this information, was to hold the British offensive in front with the cyclist company and the machine-gun company of his battalion (and if this is not an insult to that British battering-ram of 48 battalions, the word has lost its meaning) while his 2 remaining *Jäger* companies were to move round to Piétre (west) to assist in blocking the northern flank of the break-in and take in enfilade any further advance. It will be noticed how the first care of the German commanders was to block the flanks and only to fill up the centre as reinforcements became available. The brigade commander,[12] however, feared that the breakthrough might have extended to

---

11 Two of the four guns of this advanced battery, in position between La Russie and the Bois du Biez, were knocked out during the opening bombardment. The diary of this battery describes how "soon after 8 a.m. men of the *Jäger* Battalion began to fall back, first singly, then in groups, from Neuve Chapelle village. The battery officers stopped many of them and assembled them along the Bois du Biez track, behind cottage ruins, hedges and tree-stumps, and between the gun positions, to form a firing line. The two remaining guns fired direct with shrapnel bursting at 1,000 yards on the British advance."
12 The German Order of Battle is different to the British. Taking this case as an example, the division concerned was the 14th, which included infantry, artillery, engineers and divisional troops. The three infantry regiments of the division (16th, 56th and 57th with the 11th *Jäger* Battalion attached) were brigaded as the 76th Brigade under a separate brigade commander. A German infantry regiment had three battalions each of four companies, numbered from 1 to 12 in the regiment. The *Jäger* (light infantry) were organized in separate battalions and not in regiments.

south of the Bois du Biez, and he therefore ordered the whole *Jäger* detachment to meet the attack frontally. Accordingly, the cyclist company and a section of the machine-gun company were ordered to the south-eastern corner of the Bois du Biez, from where they were to command the roads leading back from the front of the 16th Regiment. The 2 *Jäger* companies and the other section of the machine-gun company were to meet the attack at the northern end of the Bois du Biez, to protect the advanced field battery there at all costs, and to work forward, if possible, to the road triangle in Neuve Chapelle village. Advancing widely extended under a heavy shrapnel fire they passed through the northern end of the Bois du Biez and reached the road that borders its western edge. There they halted in view of the leading British battalions 700 yards ahead across the flat water-meadows, the machine-gun section (2 guns) taking up position in the strong points at La Russie and at the Bois du Biez road junction, covering the bridge over the Layes brook.

Here, from 9.30 a.m. onwards, this small force, with the few stragglers from the morning attack, covered the advanced battery, and, completely isolated from the point of view of manpower, awaited the British onslaught. The morning hours passed, but while the British troops remained along the eastern edge of Neuve Chapelle village, 700 yards away, further reinforcements continued to arrive to oppose them. On the northern flank another support company (9th) of the 13th Regiment from L'Aventure strengthened the line of the 12th Company at Piétre (west), while of the two reserve companies at Herlies the 3rd still further strengthened this flank at Mauquissart and the 6th moved to the wood near Haut Pommereau in close support behind the right centre. On the southern flank 2 of the reserve companies (1st and 2nd) of the 16th Regiment marched up from Illies by way of Halpegarde—Ferme du Biez—Les Brulots and reinforced the hard-pressed 10th Company in the front line facing Port Arthur, while the other 2 reserve companies Moved to Halpegarde. At about mid-day these 2 companies were ordered to reinforce the 2 *Jäger* companies, and, at 2 p.m., came up on their right at the northern end of the Bois du Biez. Encouraged by this support, all 4 companies advanced about 200 yards across the open to the line of the Layes brook. And still the British remained along the line they had reached in the morning hours.

As the afternoon wore on the companies in corps and divisional reserve began to arrive on the battlefield. By 4 p.m. the 4th and 7th Companies of the 15th Regiment from Corps reserve at Fournes had reinforced the right and right centre, between La Russie and Mauquissart, and half an hour later 2 companies (3rd of the 56th and 4th of the 57th Regiments) with 3 machine guns from divisional reserve at Le Marais advanced through the southern part of the Bois du Biez and filled the gap between the left of the two *Jäger* companies and Les Brulots.

The British advance, when it was resumed between 5.30 p.m. and 6 p.m., was therefore faced by exactly double the strength it had to contend with in the morning assault, and with no surprise or any effective artillery preparation to support it. The attack failed and the crisis for the Germans was past.

Later in the evening the German line was further reinforced in the Bois de Biez—Les Brulots sector by four companies from neighbouring regiments further south, one each from the 56th, 57th, 104th and 133rd Regiments. The Crown Prince Rupprecht of Bavaria, commanding the Sixth Army, in his diary entry for the 11th of March, 1915 writes that it was a mistake to continue to hold and reinforce a line which actually lay in front of the line of the strong points. He would have preferred a weakly held front line based on the strongpoints, with the local reserves kept back under cover till an adequate force for the counter-attack had been assembled. Even, he adds, if the British had broken through this line they would only have offered more favourable conditions for the counter-attack. In this idea may be recognized the germ of the elastic, or mobile, defence which was to become the foundation of the German defensive battle in 1917.

Continuation of the Battle

The 11th was misty all day and the British artillery was unable to range upon, nor could the infantry accurately locate, the new German line of defence and its pivotal strongpoints. Misty or not, this same situation was to recur again and again throughout the war; the difficulty of attacking a second position after the first assault had been held up. On the previous evening First Army headquarters had ordered the continuation of the original plan, the fan out and advance on to the Aubers Ridge, on the morning of the 11th, involving the assault on a position more strongly held than had been the front breastwork on the previous day, and for which days of preparation and a systematic artillery bombardment had been given. The story of the fruitless efforts to comply with this order during the morning and afternoon of the 11th, the confusion and delays caused by the complicated chain system of command and the continued ignorance of Army and corps commanders of the actual state of affairs on the battlefront, may be read in the British Official narrative. Messages owing to the breaking of all communications back from the front battalions by the German bombardment, had to be sent back by runners taking two to three hours, so that the direction of the battle by corps commanders ceased to function throughout the morning. When, about midday, they learned that the morning attack had been checked and they decided to continue the frontal attack by both corps at 2.15 p.m., their orders to that effect did not reach the various brigade headquarters until a few minutes before the hour of assault, and battalions and companies not till an hour or more later. The afternoon attack, therefore, ended in a disjointed affair without result, except further losses. The fact that at best the advance could only penetrate still farther into the fatal bottle-neck was apparently not appreciated. Despite these failures on the 11th, and despite reports from the front-line commanders that without effective artillery preparation the prospects of an infantry assault were negligible, the First Army commander ordered the offensive, to be resumed at 10 a.m. the following morning (12th). Before that hour, however, the Germans delivered their counter-attack.

The German Counter-Attack

The German VII Corps commander (General von Claer) when, at 10 a.m. on the 10th, he heard of the loss of Neuve Chapelle, ordered its recapture to be undertaken as soon as the allotted corps and divisional reserves arrived on the battlefield. The village had no tactical value, but this order was in accordance with the underlying principle of rigid defence that no foot of ground was to be lost, and if lost was to be at once recaptured. At the same time he asked Sixth Army headquarters for assistance and the 6th Bavarian Reserve Division, in Sixth Army reserve near Lille, was thereupon ordered to move forward to the Aubers Ridge. The leading brigade[13] (14th) left its billets in Tourcoing at

---

13 At this period the normal division had two brigades each of two or three regiments (each of three battalions). Already, however, many divisions were being organized into one infantry brigade of three regiments, the brigade commander commanding the infantry of the division.

3 p.m. and went by railway to Don, four miles east of Herlies, reaching that place on the same evening where it rested.

General von Claer, when at 9 p.m. he realized that the troops in the battle line were insufficient both to hold the line and make the counter-attack, placed the leading Bavarian brigade at the disposal of the commander of the 14th Division to be in position in the Bois du Biez by 6 a.m. to participate in the counter-attack. The instruction was to assault the new British line with the bayonet at dawn without artillery preparation, in the belief that the British battalions would not have had time to consolidate the new line for defence. This belief was never put to the test, for although the two Bavarian regiments marched out of Don at 1 a.m., there were unexpected delays in an intensely dark night, and the new day was already beginning to dawn when they reached Halpegarde, a march of six miles, and it was considered too light to advance down the forward slope of the ridge to the Bois du Biez, their assembly position. The assault was therefore postponed, the Bavarians being withdrawn to Herlies and Illies. The first of the long succession of counter-attack divisions which were to be sent against the British offensives in the three following years had therefore arrived too late, as did so many of its successors, for the immediate counter-attack (*Gegenstoss*). The British would now have time to consolidate the new line in daylight and only a deliberate and methodically prepared counter-attack (*Gegenangriff*) could hope to dislodge them and to recapture the village. Crown Prince Rupprecht of Bavaria, the Sixth Army commander, in his diary entries for the 11th and 12th of March, 1915, tells of the divided opinions as to how best this should be carried out.

To begin with he had thought that General von Claer's demand, on the 10th, for a whole division as reinforcement over-estimated the British strength, but he changed this opinion when, at 2 p.m on the 11th, he was shown a captured copy of Sir Douglas Haig's Special Order of the Day (*see* above), to the effect that 48 British battalions were engaged. In addition to the 6th Bavarian Reserve Division sent up overnight from Lille to the Aubers Ridge, he thereupon ordered forward the 86th Brigade (7 battalions) to be sent forward from Roulers to Don that same night, and also all available, 20, howitzer batteries to be lent immediately to General von Claer by neighbouring divisions. After giving these instructions he went to General von Claer's headquarters at Marquillies. He arrived just after the corps order for the counter-attack had been issued, according to which the attack was to be delivered at dawn in a manner similar to the previously prepared *Gegenstoss*, except that it was to be preceded by a half-hour bombardment of the British front line. In addition, a heavy shelling was to be maintained throughout the night on the British position, on Neuve Chapelle village and the approach roads, but it was evident that such a task, added to counter-battery work, was beyond the power of the few batteries of the artillery of the 13th and 14th Divisions and the 10 available heavy batteries to fulfil effectively. Crown Prince Rupprecht pointed out the risk of making such an attack against a prepared position with so scanty artillery preparation and thought that it would be better to wait until the artillery had done its work more thoroughly. He advised postponing the attack a further twenty-four hours, until dawn on the 13th, until the artillery reinforcement now arriving could take effect. To this General von Claer replied that the British, with another twenty-four hours at their disposal, would be able to make their new line so strong that an attack taking a week or more to prepare would be necessary to recapture the village and the original position. Moreover, he doubted whether the present line could be held for that additional twenty-four hours as the British were still attacking, and to confirm that statement he telephoned, there and then, to the headquarters of the 14th Division at Illies which replied in agreement. On hearing this, Crown Prince Rupprecht gave his consent to von Claer's plan, although others present, according to General von Krafft, his Chief of Staff, thought that the commander of the 14th Division, if, instead of being asked for his opinion, had been ordered to hold on another twenty-four hours to allow for an effective artillery preparation, could and would have done so. General von Krafft adds that the general impression was that the attack was being made with undue haste and its prospects very doubtful.

The British Defence

On the British side it was fortunate that while the corps commanders were trying to give expression to the First Army commander's urge to continue the advance, the front battalion commanders had taken the more practical step of organizing the defence of the ground gained. Daybreak on the 12th found them ready, and the half-hour German bombardment which preceded the counter-attack at 5 a.m. fell wide and behind, leaving the front line practically undamaged. A mist covered the German approach until within about 60 yards, but the full firepower of the British defence—fourteen battalions held the 3,000 yards of front between the Moated Grange and the Estaires–La Bassée road—then swept it, and against it the German advance could make no headway. Opposite the Bois du Biez, from where the Bavarians attacked, listening posts gave the warning, and in this sector southward to the La Bassée highway 20 carefully sited machine guns gave evidence of their quick and devastating stopping power in the defence. The counter-attack failed on the entire front, and whereas on the 10th the German casualties had been about one-fifth of those of the British, the proportion on this day was, reversed.[14]

The British defence against this counter-attack was the real victory of Neuve Chapelle, and it was essentially a "Soldiers' battle," won by the front battalions. Corps headquarters knew little about it until some hours later, and it was not until 3 p.m., ten hours afterwards, that the First Army commander began to realize the extent of the German failure and gave orders to exploit it by means of another general attack, sending forward the 2nd Cavalry Division to cooperate. But the moment for exploitation was long past and the attack only led to further British losses and nothing gained. This was, however, the final effort. The First Army commander appreciated that further efforts to break through in the Neuve Chapelle sector could be of no avail and decided to establish the position as a new defensive line, ordering it to be wired and secured against attack.

That order, issued at 10.40 p.m., ended the battle. The Germans decided to cut their loss and accept a local defeat.

---

14 The total British losses during the battle are given as 11,652 and the German total as 8,600 (of which about 1,700 were missing and prisoners, mostly captured in the opening assault).

3

Aubers Ridge

9 May 1915

The British offensive against the Aubers Ridge on the 9th of May 1915, was faced by a more difficult proposition than was that against the Neuve Chapelle salient eight weeks previously. The plan however, was as ambitious as before. Two sectors of the German breastwork on either side of the old Neuve Chapelle battlefield were to be assaulted, a front of 2,400 yards from the Rue du Bois by the I and Indian Corps and a front of 1,500 yards opposite Fromelles by the IV Corps. After forcing two breaches in the German breastwork at those places, 6,000 yards apart, the two columns were to spread out and advance concentrically, joining up on the Aubers Ridge, about 3,000 yards distant.

1

Experience at Neuve Chapelle had taught the Germans that a single narrow breastwork was inadequate to hold back the "amateur army of tennis-players," and they had set to work like beavers to strengthen the barrier on the whole British front from Lens to Ypres.[1] The front breastwork was doubled or trebled in thickness, in places fifteen to twenty feet across, with frequent traverses and a parados. The water-level allowed a trench depth of two to three feet, and the new breastwork, built of sandbags and revetted with large-mesh wire, reached four feet above ground with a firing step at ground level. In addition, breastworks for living in (*Wohngraben*), provided with shelters and dug-out accommodation, had been made, at varying distances, 30 to 200 yards behind the front breastwork. These were about 200 yards in length behind each battalion sector (1,000 yards).

In addition there were, as at Neuve Chapelle, a number of concrete machine-gun nests (*Stützpunkte*) 700–1,000 yards behind the front breastwork and about 1,000 yards apart, to act as rallying centres for a new firing line if the front were broken through, before the counter-attack: for example, facing the Rue du Bois assault frontage were machine-gun nests at La Tourelle, at the Ferme du Bois (Apfelhof) and at the Ferme Cour d'Avoué (Wasserburg) (*see* Map). They were normally unoccupied, but were to be garrisoned by detachments of the support companies in the event of an attack. Some of the regimental commanders had wanted to connect up these support points by a continuous cover-trench (*Deckungsgraben*), beginning in this way what they called a defence in depth (*Tiefengliederung*), but this was forbidden by the corps commander "because the battle was to be fought in and for the front line, which was to be held at all costs."

From the point of view of manpower the German position was weakly held. Each regiment had 3,000 yards of front to defend with its three battalions, so that each battalion

---

[1] The facts of the German defence given in this article are taken from the following: *Das Inf. Regiment 55*, Schulz, 1928; *Das Inf. Regiment* 57, Castendyk, 1936. Both these have been published since the British official account ("1915", Vol. II) was written.

AUBERS RIDGE

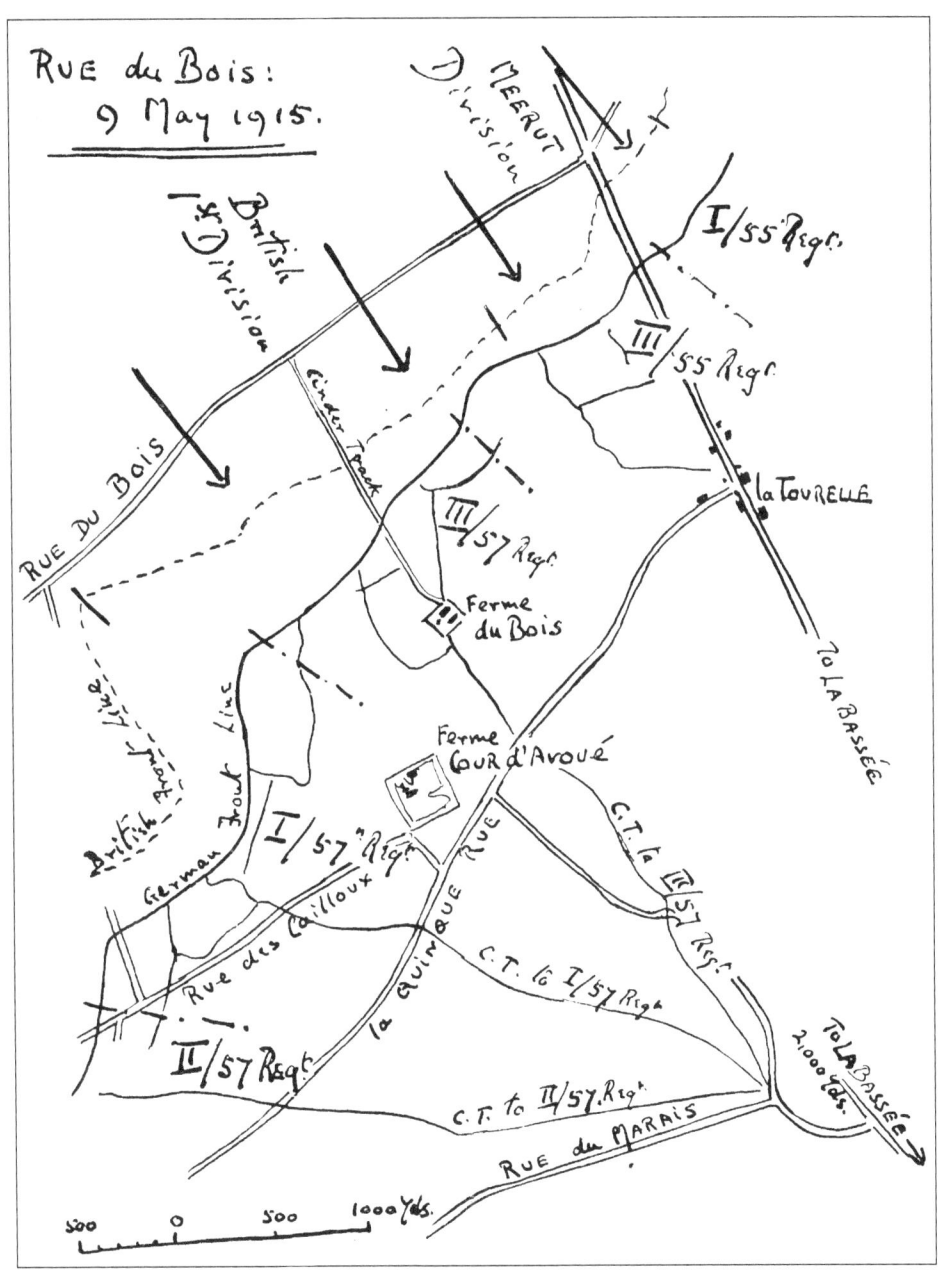

3. Aubers Ridge, Rue du Bois, 9 May 1915

had to supply its own supports and reserve on a frontage of 1,000 yards. To do this a battalion held its front breastwork with a garrison of two companies (each of about 140 rifles); it had one company in support 2,000 yards in rear and one in reserve another 2,000–3,000 yards farther back.[2]

The general-idea of the defence was to block at once the flanks of a break-in with the support companies, which were to take up a flanking position along any suitable communication trench, this flank defence pivoting on the machine-gun nests (*Stützpunkte*). The reserve companies when they arrived would, also with the help of the *Stützpunkte*, hold the attack in front and then counter-attack to recapture the front breastwork. An important improvement in the defences was the construction of communication trenches to connect the front breastwork with the living-in Trenches (*Wohngraben*) and thence back to the support companies. Near the front these communication trenches were soundly built, easily convertible into a flanking fire trench. They also had occasional concrete shelters to which the front-line garrison could hurry as soon as a bombardment began, leaving only a few sentries to watch at the front breastwork. Farther back, however, they consisted only of a double row of wattle-hurdles to give cover from view.

The artillery support consisted of six to twelve four-gun field batteries behind each division (three infantry regiments and a proportion of heavy (foot-artillery) batteries). It is interesting, to show the German system of defence at this period, that, although a second line position for the infantry was forbidden, the second line of battery positions for the artillery was already being constructed. For example, extra field battery positions were ready on the Aubers Ridge on a general line La Cliqueterie Farm—Bas Vailly—Le Willy—Gravelin about 2,500 yards behind the occupied battery positions. The general idea was that should the enemy break through to any considerable depth the batteries might have to retire temporarily, but, immediately sufficient infantry from the reserves at Lille and La Bassée arrived, the counter-attack would be delivered, and the original front line retaken. The Germans were confident that the superiority of their infantry in open warfare would enable them to do this.[3]

All this work on the German defences had not passed unnoticed by the British front garrison, which had watched and listened to its progress by day and by night, but British G.H.Q. kept to its belief, announced after the battle of Neuve Chapelle, that "with careful preparation a sector of the enemy's front line can be captured with comparative ease." The British official account says that some of the regimental officers hoped for a much greater success than Neuve Chapelle "because we have learnt its lessons and shall know what to avoid this time." But no lesson had been learnt, at least so far as concerned the direction of the battle. Tactically, it was to be fought on exactly the same lines. Once again massed manpower was to be asked to overrun a thin firing line and, even if it was overrun, no measures had been thought out to counter the problem of the concealed machine-gun nests, 800 to 1,000 yards behind, which had caused such tremendous losses and demonstrated beyond all doubt their effective stopping-power at Neuve Chapelle. The difficulties which

---

2 For example, the 3rd Battalion (57th Regiment) (*see* Map) had two companies near the front breastwork, one in support at Rue du Marais and one in reserve at La Bassée.
3 The histories of the German 7th, 22nd, 43rd, 58th Field Artillery Regiments, all published since the British Official History was written, make a valuable addition to the history of the battle for any student requiring fuller details.

that battle had shown might be expected when an attack by massed manpower enters a position defended by intelligently applied firepower had not yet been considered.

2

No cloud shaded the dawn of Sunday the 9th of May 1915, on Aubers Ridge. Skylarks circled up to greet the rising sun and peace reigned supreme while the German sentries drank morning coffee after their night's watch. Shortly before 4 a.m. a squadron of British aeroplanes flew over the German position. Twenty minutes later four shells from a British heavy battery screamed overhead and burst far behind. That interlude was followed by half an hour of quiet when suddenly, at about 5 a.m., the British bombardment opened with a mighty crash. A hundred years ago Schopenhauer wrote that the crack of a wagoner's whip was the most accursed noise he knew to "paralyse the brain, cut the thread of reflection and murder thought." Since then mankind has progressed rapidly. This sudden burst of fire from 600 British guns blasted all thought away. It sent up fountains of mud high into the air and any direct hits tore great holes in the German breastwork. In a few places all that was left to mark the line was a mound of earth and debris. The shells burst almost without cessation, making a continuous rhythm of paralysing noise. Soon a high wall of smoke, dust and splinters lay above and along the German front line, so thick that sight could not penetrate it. Except for a few sentries the garrison ran back, though not before losing many of its number, along the communication trenches, and took refuge in the concrete shelters there. But before the forty-minute bombardment had finished the men noticed that its bark was worse than its bite and began to return to their posts in the front line.

Many British officers and men, with front-line experience, must have foreseen trouble when occasionally during the bombardment a light breeze had dispersed the wall of smoke covering the German breastwork and they saw the Germans looking over the battered breastwork with rifles ready and bayonets fixed. There was no question of surprise this time. Numbers of shells were seen to be falling short[4] and great stretches of the breastwork and wire entanglement were intact. The bombardment had been no more intense on each yard of the German position than at Neuve Chapelle, and it was clearly far more inaccurate, owing to worn-out guns and bad ranging. But no cancellation order was received.

When, at 5.30 a.m., the bombardment began its final intense phase of ten minutes, the leading companies clambered out into the open of no-man's-land to take up a forward line before the assault. At 5.40 a.m. the assaulting lines, with the men extended to 3 paces interval, following at 50 yards distance, began to cross the 200 yards of flat open ground that lay between the British and the German breastworks.

3

According to the accounts given in the histories of the German 55th and 57th Regiments, which faced the attack by the 1st and Meerut Divisions from the Rue du Bois, they saw, when the bombardment had lifted to the back lines and the smoke had cleared, three lines of British and Indian troops already in no-man's land with a fourth clambering over the British breastwork and two more in rear. The sun had now risen and it was already warm. It was behind the Germans and shone in the faces of the attack, so that: "there

---

4   Many of the British shells were duds of American manufacture which when opened by the Germans were found to contain sawdust instead of explosive. (*Das Infanterie Regiment 55*, p. 86.)

could never before in war have been a more perfect target than this solid wall of khaki men, British and Indian side by side. There was only one possible order to give, 'Fire till the barrels burst.'" The first line, facing the German 57th Regiment, was already only 50 yards from the German breastwork, and it was mown down like hay before a scythe. Some reached the wire entanglement, where they were shot and remained hanging on it. The second line was enfiladed by the flanking fire of the company and machine gun on the left wing and was shot to pieces. The third line, advancing in small groups, came under the combined firepower of machine guns and rifles of the battalion as well as being enfiladed by the machine gun on the right flank of the 1st Battalion, and was practically annihilated. The fourth wave, clambering over the breastwork, was effectively dealt with by the German supporting field artillery batteries.

The attack was repulsed by the front German companies unaided and it was already beaten when the support companies, moving across country in loose formation, reached the second breastwork (*Wohngraben*) in readiness. Only at a few gaps in the front breastwork had the attackers succeeded in entering the position, and these were quickly dealt with in close fighting. For example, on the right, at the point of junction of the 55th and 57th Regiments, about fifty men broke in, of whom eight were taken prisoners and the remainder killed.[5] Some of the Indians also broke through in places and rushed at the German garrison flourishing knives, but they too were killed with the bayonet or taken prisoners.

4

Within ten minutes the attack was over, but at 6.5 a.m., hearing of the failure, the commanders of the 1st and Meerut Divisions ordered another attack after a further forty-five minutes' artillery preparation. This second bombardment was no more effective than the first, and the Germans, by propping up a large red board, gave a sign to their artillery and supporting infantry that another attack was imminent. Broken machine guns were replaced and reinforcements were sent up—for example, the 3rd Battalion of the 57th, which had most suffered in the regiment's sector, received a company (5th) from the regimental reserve to replace casualties. The second British attack, at 7 a.m., was therefore met by as strong a resistance as had been the first. The sun was well-up, the machine guns became red-hot and the gunners serving the batteries at Halpegarde, Lorgies, Illies and Gravelin streamed with sweat. The second British attack, delivered in similar manner, also failed with heavy losses. The commander of the Meerut Division suggested a third attack for 8.20, but fortunately, on hearing from the 1st Division commander that two hours would be needed to reorganize before the division could cooperate, it was postponed.

The G.O.C. First Army, Sir Douglas Haig, when he heard of the failure of these attacks, and not realizing the facts of the situation, ordered the whole operation to start again at 12 noon, but, on learning that fresh brigades would have to be put in and that the trenches were congested with dead and wounded, the hour was postponed to 4 p.m.

The Germans, who thought that the British must have had enough punishment (*die Nase voll*) for one day, were amazed to see them coming across once again in broad daylight, even with pipers (1/Black Watch) playing, as the sun lowered in the western sky. When the smoke of the bombardment had cleared the leading British troops were in some places close up to the German wire, and the whole of no-man's-land, says the history of the 57th Regiment, was again filled with extended lines of men following closely behind one

---

5   This probably refers to parties of the 1/Northamptonshire and 2/R. Munster Fusiliers.

another. On the front of that regiment the leading line succeeded in getting through the battered wire-entanglement and then over the German breastwork, where followed close fighting with bayonets and hand-grenades. All the rear lines were, however, mown down by enfilade fire from three machine guns on the left flank and rifle fire from the right of the 1st Battalion (*see* Map), as well as by the artillery fire of the 43rd Field Artillery and of two batteries of the 7th Foot Artillery Regiments. Without support, those British troops who had broken into the German position were soon overpowered. On the greater part of the attack frontage the German breastwork was not crossed. By 6.30 p.m. the battle was over. Under cover of darkness many wounded and unwounded, who had lain out in no-man's-land throughout this warm summer's day, were able to return to the British lines.

The German 57th Regiment gives its casualties at about 300 in the day's battle and those of the 55th Regiment are given as 602, chiefly from artillery fire. The losses of the British 1st and Meerut Divisions which had attacked these two regiments were together ten times as heavy, 6,340 all ranks, and those of the 8th Division, which had attacked simultaneously with no better result farther north opposite Fromelles, were 4,680 all ranks.

The diary of the German 57th Regiment refers to the magnificent courage (*ungeheurer Bravour*) with which the British had pressed their attacks, a sight which had aroused great admiration. Amazement is expressed at the repetition of the attacks in broad daylight once the first attack had so completely failed, but the Germans had at least been shown another aspect of the British character to that of an amateur army of tennis-players. They had been given a glimpse of the struggle ahead before they could be in a position to enforce their will upon that character and win through to Victory.

The battle of Aubers Ridge marked a turning-point in British tactics. From that day onwards British G.H.Q. abandoned surprise in the attack and began the long bombardment, the so-called "war of attrition." In theory the artillery now became the chief weapon of offence, and the infantry the "moppers-up." From this short account of the battle it will be seen, however, that not only was the bombardment ineffective, but the advancing British lines moved forward simultaneously without covering fire, so that the Germans were able to annihilate them at their ease, unmolested. As much as the inadequacy and inaccuracy of the bombardment, the costly failure showed the need in an attack – first, for surprise, an essential fully appreciated by the least of God's creatures, and, secondly, for improved infantry tactics. The decision of British G.H.Q. to abandon surprise and to put its faith in shell, or weight seems, therefore, to have been a questionable or, at any rate, less than half the answer to the battle. The consequence of its decision was that infantry tactics were neglected, with fateful results for the remainder of the war—and to this day. (*Vide* that parody on the science of war, "Field Service Regulations, 1935," amended date.)

4

The Fight for Hill 70

25–26 September, 1915

1

Should your footsteps ever lead you from Lens along the high road, the Route Nationale, to La Bassée, the first thing you have to do is to surmount the summit of Hill 70. From the time the road leaves the market square of Lens it rises steadily through a mile of houses and miners' cottages to the northern exit of the town and then on through another quarter of a mile of houses and cottages of the suburb, Cité St. Laurent. At the northern end of Cité St. Laurent, a local railway crosses the road at right angles and marks the limit of the housing area. South of it, behind you, row after row of miners' cottages; north of it, in front, the ground continues to rise steadily, a barren chalk slope, for 700 yards to the bare summit of Hill 70. Seventy in this case means metres and not feet, and the summit forms one of the dominant features of these foothills of the Artois plateau.

Looking ahead, once you have reached the top, the road leads straight northwards across the rolling chalk downs, leaving the Bois Hugo and Hulluch village on its eastern side, to La Bassée and the plain of Flanders. On your left, to westward, the hill slopes down at a steep gradient to the village of Loos, that lies at the bottom of a considerable depression, the ground rising again on the far side. In September 1915, on the top of this further rise, and 3,000 yards from the summit of Hill 70, lay the German front trenches facing the British, 200 yards beyond again. In rear of the German front trenches a semicircle of trenches surrounded Loos village and a redoubt had been constructed on the summit of Hill 70. The Loos defences and the redoubt were, however, only intermediary positions, and in case the front defences should be broken through, a main second line of resistance had been built on the reverse slope of Hill 70.

This was a part of the second line system of defences that had been hurriedly constructed during the summer months two to three miles behind the front line on the whole Western Front as a result of the experiences of the previous British and French offensives. The maximum wire cutting range for artillery was at that time about 2,500 to 3,000 yards, and the Germans placed their second line at such a distance that, should the first line be broken through, the enemy would have to bring forward his artillery for a renewed bombardment, which would need to be as prolonged and thorough as that against the front defences before it could be assaulted by infantry with any chance of success. The second trench system was therefore fronted by a wire entanglement equally strong and thick as the front line, and contained concrete machine gun emplacements and redoubts which could be occupied by reserve troops in case of necessity.

The German second line lay parallel to and 600 yards east of the Lens road on which you are standing, and if you turn away from Loos and look down the eastern slope of the Hill, bare and open here too, you will see Cité St. Auguste, another outlying suburb

THE FIGHT FOR HILL 70

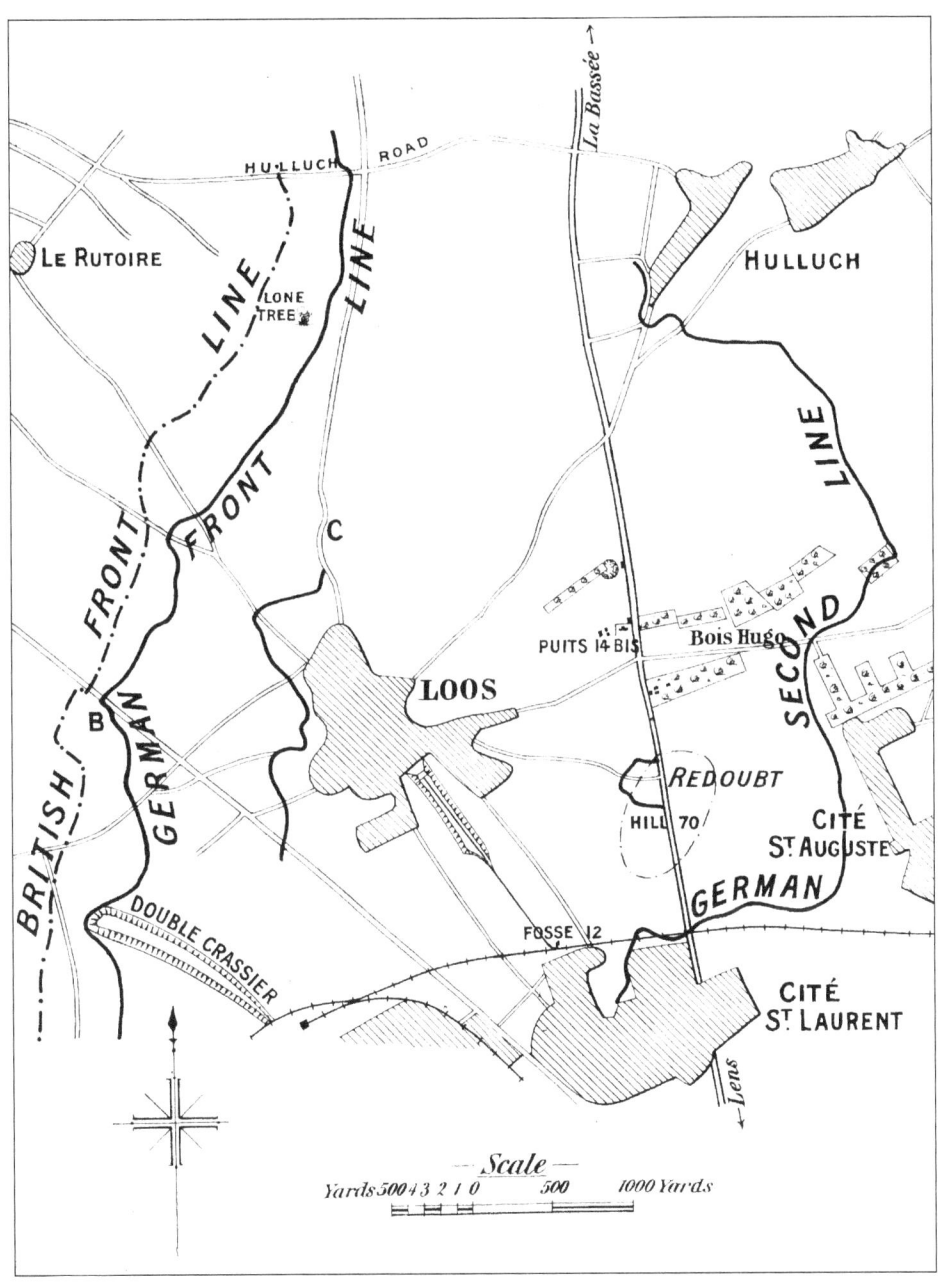

4. Loos, 25 September 1915

of Lens. The second line, passing around Hulluch village and along the eastern edge of Bois Hugo, crossed the front of Cité St. Auguste. It then turned almost at right angles westward, following the contour of the hill, and, roughly, the line of the local railway, past the northern side of Cité St. Laurent. In this sector, therefore, the second line formed a pocket around the reverse slope of Hill 70, so that any advance from the summit down the open glacis slope, either eastward against Cité St. Auguste or southward against Cité St. Laurent, could be swept by enfilade and cross fire.

2

The fight for Hill 70 formed a part of the battle of Loos, which in itself was a part of the Franco-British autumn offensive of 1915. This offensive, delivered on the 25th of September, began with great expectations. The German force on the Western Front had been much reduced during the summer to enable the operations against Russia to be completed, and the consequent superiority of men and material now at the disposal of the French and British Armies on the Western Front gave the Allied commanders every hope for a great victory. Attacking simultaneously from the Champagne towards Hirson and the line of the Meuse, and from the Artois Plateau across the plain of Douai towards the Belgian frontier, the plan was to cut off the two German Armies in the Noyon salient between Rheims and Arras, and thus to break up the German front, compelling the evacuation of the occupied territory of northern France.

The British were to cooperate in the offensive from the Artois Plateau into the plain of Douai, acting on the left of the French Tenth Army. The Lens—Liévin mining district lay in front of the point of junction of the British First Army with the French Tenth Army, and the general plan was for the two Armies to pass to north and south of this area respectively. In this manner the agglomeration Lens—Liévin would not be itself attacked, but be outflanked on both sides and eventually surrounded, the British and French troops joining hands again about Herein Liètard, six miles beyond. The British First Army, which was to carry out the attack, was therefore disposed between Lens and the La Bassée Canal. The main assault was to be carried out by four divisions, the 15th, 1st, 7th and 9th on approximately a four miles frontage. The remaining two divisions of the First Army, the 47th on the extreme right and the 2nd on the extreme left, were to form defensive flanks by swinging round to face south west and north east respectively, the 47th towards Lens and the 2nd towards La Bassée and Violaines.

On the British front the assault was preceded by an artillery bombardment lasting 96 hours, followed by the emission of a dense cloud of chlorine gas and smoke for 40 minutes from cylinders in the front trenches. Under cover of this protection the infantry was to assault the German front defences. The attacking force had a majority of 8 to 1 over the defence and, with the aid of the gas, it was hoped the assault would succeed without any great loss. The primary objective was the line of the Haute Deule Canal, six miles away.

3

On the 25th of September, 1915, the task of the 15th [Scottish] Division, the right division of the main assault and the only one with which this account is concerned, was to carry the German defences on the rising ground west of Loos, then storm Loos village and advance up the steep slope beyond to the summit of Hill 70. Leaving a battalion here to entrench and form a rallying centre, its two assaulting brigades were then to press on through Cité St. Auguste. On its right the 47th Division was to swing round and form a defensive flank between Loos and Grenay, facing Lens. On the left the 1st Division was to advance through Hulluch and Vendin-le-Vieil, side by side with the 15th, to the Haute Deule Canal.

The infantry assault took place at 6.30 a.m., following up the gas cloud. The two leading brigades, the 44th and 46th, suffered heavy losses in crossing No Man's Land, nevertheless the front defences were quickly carried and the survivors of the battalion of the German 22nd Reserve Infantry Regiment that held the line here ran back down the slope into Loos village, the Scotsmen following at their heels. After a certain amount of street fighting in the village the German resistance was again overcome. Many were killed in the fighting and a number surrendered, the remainder, some 100 in all, retiring on the second line trench at Cité St. Laurent.

The Scotsmen, elated with victory, pressed on to the farther side of the village, and, without reorganizing, began to climb up the steep slope of Hill 70. For the moment there was no further opposition and the men streamed up the Hill in leisurely fashion, giving the appearance, as one diarist says, of a Bank Holiday crowd. On reaching the summit the leading men stopped for a rest, but it was not for long. In front of the 46th Brigade on the left, men were seen running into Cité St. Auguste, 600 yards ahead, and they were believed to be other British troops about to enter the village. Those of the 46th Brigade on the summit at once sent up a cheer and pressed on down the slope towards Cité St. Auguste. As a fact, however, the men they had seen belonged to the reserve battalion of the German 22nd Reserve Infantry Regiment, who had been about to advance to reinforce their front battalion in Loos, but finding it too late were now hurriedly withdrawing to the second line position in front of Cité St. Auguste.

On the front of the 44th Brigade, on the right, a somewhat similar incident occurred. Owing to the inclination of the slope of the Hill, the leading troops of this Brigade on reaching the summit were facing southward rather than eastward, their correct line of advance, and, seeing a village in front, this was believed to be Cité St. Auguste, though as a fact it was Cité St. Laurent. Here, too, Germans were seen getting into position in the front houses, and the leading Scotsmen, some 300 in all, went on as rapidly as they could in the hope of keeping the enemy on the run.

Some senior regimental officers, on reaching the top of the Hill and seeing the situation, were able to check the remainder of the 44th and 46th Brigades and reform them behind the cover of the Hill, but 300 or 400 had already gone on beyond recall down the open slope. As they approached the German second line a heavy machine-gun and rifle fire was opened on them both from Cité St. Laurent and from Cité St. Auguste.

4

In the northern sector of the town of Lens was the third battalion of the German 178th Regiment, in reserve to its two front battalions that held the line on the left of the 22nd Reserve Infantry Regiment, opposite the French, south of Grenay. This Battalion was now ordered up to Cité St. Laurent to check the British advance which began to threaten Lens itself from the north. How this Battalion restored the situation is told in the regimental diary, which will now speak for itself.

For three days and nights the bombardment had continued without respite, and on the evening of the 24th of September, assembled in the officers' mess of the 3rd Battalion (178th Infantry Regiment) in Lens, the officers were discussing the question of the moment, when and where would the main attack come and would the battalion be sent forward from Lens? About 10 p.m. the commander of No. 11 Company, Lieut. Gieler, hurried into the gathering with important information and orders. "A French offensive is expected tomorrow morning. The Battalion will stand to arms at 4.30 a.m. at the eastern exit of Lens on the Liévin road." Orderlies were at once sent to all the neighbouring cottages, where the men were billeted, to pass round the order.

We had a restless night, but at 4.30 a.m., on the stroke, the Battalion was at the eastern exit of Lens, fully equipped for battle. To avoid risk of casualties the companies were spread about, partly on the Liévin—Angres road and partly in the suburb streets.

Dawn brought with it a cold drizzling rain, and for the moment the strength of the artillery bombardment seemed to have abated. After an hour or more of anxious waiting an order arrived, "Return to billets, but be ready to stand to arms at a moment's notice." Before we had returned our attention was drawn by an unexpected and constant rattle of machine-gun fire in the direction of the northern quarter of the town, and by a number of small white clouds of shrapnel bursting over Cité St. Laurent. Having reached the officers' quarters, an upper room of a high building in the town, we could see the reason. Away to the north, beyond Loos, a gentle easterly wind was bringing with it from the British position a greenish-yellow and black smoke-cloud towards the German front trenches. From many hundreds of small pipes the poisonous fumes could be seen gushing out in long continuous jets for some 50 yards and then uniting in one great cloud of gas which, driven by the slight breeze and held together by the damp air, moved slowly on towards the front trenches of the 22nd Reserve Infantry Regiment, holding the line on the right. The German batteries in Lens and to north of it at once opened a heavy fire, sending shells and projectiles of all kinds into the gas cloud in the hope of breaking it up and minimizing its effect. When the shells burst in it the gas was seen to rise and disperse, nevertheless the great mass of the cloud crept on unaffected and into the German front trenches.

We could now hear the continuous "tac-tac" of machine guns, showing that the infantry assault had followed up the gas cloud. Would the gas-masks prove effective? If too much of the gas laden air, sinking into the dug-outs, was inhaled the men would suffer from sickness or perhaps complete stupor, making in either case a serious defence quite impossible. From our upper room we could see through our glasses the beginnings of the attack, English and Scottish troops running across No Man's Land. Soon the ground was covered with dead and wounded. Our front line was holding. More and more extended lines of British infantry came on, however, until finally it was seen that the front trench had been overrun.

The British artillery had now lengthened its range. The hail of shrapnel bullets and the heavy shells moved farther and farther eastward until soon the barrage lay over Hill 70 and beyond, and over Lens itself. There was now a long pause, it was hoped that the remnants of the front line defenders had succeeded in holding the intermediate line about Loos village, but at 10.30 a.m. an orderly arrived from Brigade headquarters: "The Battalion will move at once by the quickest route to the northern exit of Cité St. Laurent." Other orderlies now hurried off along the streets with the order to companies: "Companies to be ready to march in five minutes." Packs were on in a moment and the various groups moved off from their billets: A quarter of an hour later all four companies were on the march along the road leading north from Lens up to Cité St. Laurent, for the most part in Indian file on either side of the road. This was to avoid observation by the enemy's aeroplanes that kept circling about over the town.

The Battalion commander, Major Gause, had gone on ahead to reconnoitre the ground and see the situation for himself. The British infantry were already in possession of Hill 70, and a few had actually reached the front houses of Cité St. Laurent, but there they had been checked for the moment. It was clear that the Battalion coming up with all speed would only be just in time to save Lens. This was of the first importance in order to cover the flank and rear of those troops opposing the French offensive on the heights of Notre Dame de Lorette and the Vimy Plateau, to the south.

Between the exit from Lens and the beginning of its northern suburb Cité St. Laurent is some 500 yards of open ground, and since both this and the road were commanded from Hill 70, the companies had to deploy and cross it by rushes in groups of half-companies. The houses of Cité St. Laurent were still under shell fire, but the companies kept away from the road and, moving by sections through the gardens of the houses, were able to reach the northern side of the suburb unnoticed and with little loss. Here Major Gause and Adjutant-Lieut. Ryssel had made Battalion headquarters. The 10th and half the 11th Companies were to move forward to the second line trench to left, west, of the road and from there advance with the idea of carrying out an enveloping attack from the left flank against the extended line of British infantry that could now be seen lying out on the Hill. The 9th and 12th Companies were ordered to occupy the second line of trench to the right, east, of the road, and from there support with machine-gun and rifle fire the advance of the left companies.

After brief instructions from the company commanders, companies moved off to their positions. The 9th and 12th Companies, extending out to right of the road, suffered some casualties in crossing the railway embankment, but reached the second line trench, 50 yards beyond, without further incident. Here they reinforced the scattered remnants of the 22nd Reserve Infantry Regiment. In front a number of Scottish troops had worked forward to within 100 yards, but from there they could see the formidable wire entanglement in the front, and as they were being fired at heavily both from Cité St. Laurent and Cité St. Auguste, they had halted and were now digging into the ground like moles. The hard chalk soil made this work slow and difficult for them in a lying position.

The 10th Company creeping along ditches and running across open bits of ground also reached the second line trench, occupying the sector of 300 yards between the Lens road and the point where the railway cuts across the trench. Half the 11th Company was held back in Battalion reserve in Cité St. Laurent, the other half following the 10th Company and extending its left by moving under cover of the railway embankment that leads on to the pithead of the coal mine, Fosse 12. Twelve to fifteen feet high at this point, the embankment gave good protection, but as the men lined up and looked over the top they saw the heads of Scotsmen 15 yards away already in position and entrenching on the other side of it.

These positions had been taken up by 12 noon, and it was now possible to appreciate the position and strength of the enemy. It appeared that a number of troops had advanced down the slope of Hill 70 towards Cité St. Laurent until their triumphal progress had been held up in front of our second line trench. It was clear, however, that a large number of the enemy were assembled on the far side of Hill 70, about 800 yards away. All our troubles and the long waiting were now forgotten as we prepared to get to grips with the British. The constant machine-gun and rifle fire was kept up against the Scotsmen in front wherever they could be seen, and at the same time some of our men crept forward to cut narrow gaps in the wire entanglement preparatory to our advance.

The machine-gun fire from the railway embankment on the left flank was most effective, as it was able to take much of the enemy's line in enfilade, the shallow scrapings they had made in the hard chalky soil giving little protection. To increase this effect, reinforcements were sent from the two right flank companies to the left, ready to add to the weight of the attack which was already starting from the left flank. At 1.30 p.m. a few Scotsmen began to leave their cover, at first crawling and then breaking into a run in an effort to reach the shelter of Hill 70 again: The gradual breaking up of the enemy's resistance was now evident. Seeing, apparently, the hopelessness of their advanced position, more Scotsmen began the fruitless effort to get back over the 600 yards of open glacis slope, but there was no cover and they were shot down. The feeling of victory in the German troops could now no longer be held in. check. On the left they rushed across the railway embankment bayoneting or taking prisoner any Scotsmen who had remained on the far side and then followed close on the heels of the remainder towards the summit of Hill 70, here and there a man stopping to fire a shot standing at the Scotsmen as they topped the crest of the Hill. The cheers of the troops advancing on the left infected the others, east of the Lens road, who now without any orders got up from the trench and passed through the gaps in the wire entanglement. The whole Battalion, taking with them the remnants of the 22nd Reserve Infantry Regiment, now rushed wildly forward on a broad front of 700 to 800 yards towards the summit of Hill 70. Their cheers filled the air as they ran forward, passing over the shallow trenches that had been dug by the Scotsmen, and in which were many dead and wounded and a number of unwounded who were taken prisoner.

To those who took part, this charge up the slope of Hill 70 will be an unforgettable experience, while to those who watched it, it was a war picture such as will seldom recur. Adjutant-Lieut. Ryssel was mortally wounded by a shell splinter during the charge, his last words as he lay dying being: "We have it, hurrah."

By 2 p.m. the important task that had been set the Battalion was accomplished, and Hill 70, the height that dominated the town of Lens, was again in German possession. The redoubt was reoccupied and a general line taken up near the crest. The next thing to be done was to hold it against the great superiority of British troops who were already entrenched on the farther slopes, both to the west towards Loos village and to the north towards Bois Hugo. Beyond Bois Hugo it was seen that the enemy had succeeded in crossing the Lens—La Bassée road on a narrow frontage between the wood and Hulluch village. The wood itself so teemed with Scotsmen that the men at once named it "Scots Wood" (*Schottenwald*), a name which it retained throughout the war. Two machine guns were brought forward from Cité St. Laurent and placed in position, one in the redoubt and one in a solitary house by the roadside on the summit of the Hill. At the same time, since the enemy's reinforcements were seen moving into Loos, the remaining half of the 11th Company was ordered forward and took up a position to left of the redoubt, making use of the shell holes for cover. Further British attacks during the afternoon were repulsed, but the British artillery continued to shell our position spasmodically, and during the evening the solitary house by the roadside was destroyed by a direct hit.

Since no further German troops arrived on the Hill during the afternoon and evening, it was not possible to attempt a farther advance down the slope either towards Loos or Bois Hugo, and that night entrenching tools were brought up and the position consolidated to right and left of the redoubt, the redoubt itself being strengthened and wired.

5

Leaving the German diarist for a moment we will return to the British side of the battle front. The 44th and 46th Brigades had failed to hold Hill 70, and at nightfall the 45th Brigade, the reserve brigade of the 15th Division, moved forward into Loos village and relieved a number of the battalions on the Hill.

On the left the 1st Division had been unable to progress beyond the Lens—La Bassée road, and during the night the 21st and 24th Divisions advanced from Vermelles and Philosophe across the Loos valley, relieving the 1st Division in the early hours of the 26th.

General Haig's appreciation of the situation at this time was that the Germans, beaten and driven from their main line of defence in this sector of the battlefield, were now holding on to a thin back line, and he believed that a determined attack by the 21st and 24th Divisions between the Bois Hugo and Hulluch would be able to pierce this back line and thereby turn the German positions to north and south, including perhaps the town of Lens itself.

It was decided that since an advance by the 21st and 24th Divisions beyond the Lens—La Bassée road could be observed in every detail and enfiladed from the German redoubt on the summit of Hill 70, the troops about Loos, particularly the 45th Brigade, should attack the redoubt at 9 a.m. and gain possession of the summit before the main assault of the 21st and 24th Divisions, which was timed for 11 a.m.

During the night, however, the Germans had reinforced their line and their fears of a complete break through were temporarily set at rest. The, result of the first day's fighting was that the British had been unable to press their offensive beyond the Lens—La Bassée road, and the second line trench was everywhere intact and in German hands. Southward again between Lens and Arras the German IV Corps had been able to hold in check the assault of the French Tenth Army against the defences on the Vimy Plateau.

Time was thus given to reinforce the most threatened points, and of these reinforcements 4 battalions were sent from Lens and Douai to occupy the German second line position on the front Cité St. Laurent – Cité St. Auguste – Hulluch.[1]

Such very briefly was the situation about Hill 70 on the early morning of the 26th. We will now return to the German diary.

6

The early hours of the following morning, the 26th of September, were misty, but after a heavy bombardment of the Hill the British attacked up the slope from Loos. The infantry in several extended lines came up time after time against the redoubt and the trenches to right and left, but were beaten back with heavy loss. In places they entered our trench, but after hand-to-hand fighting these isolated parties were driven out again, all the assaulting troops eventually falling back to the original line of trenches half way down the Hill.

Later in the morning bright sunshine dispersed the mist and a good bird's eye view of the whole battlefield was obtained. To northward the British line formed a salient into the German position, their front extending from Loos along the slope of Hill 70 to Bois Hugo and thence along the La Bassée road towards Hulluch. It could be seen, too, that the German second line, which had now become the front line and some 800 yards from the British, was amply occupied by fresh German troops who had come forward during the night.

At 2.30 p.m. the Scotsmen, supported by a heavy artillery bombardment, attacked the right of our position on the Hill, between the redoubt and Bois Hugo, but this was also repulsed by our fire, the attacking lines being taken in enfilade from the redoubt on the summit. Shortly afterwards, the enemy near Bois Hugo appeared to be moving back, while the German regiment on our right was seen to be advancing towards the opposite, eastern, side of the wood. This raised once more our offensive spirit and a number of men under Lieut. Franke moved down the Hill, keeping east of the La Bassée road and reached the Bois Hugo before the other regiment. Corporal Diese, a well-built, broad-chested Saxon, was the first to enter it, but after a few steps through some dense undergrowth he suddenly crouched. Ten paces in front of him, in a small clearing, stood a group of six Scotsmen[2] looking anxiously about them.

Some of them seeing Diese raised their rifles, but before they could aim and fire, Diese still crouching, threw his entrenching tool at the group, the axe-part hitting one of them in the forehead and blinding him. This so alarmed the others

---

1   One battalion of the 27th Infantry Regiment marched from Noyelles-sous-Lens through Lens to the second line about Cité St. Laurent. One battalion of the 26th Infantry Regiment was brought up from Liévin through Lens to Cité St. Auguste, and during the night occupied the second line position from north of Bois Hugo as far as Hulluch. Both these battalions were the reserve battalions of their respective regiments, the remaining battalions staying in position to oppose the French. In addition, two battalions of the 93rd Infantry Regiment belonging to the 8th Division, the reserve division of the IV Corps, were sent by rail from Douai immediately the news arrived of the British breakthrough north of Lens. They had trained from Douai at 11 a.m. to Billy-Montigny, east of Lens, and thence marched to Cité St. Auguste, reinforcing early in the evening the battalion of the 22nd Reserve Infantry Regiment that had been in position there throughout the day.

2   These probably belonged to the 6th Camerons, who made determined and repeated efforts during the afternoon to regain the Bois Hugo.

that instead of firing they ran towards cover in the undergrowth. Taking advantage of this, Diese at once rushed forward shooting one and bayoneting another. While doing so, however, one of the Scotsmen came up behind him and hit him over the head with the rifle-butt, felling him to the ground. In the meantime, the forty others under Lieut. Franke had come forward to Diese's assistance, and the latter, quickly recovering consciousness, as his helmet had taken the worst part of the blow, went on with the party towards the western edge of the wood. The other regiment now came up and, driving the rest of the Scotsmen in front of us, the whole wood was gradually cleared. The enemy retired across the Lens—La Bassée road and we reoccupied the mine shaft Puits 14 bis on the far side of it.

The gap that had been threatened in the German position between Loos and Hulluch was now restored. Sufficient reserves were at hand and a new position was taken up from Fosse 12 across the summit of Hill 70 and thence along the La Bassée road, past the western end of Bois Hugo towards the western side of Hulluch village. During the afternoon five more attacks were made by British troops from about Loos against our position between Hill 70 and Bois Hugo. At times eight, ten and more extended lines of men were advancing simultaneously one behind the other up the wide open slope of Hill 70 against our trench.[3] More and still more lines seem to come out of the ground and move forward against us, but in vain. Met by a heavy shell fire and by a hail of bullets one British battalion after another was riddled and shot to pieces. The lines never reached our trench, and finally the whole British attack fell back across the Loos valley in the utmost disorder.

Our small force had achieved the apparently impossible. The advance of vastly superior numbers had been definitely checked and our Battalion justly claims a lion's share in the victory of Loos. This is all the greater when it is considered with what endless care the British had made their preparations for the offensive, and what an enormous supply of ammunition had been assembled.

The Battalion almost exhausted from want of food, drink and sleep was now relieved and went back to billets in Cité St. Laurent. It had lost about half its strength in casualties, and the dead were carried in procession through the suburb for burial in Lens cemetery. Our position around Lens itself had, however, been saved. For months afterwards French and British shells continued to burst over the Town, but neither we nor the local inhabitants paid much attention to them; we were by now accustomed to the conditions of war. The children, in particular, cared for none of these things. They went on playing in the streets, regardless, and singing their famous song:

C'uest la guerre
nix pomme de terre
beaucoup, beaucoup militaire.

---

3   These were the successive attacks made without success by the 21st Division and part of the 15th Division.

5

The German Attack at Vimy Ridge

May 1916

The British relief of the French Tenth Army in the line south of Loos, undertaken as a result of the German pressure at Verdun, was completed early in March 1916. Thus we took over the positions on Vimy Ridge so hardly won by the French troops during the Battles of Artois of the previous year, when the Germans were driven from the heights of Notre Dame de Lorette, and across the Souchez river to the ridge beyond.

Subsequent reorganization of the line allotted to our 47th (London) Division—IV Corps, First Army—the Berthonval and Carency sectors. On its immediate right was the 25th Division—XVII Corps, Third Army. Here, on either side of the junction of the two Armies, our trenches ran along the western slope of the highest part of Vimy Ridge. Thence they traversed the northern slopes, running down towards the Souchez river between the villages of Souchez and Givenchy-en-Gohelle.

Neither British nor German had command of the crest, and neither viewed his front defences with any satisfaction. Immediately to the south of the Berthonval sector it had been our intention to hold the front line as the main line of resistance, in order to keep the Germans as far as possible from the Talus des Zouaves, a narrow ravine running up from the Souchez valley about 800 yards behind the front trenches. Along this ravine the Germans were in the habit of placing heavy and accurate barrages, which threatened to isolate the forward positions of both our 25th and 47th Divisions. But the enemy had obtained such a good start in their mining operations that it was extremely dangerous to hold this front line in strength. Consequently it had to be held by posts, and all efforts were concentrated upon the consolidation of the support system. Our 25th Division had come to regard this sector as a most difficult one: constant bombardment and mine warfare had made the front area a maze of shell holes and craters, whilst a ceaseless struggle had to be waged both above and below ground.

The right portion of the Berthonval sector was also in a bad state. There was little wire out, and the communication trenches were under observation of the Germans holding advanced posts in mine craters. Between the front line and the support trenches were small isolated posts, and the German artillery fire made movement by day almost impossible.

Generally, as regards observation, the Germans were at a decided disadvantage. From the eastern side of the Lorette spur—beyond the river and some 1,500 yards north-west of Souchez village—extensive views could be obtained of the ground behind the German line.

On the German side it is interesting to find that their attack had its origin in the fear that our mining operations would make their forward positions untenable. It was therefore considered necessary to advance and get possession of our mine shafts.[1] The 86th Reserve Regiment assumed that a large portion of its trenches was undermined. "We

---

1 "History of the 163rd (Schleswig-Holstein) Regiment."

THE GERMAN ATTACK AT VIMY RIDGE 45

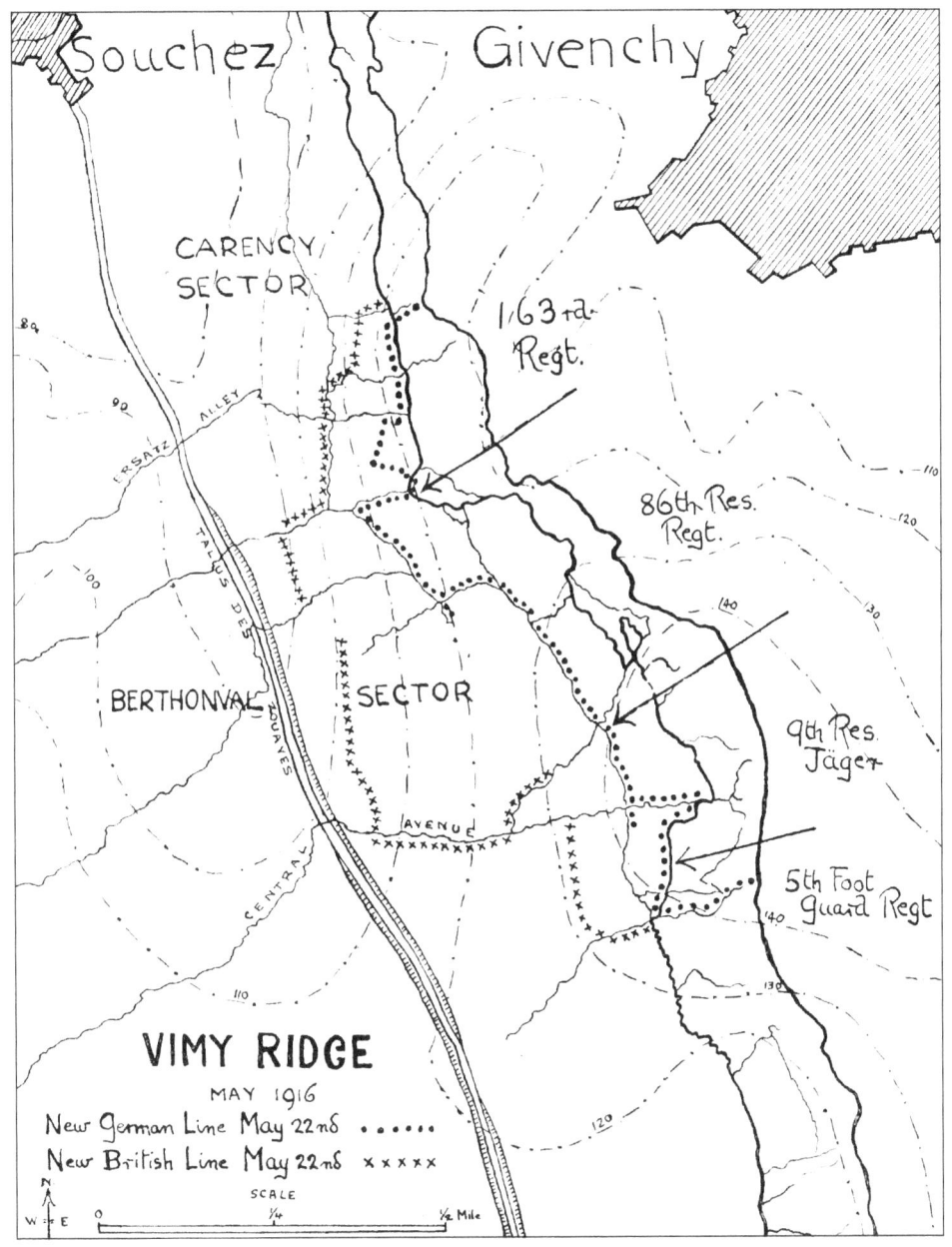

5. Vimy Ridge, May 1916

could not fight the enemy with the same weapons, as he was superior to us in both men and material." The only possible counter-measure was, therefore, an advance which would take possession of the entrances to our mine galleries "and thereby obtain a respite from underground warfare."[2] The 4th Guard Division (Guard Reserve Corps), which relieved the 1st Bavarian Division on the front opposite our 25th Division early in May, found that mine warfare was on the increase. The pioneer companies had to be augmented by *Bergmannszüge* (Mining Sections) formed by men of other units, and Bavarian pioneers who were familiar with the sector remained behind to assist the newcomers.[3]

North of the 4th Guard Division the German IX Reserve Corps had the 17th Reserve Division in the line. From a point approximately opposite Central Avenue, the junction of our 25th and 47th Divisions, the troops holding the front consisted of the 9th Reserve Jäger Battalion, the 86th Reserve Regiment, and the 163rd (Schleswig-Holstein) Regiment, the last-named formation overlapping the right front of our Carency sector.

The German attack was under the direction of Lieutenant-General Freiherr von Freytag-Loringhoven.[4] In it the 163rd Regiment was to be the predominant partner, and the operation was officially named "Schleswig-Holstein." Preliminary orders were issued as early as the 9th of May for "the middle of May," but the attack was eventually postponed till 9.45 p.m. (7.45 p.m. British time)[5] on the 21st.

The assault was to be delivered from an eight-company frontage which embraced our Berthonval sector, the right battalion front of the Carency sector to the north, and the left of the 25th Division to the south. This portion of our line was held as follows:

Left of 25th Division: 10th Bn. Cheshire Regt. (7th Brigade).
Berthonval sector } 1/7th London (City of London) (140th
(Central Avenue } 1/8th London (Post Office Brigade)
to Ersatz Alley) } Rifles)
Carency sector: 1/20th London (Blackheath and Woolwich) of 141st Brigade.

Our 47th Division had barely taken over the Berthonval sector from the 25th Division, the 140th Brigade completing the relief in the trenches on the night of the 19th/20th of May, whilst the artillery relief was fixed for the night before, and the actual night of, the attack.

The German organization for the assault is available in detail.[6]
Northern sector: Lieut.-Colonel Sick.
  Nos. 5 and 8 Coys. 163rd Regt. to assault.
  268th Pioneer Coy.
  5 machine guns, 71st Machine-Gun (Schützen) Section.
  7 machine guns, 163rd Machine-Gun Coy.
  One company 163rd Regt. in local reserve.

---

2 "History of the 86th Reserve Regiment."
3 "History of the 4th Guard Division."
4 The well-known military writer. He was deputizing for the commander of the 17th Reserve Division, Major-General von Zieton, who was away on leave.
5 Hereafter only British times are mentioned.
6 Histories of the 163rd Regiment, the 86th Reserve Regiment, and the 9th Reserve Jäger Battalion, from which this account is mainly compiled.

THE GERMAN ATTACK AT VIMY RIDGE   47

      Nos. 6 and 7 Coys. 163rd Regt.   } Regimental reserve in and
      with 2 machine guns.   } near Givenchy.
      Nos. 9 and 10 Coys. 163rd Regt. at La Coulotte.
      Nos. 11 and 12 Coys. 163rd Regt. at Sallaumines.

The troops at La Coulotte—near the main Arras—Lens road, more than two miles north-east of Givenchy—and at Sallaumines—a further two miles away in the same direction—were designated "brigade reserve."

      Centre sector: Colonel von Wurmb.
          On right—Nos. 1, 3 and 2 Coys. 86th Reserve Regt. followed by Nos. 6, 5 and 4
          Coys. to carry material.
          Half No. 1 Coy. 9th Reserve Pioneers.
          No. 1 Coy. 12th Bavarian Pioneers.
      On left—Nos. 4 and 1 Coys. 9th Reserve Jäger Battalion.
      Nos. 13 and 15 Coys. 86th Reserve Regt.
      No. 10 Coy. Bavarian Reserve Pioneers.
      293rd Mining Coy.
      No. 2 Coy. 9th Reserve Jäger Battalion.
      No. 3 Coy. 9th Reserve Jäger Battalion and machine-gun reserve.
      No. 14 Coy. 86th Reserve Regt. in brigade reserve.

The Jägers had been reinforced by the arrival of a cavalry machine-gun section armed with captured Russian weapons. The left-centre assault column occupied a depth of nearly 1,100 yards.
      Left sector: Nos. 5 and 8 Coys. 5th Foot Guard Regiment.
      The night of the 20th/21st of May was utilized to get the assaulting troops into positions of assembly, and all were ready by daybreak.

The Attack

No signs of the projected German attack appear to have been noticed by our troops before 3.40 p.m. on the 21st of May, when an artillery barrage was put down on the whole front of assault. Our communication trenches leading up to the Talus des Zouaves were also shelled, and forward communications were cut. German artillery fire was heavy on back areas and battery positions, the latter being deluged with gas shell. This was used, too, on our front defences; and a change of wind blew the gas back over the German troops waiting to assault, but little harm was suffered thereby.
      All the guns of the IX Reserve Corps were employed in the operation, supplemented by the artillery of the IV Corps and Guard Reserve Corps, six heavy howitzer batteries, and nine mortar batteries—80 batteries in all. Six heavy, nine medium, and eight light Minenwerfer were also in action. The counter-battery work, with air observation, proved most effective and no less than 83 British batteries were located. The ammunition allotment per battery for the preliminary bombardment averaged 200 rounds an hour.[7]
      The British artillery fire opened in retaliation was heavy but erratic (planlos), and slackened about 5 p.m. to increase again about two and a half hours later. A heavy battery

---

7 "History of the 9th Reserve Jäger Battalion."

firing from Bully Grenay was able to do considerable damage to the troops assembled on the extreme right of the attack, where the German trenches, on the north-western slope of the Vimy crest in front of Givenchy, lay open to the view of the British farther north.

At 7.45 p.m. the German guns lifted from the British front line to about 170 yards beyond, and the infantry advanced a moment later. On the extreme right No. 5 Company of the 163rd Regiment at once encountered artillery and trench-mortar fire, and soon suffered casualties from rifles and machine guns defending a crater in advance of the British line which was 450 yards away. The bombardment did not appear to have done much damage, and it was difficult to negotiate the British wire; but Lieutenant Hilmers led his men forward with great resolution, and was the first to enter the British trench. There was some hand-to-hand fighting before the defenders fell back to their second position, which they seemed content to hold, for no counter-attack developed on this part of the front. A platoon of No. 8 Company came forward to link up the new line with the assaulting troops on the immediate left.

The centre of the 163rd Regiment's attack had only reached its own wire when it was enfiladed from the right by rifles and machine guns, but this did not stop the advance, although a company commander, Lieutenant-of-Reserve Schulz, fell badly wounded. The British wire, which proved to be only slightly damaged, was cut by hand and the British were bombed in their trench, which was eventually captured after bloody hand-to-hand fighting.

On its left front the 163rd found that the artillery preparation had been so effective that it was impossible to locate the British defences amongst the chaos of shell holes. Here the British shells were bursting too high and too far behind to hinder the stormers, who, unable to recognize their objective, over-ran it and approached a trench several hundred yards beyond. Lieutenant Köhler, who led his company walking-stick in hand, was badly wounded, but this trench was captured. Lieutenant-of-Reserve Marpmann, who assumed command, soon realized that he was too far forward. He was being shelled by his own artillery, whilst a white signal rocket showed that the remainder of his Regiment, on the right, were over 400 yards in his rear. There seemed nothing to do but to get back into the general line, and this retirement was carried out, except upon the extreme left, where a platoon under Lieutenant-of-Reserve Wohlers still hung on to the forward position, having got into touch with the right wing of the 86th Reserve Regiment.

Now the British came on again and occupied the trench which had been vacated. Marpmann led another advance and recaptured the position he had abandoned. Here he proceeded to consolidate, and, by means of green signal lights, managed to prevail upon the German gunners to lengthen their range. The neighbouring company of the 86th Reserve Regiment soon afterwards sent over a message to ask that the position should be held, as it also had over-run its objective. But the difficulty was to link up with the troops on the right.

An endeavour was made to throw back the right flank, but the distance was too great to be covered; it was the opportune arrival of a platoon of No. 8 Company which enabled the gap to be filled. This platoon had been sent forward by Captain Weede, commanding the assault troops of the 163rd Regiment. Consolidation of the captured line could now proceed and much progress was achieved during the night, a start even being made on the construction of new dug-outs.

The prisoners amounted to 5 officers and 44 other ranks, belonging to the 1/6th,[8] 1/7th, 1/8th and 1/20th London Regiment, and no less than 240 British dead were found in and near the captured trenches. The Regimental casualties suffered in the assault amounted to one officer and 44 others killed; 4 officers and 208 wounded; and 11 men missing. Among the spoils of victory the 163rd Regiment counted two machine guns, three trench mortars, about 50,000 cartridges, "thousands of hand-grenades," numerous rifles, and a quantity of equipment, including greatcoats and gum boots.

The 86th Reserve Regiment claims an easier victory. Before the hour of the assault a shell of large calibre burst in a crater on the left and inflicted heavy casualties on the stormers assembled there. The company on this flank had great difficulty in deploying, owing to the many craters in its path, and was obliged to begin its advance upon a frontage of 75 yards. Then a British forward post, undamaged by the bombardment, had to be taken by bombers who were sent on ahead of the first wave of the attack. But after these early difficulties had been surmounted, the British front trench was captured without much fighting, most of the defenders coming forward with their hands up. Carrying on the advance the British main line of resistance was taken by surprise, most of its garrison being found in the dug-outs, where they fell an easy prey. Many prisoners were thus captured, and consolidation of a very much damaged trench was put in hand. Four machine guns which had been buried by the bombardment were dug up.

The Regiment made similar good progress along its whole front, though hindered everywhere at first by machine guns which had to be put out of action by parties of bombers. It reaped the full benefit of the German bombardment, and its machine guns, which came forward with the second wave and were handled with great bravery and tactical skill, did very effective work. Failing to identify their objectives, which, for the most part, had been battered and blown out of all recognition, the companies advanced even farther than the left company of the 163rd Regiment. Caught at last in the barrage of their own artillery, the troops were drawn back some distance and set to dig a new line, which was considered an easier task than it would have been to consolidate the damaged British trenches. So little resistance had been offered that a much farther advance was believed to be feasible here.

Farther to the left the 9th Reserve Jäger Battalion only succeeded after a sharp hand-to-hand struggle, for in many places the British (our 1/7th London Regiment) fought to the last man. Three prisoners were taken, and these stated that it was the general belief that the attackers were Bavarians who gave no quarter. From this it would seem that the relief of the 1st Bavarian Division by the 4th Guard Division at the beginning of May was not known to our troops; or the presence of the Bavarian pioneers retained in the line may have created a false impression.

After reaching their objectives the Jägers had trouble on both flanks. On the left it was difficult to get touch with the 5th Foot Guard Regiment, though this was eventually accomplished in spite of the broken and chaotic condition of the trenches. On the right the 86th Reserve Regiment, by going forward too far, caused No. 4 Company to do likewise in order to conform. This company soon became involved in heavy fighting in the British third line where the German barrage fell upon it. No. 1 Company, and the Foot Guards beyond it on the left, mistook No. 4 Company for British troops and opened fire with

---

8   One company of this battalion was sent up to reinforce the 1/7th London after the attack commenced.

rifles and machine guns, causing many casualties. The night was well advanced before the necessary withdrawal and readjustment of the line could be made.

Consolidation and the British Counter-Attacks
The 5th Foot Guard Regiment, which had used two companies of its second battalion in its successful assault, was heavily bombarded in its new position, and states that "several counter-attacks" were repulsed. In this sector—the extreme left of our 25th Division—the 10th Cheshire fought very stoutly, and received substantial support.

The 9th Reserve Jäger Battalion makes no mention of any counter-attack. The British artillery was not, at first, directed upon the captured trenches, but those in rear, and especially communication trenches, were heavily shelled. The avenues of approach to the new position led downhill, and were thus under British observation. When daylight came the work of consolidation was suspended by general order with the idea of not betraying the position of the new line which, judging from the fall of their shell, the British had not yet been able to locate. The British artillery seemed to have been re-grouped, and the misty weather hindered the German gunners in their counter-battery work.

The front line companies of the Jägers were relieved on the night of the 23rd/24th of May, by which time casualties had grown appreciably heavier, the British bombardment making it difficult to get the necessary material for consolidation up to the front line. This was now shelled with accuracy by the help of air observation, the British machines swooping low over the German trenches. In the evening of the 24th the Jägers were replaced by troops of the 162nd Regiment. With the battalion casualties are included those of the fourth battalion of the 86th Reserve Regiment and of the attached Bavarian pioneers. They are given as one officer and 41 others killed; 8 officers and 179 wounded; and 6 men missing.

Local counter-attacks are mentioned as having been delivered upon the left flank of the 86th Reserve Regiment at 8.00, 9.00 and 10.00 p.m., on the 21st of May. It was not until after midday on the 22nd of May, when some German shells fell short and a green light was sent up from the trenches as a signal to the artillery to lengthen their range, that the British discovered the exact position of the new line. Soon afterwards it was heavily bombarded, and the British fire did not slacken upon the area in rear. The old fire trenches and communication trenches were practically destroyed, for they could not be repaired whilst this heavy shelling continued night and day.

Cables were laid in this sector, but were so often cut by the British artillery fire that air lines were employed as being easier to repair. But eventually the task was given up as hopeless, and the telephonists were used as runners.

From messages received at Regimental headquarters it had become apparent that the Regiment was still out beyond its objective, and orders were therefore given by Colonel von Wurmb that the correct line was to be taken up at 1.0 p.m. on the 22nd. But the company commanders could not identify anything—the shattered ground bore no resemblance to the map—and the whole area was so heavily shelled that movement by daylight was impossible. In the evening the British used gas shell.

At 2 p.m. on the 23rd of May "the enemy suddenly attacked the ruins of our position," but this attempt was driven off was by artillery fire. At night a battalion relief was carried out. It was necessary for the incoming troops to move up across the open in extended order, for there were no trenches left which were usable. So, shrapnel and machine-gun

THE GERMAN ATTACK AT VIMY RIDGE 51

fire took their toll, and casualties were so heavy that the task of evacuating the wounded proved beyond the efforts of the medical personnel, which itself suffered serious loss. One aid post, established in a dug-out, was buried by a heavy shell. Numbers of wounded lay out under heavy fire all next day.

It was at 8 p.m. on the 23rd of May that "the enemy left his trenches to rob us of our spoils."[9]

There is a tale of bitter fighting—of bombing, short-range rifle and machine-gun fire—which continued most of the night. There were probably many alarms. Casualties mounted so rapidly from artillery fire that two of the company commanders decided to hold their portion of the front line with weak posts, the intervals being covered by the flanking fire of machine guns. This decision they reported to Divisional headquarters, but the message was imperfectly received. The Division judged it necessary to send up additional troops to cover the new gaps in the line, and this movement, carried out over the open as it had to be, caused serious and unnecessary loss.

The British fire had not slackened in the least when the regiment was relieved on the evening of the 25th of May, by which time it had lost 7 officers and 68 other ranks killed; 8 officers and 456 wounded, and 25 men missing.

On the new front of the 163rd Regiment the process of consolidation had proceeded apace, and a considerable quantity of wire was put out. The attack was considered to have been completely successful, the bravery and devotion of all ranks being supplemented by their excellent training and by the splendid organization of the operation.

The *Granatenwerfer* detachments had rendered admirable service by keeping under fire certain craters in the British line before, during, and after the assault. One detachment was buried by the burst of a heavy shell, but soon succeeded in coming into action again. Cables which were unreeled by signallers who went forward with the storm troops provided a reliable means of communication: it was soon possible to telephone to the new front line. The persistent shell fire caused frequent breaks, but all were promptly repaired. The stretcher-bearers, using tent-squares slung on poles instead of stretchers which would have been impossible to handle and carry over the broken ground, displayed remarkable devotion. Rations were got up to the fighting troops in spite of all difficulties. Before the attack every one received hot food and coffee, and one company was specially detailed to carry hot meals to the front line next day. A good supply of seltzer-water had been placed in the trenches, and each man was given a half-bottle of claret.

There were three counter-attacks early in the night of the 21st of May, and during the first of these a British officer entered the front trench, but was killed instantly. Later the British managed to get in on the right of the line, and were only driven out after a sharp bombing encounter in which Lieutenant-of-Reserve Rottgardt was killed. At 2.45 a.m. the British came on again, this time in two thick waves, but heavy rifle and machine-gun fire brought them to a standstill some thirty yards from the position. Half an hour later another effort was repulsed in similar fashion, captured bombs, rifles and cartridges proving invaluable as all the German supplies had by this time been expended. It is calculated

---

9   There is no British evidence that a counter-attack was delivered on the 86th Reserve Regiment at this time. A counter-attack been fixed for 8.25 p.m., but our 99th Brigade in this sector did not advance.

that at least one company of British was concerned in this last counter-attack. Strange to say, the losses of the Regiment in all these encounters amounted to only two men killed.[10]

Towards morning the British shelled the forward positions with gas, and the work of consolidation was interrupted while everyone put on his gas-mask. From dawn onwards the trenches in rear were kept under constant and heavy fire which did not slacken during the whole of the 22nd. After reorganization the front line was held by five platoons with four machine guns.

In the afternoon a counter-attack appeared to be threatening opposite the left, so a barrage was called down and rifles and machine guns opened. There were no further signs of a British advance. It was noteworthy that the captured trenches received little bombardment, the efforts of the British gunners being concentrated upon the trenches and communications in rear. This fire was so heavy that the battalion relief arranged for the following night, the 22nd/23rd of May, was only carried out with great difficulty and considerable loss.

The bombardment grew even heavier during the afternoon of the 23rd of May, and about 7 p.m. the sentries in the centre and left of the regimental front observed considerable movement in the British lines. The Holsteiners everywhere stood to arms, and about an hour later a counter-attack was launched.

It did not appear to be pressed on the right, where small parties were easily driven off by fire. On the left the barrage prevented the British from closing, but at one point the attackers did get within "throwing distance" of the position, and were only repulsed after some vigorous bombing by No. 4 Company.[11]

The most serious threat was to the centre of the front held by the Regiment, and here the machine guns in the right sector were able to give valuable assistance with flanking fire. The first wave of the British was repulsed, but the second entered the trenches on the right and in the centre of the company front. There were fierce bombing encounters and much hand-to-hand fighting during which Lieutenant Kaiser was killed. A machine gun received a direct hit from a trench mortar shell which destroyed both gun and detachment, and the situation was critical when the arrival of a platoon from No. 11 Company turned the tide. The British were then driven out and retreated under heavy fire.

Another attempt to advance was frustrated by flanking fire from the left, which had not been seriously involved. But on the right the British still hung on in one place where a post under Lieutenant-of-Reserve Arens had been cut off. This officer was wounded in two places, but continued to encourage his men, who fought stoutly with rifle and hand-grenade until the British were driven back. This was not done until another platoon of No. 11 Company had been brought up. A platoon of No. 3 Company, employed to carry bombs and ammunition, also pressed into the fight: its commander, Lieutenant-of-Reserve Wohlers, led his men gallantly until he was killed.

Three further attempts to counter-attack were dealt with by the artillery barrage, and the fighting then, died down. The Regiment had lost 43 killed and 102 wounded, but the British must have suffered very heavily, for numerous dead lay in and around the position.

---

10 Our records show that one company each of the 1/8th London and the 1/15th London delivered counter-attacks from the left of the Berthonval sector. The 1/15th London relieved the 1/8th before dawn.
11 The counter-attack was delivered by our 142nd Brigade, whose frontage did not extend so far as the right of the 163rd Regiment. And the extreme left of the latter was opposite the left of our 99th Brigade, which did not advance.

The intensive fire of the British heavy artillery continued until the afternoon of the 24th of May. In the evening of that day it was at last possible to evacuate the wounded, bury the dead—the German dead were taken back and interred at Sallaumines—and proceed with the reorganization of the position.

The 163rd Regiment took a special pride in the "Schleswig-Holstein" operation. Farther to the north, east of the Souchez river, in February 1915, it had — for the first time as a complete regiment — delivered a successful assault when it captured the "Giessler heights" from the French. But this action on Vimy Ridge was regarded as a greater exploit. The troops had advanced against trenches and wire much less damaged than was their objective in the previous action; and it was considered that the British were much more dogged in defence and more spirited in attack than the French had proved to be.

6

The German Defence during the Battle of the Somme, July 1916

Part I

A number of German regimental histories, German individual diaries and other papers have recently been published dealing with the fighting on the Somme in the summer of 1916, and together they give a vivid picture of the German defence throughout the various stages of that long-drawn-out battle. The following collection of notes and extracts, made on reading such of those publications[1] as deal particularly with the opening offensive of the 1st of July and the seven days' bombardment which preceded it, may be of interest.

Introduction
The immediate object of the offensive undertaken by the French and British Armies on the Somme Plateau in July, 1916, was, first, to relieve the German pressure on Verdun; secondly, to prevent the further transfer of German troops to other theatres of war; and thirdly, to wear down the German strength on the Western Front. The plan of operations to achieve this purpose had undergone considerable changes. At first, the main offensive was to be delivered by the French on a front of 35 miles astride and south of the Somme, while the British Fourth Army, holding the right of the British battle front, was to make a subsidiary attack on a front of some twelve miles between the Somme and the Ancre. The course of events on the Verdun front had, however, necessitated sending further considerable reinforcements to that area with the result that the extent of the French offensive had had to be modified. By the middle of June 1916, the French strength in the Somme district had been reduced by more than a third and they found themselves unable to sustain an offensive on a front greater than 9 miles. So it gradually came about that the importance of the French and British attacks was reversed. The originally intended subsidiary operation of the British Fourth Army gradually became the main operation, and the French offensive the subsidiary operation.

The British Fourth Army was to break through on a frontage of 18,000 yards between the French left at Maricourt, on the northern bank of the Somme, and Serre, north of the Ancre. It was then to press forward eastward across the rolling uplands of the Somme, a great open expanse of chalk downs, and secure the line Bapaume—Guillemont, an advance

---

1   *Die Schwaben an der Ancre*: Gerster, Heilbronn, 1920. *In Stahlgewittern:* Jünger, Berlin, 1922. *Die Bayern im Grossen Kriege, 1914–1918*: Bayerischen Kriegsarchiv, Munich, 1923. *Das Wurttemburg. Res. Inf. Regt. Nr. 119 im Weltkrieg, 1914–1918*: Gerster, Stuttgart, 1920. *Das Wurttemburg. Res. Inf. Regt. Nr. 121 im Weltkrieg, 1914–1918* : Holtz, Stuttgart, 1922. *Die 26 Res. Division, 1914–1918*: Stuttgart, 1920 (mostly photographs). *War Diary of the German 55th Res. Inf. Regt. from the 24th of June to the 2nd of July*, 1916: captured during the Somme fighting.

THE BATTLE OF THE SOMME, JULY 1916   55

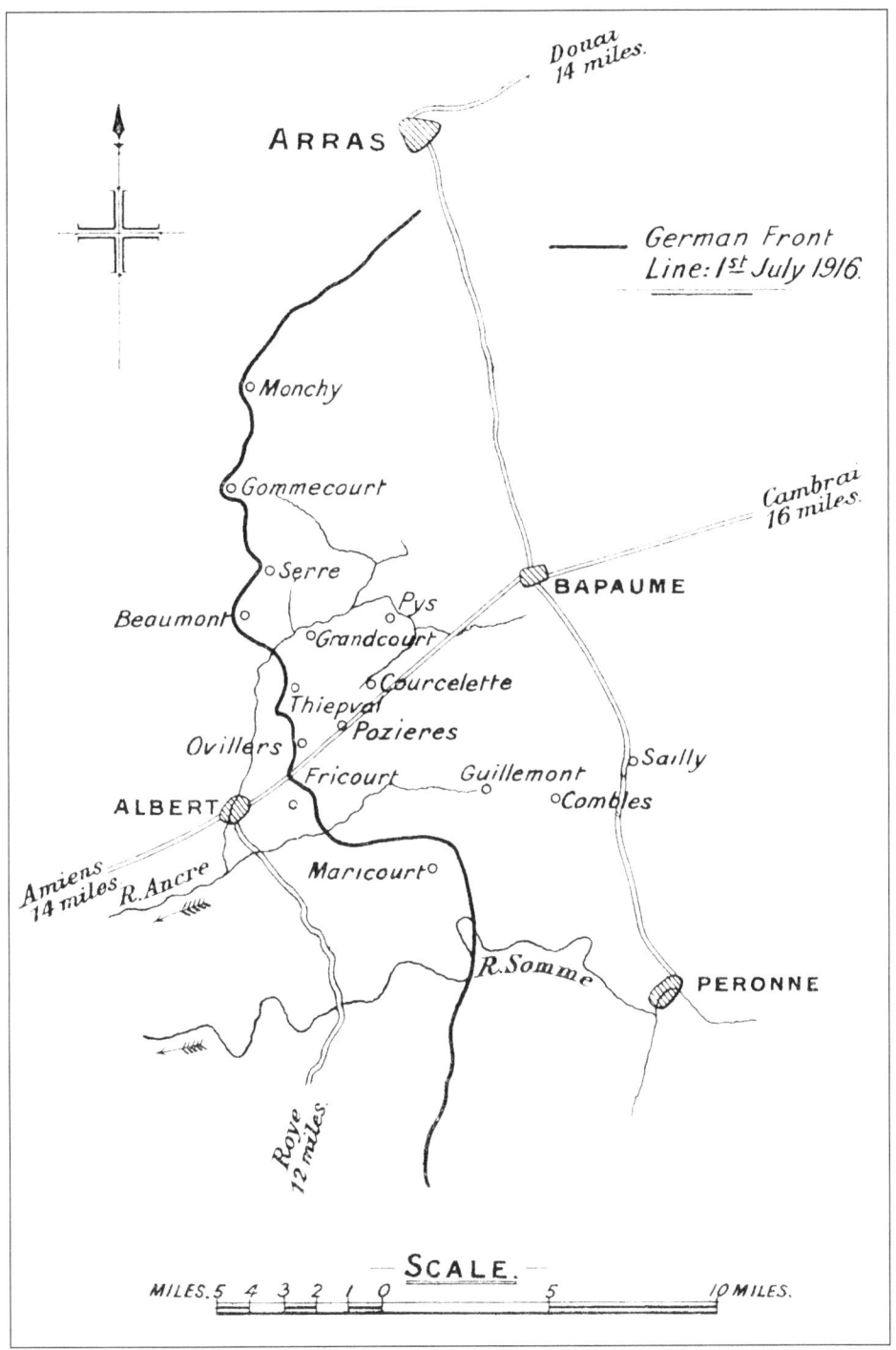

6. German Front Line, 1 July 1916

of 6 to 7 miles. From here it would advance to the Bapaume—Peronne road keeping touch with the French who were to advance on the right to a front Sailly—Saillisele—Rancourt—Peronne. The establishment of a position on the Bapaume—Peronne road would conclude the first stage of the operation. Efforts would then be made to work northward up the German defences between the Ancre and Arras and to press on eastward down into the plain of Douai capturing the important rail and road centres of Douai and Cambrai.

The offensive was to begin with a prolonged bombardment lasting five days, the infantry assault to be delivered on the 29th of June. On the 28th, however, the French reported that their preparations were not complete and at their request, and for the additional reason of the bad weather, the infantry assault was postponed for 48 hours,

For the preliminary bombardment on the British front and for covering the attack 1,513 guns and howitzers had been placed in position behind the battle front, averaging a field gun to every 20 yards and a heavy gun to every 60 yards of front. Nearly two million shells[2] were collected in the ammunition dumps behind the battery positions. For the main assault itself, thirteen infantry divisions had been assembled in and behind the British front line.

Prelude to the Battle

The German position was of great strength, the result of the experiences gained in the various defensive battles on the Western Front in 1915. After the fighting in the Champagne and the Battle of Neuve Chapelle in the spring of 1915 the original single fire trench had developed into a defensive zone, a series of three trenches 150 to 200 yards apart. The French offensive on the Vimy ridge in May and June 1915 proved this to be inadequate owing to the increasing size and quantity of the French and British artillery, and in July and August of that year a second defensive system was hurriedly constructed on the whole of the Western Front, 1½ to 2 miles behind the front defensive zone. This second position was as strong and heavily wired as the front one, so that it could not be rushed by the first infantry assault. It was, therefore, considered that the Allied artillery would have to be brought forward to new positions to prepare the way for a fresh assault, and that time would be given for German reinforcements to reach the threatened zone.

In September 1915, this second defence system had been put to the test and had successfully withstood the French and British offensive in Artois and the Champagne at the end of that month. Nevertheless, the preparations by the Western Powers for an offensive operation on a still greater scale in 1916 led to the construction by the Germans, in February of that year, of a third line of defence some two miles in rear again. It was not until May, 1916, four months later, and shortly before the outbreak of the Somme fighting, that this third line was finally completed.

The German position thus consisted of three defensive zones connected one with another and extending back to a depth of 4 to 5 miles.

---

2   1,628,000 rounds of ammunition were fired by the British artillery during the preliminary bombardment and the first day of the assault.

The Germans, as far as, possible, had kept units in the same part of the line throughout the war, so that companies, battalions and regiments competed with each other for the strongest wire entanglement and the best trenches and dug-outs. Great importance had been given to the wire entanglement since, as it protected the front trench from surprise attacks and minor enterprises, it enabled a considerable reduction in the trench garrisons. The original wire entanglement, broad wire on wooden posts or framework 5 to 10 yards in breadth, had now grown into 2 great belts of entanglement, each some 30 yards in width and 15 yards apart. Masses of barbed wire of double and treble thickness were interlaced to iron stakes and trestles, 3 to 5 feet high, and made an impassable barrier except for small gaps left here and there for German patrols to pass through.

The increasing weight and quantity of the French and British artillery had also necessitated a strengthening of the front trench itself and of the shelter for its garrison. For this reason traverses 10 yards thick had been built across the trench at frequent intervals so as to localize the bursts of the heaviest shells and mortar bombs, and concrete recesses had been dug deep into the parapet from which the sentries could observe either directly or with a periscope. The dug-outs, instead of the original 6 to 9 feet below ground in the spring of 1915, had now been tunnelled to a depth of 20 to 30 feet and at intervals of 50 yards, each capable of holding some 25 men. These were adequate to contain the whole garrison of the front trench in the event of an artillery bombardment. At each end of these tunnelled dug-outs (*minierte Stollen*) wooden steps led up a steep shaft to daylight and directly into the front trench.

Since for many months past no offensive had been contemplated by the German commanders on this front, measures for defence had been thought out in every detail, particularly as regards the cooperation of artillery. The whole front was divided into barrage sectors (*Sperrfeuerstreifen*) and every officer in the front line was supposed to know both those batteries which were ready to form a barrage in front of his trench and also those detailed to take on any targets suddenly appearing on his front. An extensive telephone system, which for 5 miles behind the front line was buried at a depth of 6 feet or more below the surface, connected the front trench direct with these batteries, and special fire-direction tests were constantly practised. This soon led to a mutual cooperation and confidence between the two arms which was to become the foundation of the defence during the Somme fighting.

For eleven months the Somme district had been a place of peace, so much so that the German divisions there had earned the name of the "Sleeping Army." Early in May, however, an ever-increasing activity behind the British line showed that this peace was merely a calm before the storm. By day long lines of motor lorries and wagons could be seen in constant movement on the roads behind the British lines, and by night continual digging and the unloading of material could be heard near the British trenches, combined with the incessant rolling of heavy goods trains apparently carrying ammunition. Fresh entrenchments gradually appeared, and sand-bag revetments, at close intervals along the front storm-trench, showed that it was being prepared for gas cylinders and generally strengthened. The woods near the battle zone, became daily more full of life and activity.

The German artillery was unable seriously to interfere with these preparations, for whereas the British seemed to observe every movement with a thousand eyes, the German eyes were completely blinded. All along the western horizon, the British captive balloons hung in great clusters, like giant mushrooms on thin stalks, directing the fire of their heavy guns and observing every movement behind the German lines. British aeroplanes flew over the German positions at will, reconnoitred the main lines of communication, photographed the infantry trenches and the German positions and strong points, dropped bombs on the big shelters behind the lines and on the heavy batteries, and attacked the gun detachments with machine-gun fire. If a German aeroplane or a captive balloon dared to ascend for a moment, British aeroplanes fell upon it like a mass of angry hornets and destroyed it.

In view of these many portents of an offensive in the Somme district, the German front was strengthened towards the end of May. Between Arras and Gommecourt, north of the Ancre, the Guard Corps (3 divisions) was in position, the XIV Reserve Corps (2 divisions) held the front from Gommecourt southward to the Somme, while the XVII Corps (3 divisions) carried it on astride the Somme and south of the river. There were thus 8 German divisions on a frontage of 60 miles between Arras and Roye, while behind this front 3 more divisions stood in reserve.

It was already anticipated that the front of the offensive would probably be delivered against the XIV Reserve Corps, in the centre, and the Guard Corps, therefore, took over the northern sector of its front facing Gommecourt and Serre. This enabled the XIV Reserve Corps to close up from a frontage of 30,000 yards to 20,000 yards and its 2 divisions were now (23rd of May) reorganized, the 26th Reserve Division on a front Serre—Thiepval—Ovillers and the 28th Reserve Division from Ovillers by Fricourt to Maricourt. The recruit battalions of each division were at this same period moved forward nearer the front, ready to occupy the second and third line defences if necessary.

The 13 divisions of the British Fourth Army, assembling in the zone Serre—Albert—Maricourt, were thus opposed by the 2 divisions of the German XIV Reserve Corps, while the 2nd Guard Reserve Division faced the left of the British Third Army about Gommecourt. In artillery the Germans were at an even greater disadvantage, there being approximately 240 guns and howitzers in rear of the battle zone, less than a sixth part of the quantity of British artillery opposed to them.

Apart from strong patrol attacks early in June there was little actual fighting or artillery activity until, on the 20th of June, British heavy guns began to bombard the. German rear communications and the villages behind the German front as far as Bapaume. This continued intermittently till the evening of the 22nd, but, on the 23rd, all was again quiet, a last breathing-space before the great onslaught. It was the eve of the Somme Battle.

The Preliminary Bombardment

The night of the 23rd–24th of June passed quietly and day broke clear with the promise of a Sunday of blue skies. The Germans in their deep tunnelled dug-outs in the front line had finished their morning coffee and the night sentries had been relieved when, suddenly, at 6 a.m. a great mass of shells burst with a thundering crash on and along the whole front. The day sentries, looking out from their bomb-proof shelters towards the British trenches, saw no movement there and the British wire entanglements appeared normal, showing that no immediate attack was to be expected. Above the German lines, however, hung a mass of small white clouds as the shrapnel burst, their bullets clattering into the German trenches and on to the roofs and walls of the ruined villages nearby. This violent tornado lasted some hours and the Germans, safe in their deep shelters, smiled at the thought of the British trying to prepare the position for assault with shrapnel. About midday the shelling changed to a steady well-regulated and carefully-aimed fire, as if the British batteries were competing with one another in a shooting tournament, but during the afternoon the strength of the bombardment increased again, being concentrated especially upon the Thiepval sector. The rumbling of heavy batteries now mingled with the noise of the field guns, their great shells sending up massive fountains of earth and smoke. Towards evening the sky clouded over and a light rain fell, laying the dust and making the ground about the trenches, churned up by the shells, a sea of mud.

During the following day—25th of June—the fire of the British heavy batteries increased and whereas on the previous day nine-tenths of the fire had been shrapnel or from guns of small calibre, the heavy batteries were now in the majority. Their shells, hurtling through the air, crashed into the German trenches. The ground shook and the shelters and dug-outs tottered. Here and there the sides of a trench fell in, completely blocking it. Masses of earth came tumbling into the deep dug-outs, obstructing the entrances to many of them. By evening some sectors of the German front line were already unrecognizable and had become crater-fields.

From the intensity of the fire in certain places, particularly astride the Ancre, north and south of Thiepval, about Ovillers, Fricourt and Mametz, it could be roughly foretold at which points the British intended to assault, and that night the brigade and divisional staffs made their defensive preparations accordingly and ordered the second line of defence to be garrisoned. The fire slackened somewhat during the night, but, early on the 26th, increased again. In the early hours, about 5 a.m. clouds of chlorine gas crossed No Man's Land from the British trenches north of the Andre towards Serre and Beaumont, and again, about 11 a.m., a thick yellow-brown mist of gas and smoke moved from the British line towards Fricourt on the southern part of the front. The dense fumes reached the German position and, being heavier than air, filled every crevice in the ground. They crept like live things down the steps of the deep dug-outs filling them with poison until sprayers negated their effect. At midday the bombardment increased to a still greater intensity in the central sector about Thiepval and then suddenly stopped as if preliminary to an infantry assault. The German sentries, looking towards the British trenches, saw, however, no sign of infantry, but instead another dense cloud of gas moving slowly forward towards them. This, together with the previous bombardment, led them to believe an infantry attack to be imminent. "Gas-attack!" they shouted down the dug-outs. Gas masks were hurriedly put on and in a few moments fantastic shapes climbed up out of the earth and lined the edges of the craters and what remained, of the German front trench. Red rockets hissed into the air giving the signal to the German artillery which quickly placed a barrage of shells in No Man's Land to check a possible infantry advance behind the gas. The yellow fumes passed over the German line closely followed by reddish-brown smoke clouds and the battle zone was enveloped in a dark, muddy fog, but there was still no sign of an infantry attack. The fantastic shapes crawled back again into the depths of the earth.

During the afternoon aerial torpedoes, fired from heavy mortars in the British front line, made their first appearance. Coming down almost perpendicularly from a great height, these monsters bored deep into the ground and then burst. Tons of earth and great blocks of chalk and rock were hurled into the air, leaving craters some 12 feet deep and 15 feet in diameter. Only deep dug-outs of great strength could stand the shock and the weaker ones were crushed to atoms with all that they contained. The Germans, who up till now had endured the inferno outside almost with indifference, began to feel alarmed. Every nerve was strained as they sat listening to the devilish noise and waited for the dull thud of the next torpedo as it buried itself in the ground and then the devastating explosion. The concussion put out the candles and acetylene lights in the deepest dug-outs. The walls rocked like the sides of a ship and the darkness was filled with smoke and gas fumes.

A fresh note, too, now mingled with the thundering of the heavy guns, as the shells from a British rival to the German "Big Bertha" shrieked through the air and spent their weight against the redoubts and principal strong points in and behind the German lines. A hail of shells of lesser calibre was also poured into the villages near the front, such as Miraumont, Irles, Grandcourt, Courcelette, Pys and Pozières, the ruin of which was quickly completed. The roofs and walls of the cottages collapsed, blocking the streets, and the foundation of the roads was torn up, the deep craters preventing any traffic along them. Some of the villages near the front were also badly affected by the gas that swept over them from time to time from the British trenches. Any remaining shrubs and plants were withered by it. Rats, mice, moles and much else came out of holes and corners and lay dead about the place. Civilians with streaming eyes and choking for breath implored the Germans to give them gas masks, but instead, they were at last compulsorily transported from the danger zone. As the cellars gave little cover against the heaviest shells the villages were also gradually evacuated by most of the troops sheltering in them.

The 27th and 28th of June brought a similar picture of continuous devastation which was increased by heavy rains. The bombardment continued to appear without method, an intense and apparently wild shelling, then carefully observed heavy artillery fire by individual batteries, then trench mortar bombs and aerial torpedoes or gas-attacks, or again a sudden tornado of shells, with occasional periods of complete quiet. During calm intervals at night patrols would move forward from the British trenches across No Man's Land to inspect the damage done and to see if any Germans were still alive. Some of these patrols were captured and, from statements made,[3] it was concluded that a combined French and British attack was to be delivered on both sides of the Ancre and the Somme at 5 a.m. on the 29th of June. At that hour the whole German line stood to arms, all units were ready at their posts, reinforcements had been brought up during the night and the artillery ammunition comparatively replenished. The morning, however, passed quiet and no attack developed. In the afternoon the British bombardment was resumed with all its former violence, swelling at times to gigantic proportions and then falling off, only to concentrate the more intensely on some small sector of the front. Then suddenly it would begin again along the whole line and move slowly eastward towards the rear defences, settling for a time on the villages, redoubts and battery positions. The British gunners, whom the Germans imagined sweating through the heat of the day at their work of destruction, appeared to be indefatigable. Now and again the storm of shells would be followed by a gas attack, with occasionally a small infantry advance, as if once more to test the strength of the German defences. In most cases, however, the trench garrison sufficient warning from the sentries with their periscopes, either in the concrete recesses,

---

3   In the regimental history of the 119th Reserve Infantry Regiment it is stated that this information was given by a Polish Jew [British regiment not given], captured by their 10th Company.

or, if these had been destroyed, from the dugout entrances, and a heavy machine-gun and rifle fire greeted the attacks. Few reached the German position.

The 30th of June was a repetition of the previous six days. The German front defences no longer existed as such. Wire entanglements had been swept away; iron stakes and posts dotted along about the front, with thick strands of barbed wire knotted around them, were all that remained to mark the position of this first, and exceedingly strong, protection of the front trench system. The trench itself had gone. A succession of shell-craters replaced it, and half-closed holes in the earth marked where the exits from the deep dug-outs had still been kept open. The steps down to them were, however, buried in the fallen earth and stones, so much so that it was difficult to get a footing to climb up the steep slope to daylight. In some cases both entrances to a dug-out had been completely blocked up and since there was no underground gallery to connect one dug-out with another the men inside were suffocated.[4] The look-out shelters and bomb-proof observation posts now a heap of ruins, a mass of twisted steel rails and broken blocks of concrete. All the communication trenches had also been blocked and many of them completely destroyed.

The First Assault: 1st of July 1916

The colossal expenditure of money, guns, ammunition and human energy had done its work and the German position now indeed seemed ready for assault. Every yard of ground was churned up and churned again, the land being reduced to a desert of mud and shell-craters. Trees were uprooted and slashed to pieces, houses and cottages were razed to the ground and their ruins crushed to powder, so that whole villages were no longer recognizable. In spite of the devastation and chaos on the surface, the majority of the defenders in those of the deep underground dug-outs still intact had, however, survived the ordeal. For seven days and nights they had sat on the long wooden benches or on the wire beds in the evil-smelling dug-outs, some 20 feet and more below ground. The incessant noise and the need for constant watchfulness had allowed them little sleep, and ever-present, too, had been the fear that their dug-outs might at any time become a living tomb from which escape would be impossible. Warm food had seldom reached them during the bombardment, so that they had had to live on the supplies, three dumps each of 2,000 rations in each company sector as well as supplies of chocolate and mineral waters, previously stored in the front line.

After a restless night, during which the British artillery concentrated its fire chiefly against the rear defences and communications, the 1st of July broke clear and cloudless. With the first light of day British aeroplanes filled the air and captive balloons ascended all along the western horizon. The early hours between dawn and sunrise were comparatively quiet apart from isolated shell bursts. At 6.30 a.m., however, a bombardment of an intensity as yet unparalleled suddenly burst out again along the whole front. At first it was most severe in the centre, about Thiepval and Beaumont, but it quickly spread over the entire line from north of the Ancre to south of the Somme. For the next hour continuous lines of great fountains of earth, rocks, smoke and debris, played constantly into the air and, as one German describes it, it seemed as if all the fiends of the infernal regions had been loosed to tear up and destroy the entire district. The giant explosions of the heaviest shells

---

4   As a result of the experiences during this bombardment, the German dug-outs were afterwards connected in series by underground galleries.

were the only distinguishable noises in the continuous thunder of the bombardment and the short regular intervals of their bursts gave it a certain rhythm.

All trace of the front defence system was now lost and with only a few exceptions all the telephone cables connecting it with the rear lines and batteries were destroyed, in spite of the depth at which they had been laid. Through the long trench-periscopes held up out of the dug-outs could be seen a mass of steel helmets above the British parapet. The storm-troops were evidently ready, standing shoulder to shoulder, and there was little doubt that the infantry assault was imminent. The Germans in their dug-outs, each with a beltful of hand-grenades, therefore waited ready, rifle in hand, for the bombardment to lift from the front defence zone to the rear defences. It was of vital importance not to lose a second in reaching the open before the British infantry could arrive at the dug-out entrances.

At 7.30 a.m. the storm of shells ceased as suddenly as they had begun. The Germans at once clambered up the steep shafts to daylight and ran to the nearest craters, singly or in groups. Machine guns with their heavy ammunition boxes were pulled up out of the dug-outs and hurriedly placed in position and a rough firing line was thus established. The various German diaries, as also statements made by German prisoners taken at the time, show that the shell-craters were considered as good or better for defensive purposes than the original trenches. In the latter the men's positions were always known, but, when they were posted among the craters, it was impossible to locate the machine guns and rifles. The defence was also made more mobile as the men could rapidly take up fresh positions in other shell holes either in front, in rear or facing the flank.

It seems, from reading the German accounts that the success or failure of the attack depended in great measure on the closeness with which the advancing lines of infantry followed the artillery barrage, a matter that apparently was not carried out uniformly by the British assaulting divisions. In some cases, particularly on the southern part of the front about Montauban, Mametz and Fricourt, the leading assaulting lines had advanced 15 to 20 minutes before the conclusion of the first period of the bombardment and lay out in the open close to the German position, so that when, at 7.36 a.m., the artillery lifted from the rear defences they had reached the entrances to the German dug-outs before the Germans had had time to clamber up out of them. Where this was done the assaulting lines were able to cross No Man's Land and through the German first defence zone with little loss. In some other parts of the front, however, the infantry advance did not leave the British front trench till the first artillery lift, at 7.30 a.m., and the Germans were thus given time to get into position among the shell-craters.

Instances of both cases are to be found on the front of the German 26th Reserve Division which, with the 28th Reserve Division on its left, bore together the full weight of the British assault. The 26th Reserve Division, the accounts of which are more complete, held from Ovillers past Thiepval and across the Ancre to Beaumont and Serre, a frontage of 9,000 yards. All its 4 regiments were engaged, each with 2 battalions in the front line and 1 in support with the recruit battalion in reserve. The left, between Ovillers and Thiepval, was held by the 180th Infantry Regiment, with the 99th Reserve Regiment between Thiepval and the Ancre. North of the Ancre to Serre, the line was continued by the 119th Reserve and the 121st Reserve Infantry Regiment. The attack of the British X Corps, the central assaulting corps of the Fourth Army, on the front Ovillers—Thiepval—Beaumont, therefore, came up against the 180th and 99th Reserve Infantry Regiments, its 32nd Division against the 180th Infantry Regiment, and its 36th (Ulster) Division against the 99th Reserve.

To take first a description of the fighting on the front of the German 180th Infantry Regiment. The account will be given practically as it stands and the natural German bias must be pardoned. While the Germans were running out from the dug-outs and taking up their positions in the craters nearby, a series of extended lines of British infantry began to move forward from the British trenches. The first line appeared to continue without end to right and left. It was quickly followed by a second line, then a third and a fourth. They came on at a steady, comfortable pace, as if expecting to find nothing alive in the front trenches and only perhaps a weak resistance in the second and third line trenches. Some appeared to be carrying kodaks and stopping to take photographs that would perpetuate the memory of their triumphal march across the German defences. The front line, preceded by a thin line of skirmishers and bombers, was now half-way across No Man's Land. "Get ready!" was passed along the German front from crater to crater, and heads peered over the crater-edges as final positions were taken up for the best view and machine guns were mounted firmly in place. A few moments later, when the leading British line was within 200 yards, the rattle of machine-gun and rifle fire broke out along the whole line of craters and a hail of lead swept into the advancing lines. Some fired kneeling so as to get a better target over the broken ground, while others stood up in the excitement of the moment, regardless of their own safety, to fire into the crowd of men in front of them. Red rockets sped up into the blue sky as a signal to the artillery and immediately afterwards, a mass of shells from the German batteries in rear tore through the air and burst among the advancing lines. Whole sections seemed to fall, and the rear formations, moving in closer order, quickly scattered.

The advance rapidly crumbled under this hail of shells and bullets. All along the line men could be seen throwing their arms into the air and collapsing, never to move again. Badly-wounded rolled about in their agony and others less severely injured crawled to the nearest shell holes for shelter. The British soldier, however, in the words of the author of *Die Schwaben an der Ancre*, has no lack of courage and once his hand is set to the plough he is not easily turned from his purpose. The extended lines, though badly shaken and with many gaps, now came on all the faster. Instead of a leisurely walk they covered the ground in short rushes at the double, halting for a moment where the ground gave cover. Within a few minutes the leading troops had reached within a stone's-throw of the German crater-line, and, while some Germans continued to fire at point-blank range, others threw hand-grenades among them. The British bombers answered back, throwing grenades into the craters, while the infantry rushed forward with bayonets fixed. The noise of battle now became indescribable. The shouting of orders and the shrill British cheers as they charged forward could be heard above the violent and intense fusillade of machine guns and rifles and the bursting bombs, and above the deep thunderings of the artillery and the shell explosions. With all this was mingled the moans and groans of the wounded, the cries for help and the last screams of death. Again and again the extended lines of British infantry broke against the German defence like waves against a cliff, only to be beaten back and then to be brought forward again by fresh waves of men, which in their turn were decimated and checked by a hail of lead. It was an amazing spectacle of unexampled gallantry, courage and bulldog determination on both sides. Only in one sector, that of the 9th Company (3rd Battalion) immediately south of Thiepval, did the

British succeed in breaking through, and here so many of the dugouts had been broken in by the bombardment that few of the company had survived. The adjoining companies were, however, quick to see the danger and placed flanking parties of bombers to prevent an extension of the gap. Moving straight to its front the British force which had broken through approached the second line trench, but a German reserve company, hurried forward, was in time to save it and held up the advance. Fresh British troops were now sent into the gap, but they were taken under cross machine-gun fire from either flank and, suffering heavily, were unable to pass through. A detachment of 150 to 200 men, approaching by a sunken road in close order was seen by a German machine-gun crew in a forward crater and annihilated, only 15 getting away. The German bombers gradually advanced from the flanks, moving forward from crater to crater until they had formed a line cutting off the retreat of the British force still in front of the second position. At about midday the latter, finding itself unsupported, began to move back. The reserve company at once advanced and, attacked in front and rear, the whole British force was surrounded. By the evening the attack had come to a standstill and the 180th Infantry Regiment was again in possession of the whole of its original front.

Turning to the diary of the British 32nd Division which attacked the front south of Thiepval, one finds that: "At 7.30 a.m. when the artillery lifted on to the German support line, the infantry advanced to the attack. ... They [the 96th Brigade] were unable to gain the enemy's trenches, as from the moment that they left the shelter of their front line they came under heavy machine-gun fire. Cover was taken in shell holes in No Man's Land and although further advance was impossible, many of the Germans who exposed themselves freely in their endeavour to get targets, were shot by rifle and Lewis-gun fire." And then, regarding the breakthrough in one place: "The 15th Lancashire Fusiliers [96th Brigade] advancing in two extended columns, through woods and broken ground, made rapid progress. At 9.10 a.m. its leading troops were seen east of Thiepval, beyond the German front defences. At 9.15 a.m. the 16th Lancashire Fusiliers moved out from our front line to support the 15th. As soon as they got into No Man's Land they were met by heavy machine-gun fire and were forced back into our line with heavy loss. ... At dusk the situation was that some of the 96th Brigade were believed to be east of Thiepval and cut off."

The German 99th Infantry Regiment, which held a front from Thiepval to across the Ancre has, however, a different tale to tell. One reads in their account that the British overran their position in the first rush and overcame the weak resistance. Before the Germans had time to emerge from their dug-outs, British sentries were standing on guard at the entrances with apparently no inclination to descend. They feared, says the German account, the unknown world of the dug-outs and contented themselves with throwing down hand-grenades and stink-bombs from time to time. In the meantime the remainder of the British advance pressed on across the open through the Schwaben Redoubt towards Grandcourt, 3,000 yards, beyond. There ends the story of the defence of the German front line position.

Turning to the diary of the 36th (Ulster) Division to find some reason for the great difference between the two attacks, its own north of Thiepval and that of the 32nd Division south of Thiepval, one reads: "The troops began to leave their assembly trenches about 7 a.m. and by 7.30 a.m. the leading battalions were lying in the open within 200 yards of the enemy's front trench. No difficulty was experienced in this. At 7.30 a.m. the troops assaulted and captured the enemy's front and support lines with practically no fighting and very few casualties. At 8.55 a.m. the enemy's third line was reached."

Part II

The previous article of this series contained an account from the German point of view of the seven days' bombardment prior to the Somme offensive of the Franco-British Armies on the 1st of July, 1916, followed by an account of the first assault by the British divisions. The opposing forces were at a comparative strength of one British division (averaging 14 battalions) to one German regiment (3 battalions), each on a frontage of some 2,000 yards, the sectors roughly corresponding. The left flank regiment, the 180th, of the German 26th Reserve Division, holding south of Thiepval between Thiepval and Ovillers, was attacked by the British 32nd Division, but the assaulting lines started too late behind the artillery barrage and were held up by machine-gun and rifle fire in No Man's Land. North of Thiepval, the 36th (Ulster) Division, advancing immediately behind the artillery barrage, had, however, broken through the central sector of the 99th Reserve Infantry Regiment.

On the Front of the British 36th Division

The capture of the German front trench by the British 36th (Ulster) Division in the first rush of its two leading brigades, 108th and 109th, enabled the successive lines to press on at once, leaving small parties to watch the dug-out entrances in the front trench and to capture any Germans who still survived.

Beyond the German front line the ground continues to slope upwards at a steep gradient, rising 250 feet in the 1,000 yards that lie between it and the summit of the Thiepval ridge, one of the many dominating features in this great expanse of rolling upland. In front of the Ulster Division lay the northern end and highest point of this ridge, and on it the Germans had constructed the Schwaben Redoubt (*Feste Schwaben*), a great parallelogram of trenches with a front face of 600 yards. This work had a fine command over the surrounding country. To north and west the ground fell steeply to the deep-cut valley of the Ancre, while to eastward it overlooked the German battery positions and the communications leading back to Bapaume. Some 400 yards back was the eastern side of the Redoubt, and 600 yards beyond again was the German second line position, the Grandcourt line, that lay north and south through Grandcourt and Pozières, with a strong work, the *Feste Staufen*,[5] midway between those two villages.

The 108th and 109th (Ulster) Brigades, advancing up the slope at a rapid pace, reached the summit before 8 a.m. and rushed the Schwaben Redoubt. Its small German garrison, a support company for the front defences, taken by surprise, had not manned the Redoubt before the British were in among them, and they surrendered without any organized resistance. The two brigades had reached their objective and in their advance had annihilated the centre battalion of the 99th Reserve Infantry Regiment, capturing over 500 prisoners.[6] The 107th Brigade following, in support, now passed through the two assaulting brigades and began its advance on the German second position, the Grandcourt

---

5   Named by the British "Stuff Redoubt."
6   A number of these prisoners belonged to drafts from the depôts of other regiments and had not yet altered the numbers on their shoulder straps, a fact that apparently led to the belief by local commanders that a considerably stronger force held the front than was actually the case.

line. Instead of waiting till 10 a.m., as originally ordered for this movement, the Brigade pressed ahead and thus overtook the artillery barrage. The leading lines carried on into the barrage now about the Grandcourt position, and lost very heavily, the remainder falling back to the eastern side of the Schwaben Redoubt and the Hansa line, an intermediary trench leading from the eastern side of the Redoubt down the northern, edge of the ridge to the Ancre valley. "Had it not, been for this barrage," writes a diarist (107th Brigade), "we could have taken the Grandcourt line sitting."

The situation as reported to British X Corps headquarters by 9 a.m., was that the 36th Division had crossed the German front defences and was in possession of the Schwaben Redoubt; that the 32nd Division, on the right opposite Thiepval, had failed to capture the front position[7] and was held up in No Man's Land; and that the advance of the 29th Division, on the left north of the Ancre, was also checked. In these circumstances it was clear that, if the 36th Division continued to advance farther into the enemy's defensive system, its leading troops would be threatened with envelopment. At 9.16 a.m. a message had been sent, therefore, to the 36th Division to stay the advance of its 107th Brigade on the Grandcourt line until the situation on the flanks had improved. The only means of forwarding this order was by messenger, and by the time it arrived at 107th Brigade headquarters the battalions had already advanced beyond recall and were committed to the attack of the Grandcourt line.[8]

The fate of this venture of the 107th Brigade on the further slope of the Thiepval ridge, with both flanks in the air and unsupported, is best watched from the German side of the battle front. The line from Ovillers through Thiepval to the Ancre was held by the 52nd Reserve Infantry Brigade (26th Reserve Division XIV Reserve Corps), all Württemburg troops. The 180th Infantry Regiment was defending successfully the front position from Ovillers to south of Thiepval. Thiepval itself was still held by the left battalion of the 99th Reserve Infantry Regiment, but the centre and right of that regiment, holding from Thiepval to the Ancre, had broken, most of the defenders being taken prisoner before they could emerge from their deep dug-outs, the supporting companies in the Schwaben Redoubt and the Hansa line being also overrun. Owing to the smoke and dust of battle which hung along the ridge in the still morning air, it was not clear to the German observers in the Grandcourt line whether the troops they could see forming up and reorganizing in and near the Schwaben Redoubt were friends or foes, so at first no action was taken. It was not until the fresh British battalions (107th Brigade) began to move out from the Redoubt and advance towards them that all doubts were put at rest. The only force available to occupy this sector of the Grandcourt position was the recruit battalion of the 180th Infantry Regiment and one machine-gun company, in and behind Grandcourt, and as soon as the artillery barrage lifted from the Grandcourt line they manned that sector of it in and south of the village. The British now tried to advance again from the eastern face of the Redoubt, but this time they were met by heavy machine-gun and rifle fire; nevertheless, some fifty men were able to reach the emplacements and covered trenches of the German 5th Field Battery in a fold of ground, Battery Valley (*Artilleriemulde*), 100 yards in front of the Grandcourt position, whilst others, farther south, were able to enter the position itself at a point where it was unoccupied south of the Grandcourt—Thiepval road crossing.

---

7 See Part I of this chapter.
8 See 36th Divisional and Brigade Diaries, July 1916. *History of the 36th (Ulster) Division.*

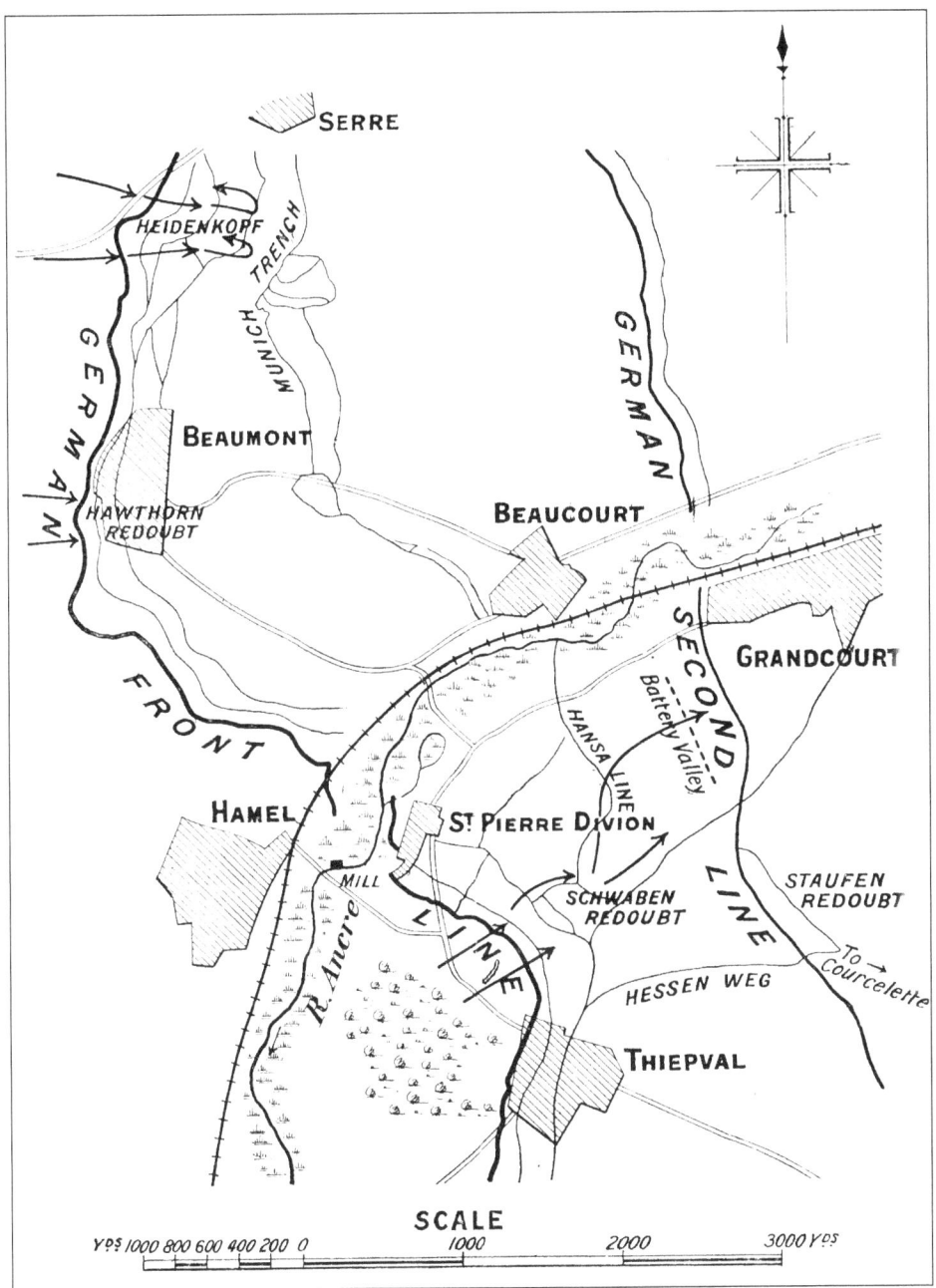

7. Somme, 1 July 1916 – Position of German 26th Reserve Division

By 10 a.m. the situation on the front of the 26th Reserve Division was critical. Although the 119th Reserve Infantry Regiment on the north bank of the Ancre still held and the line from Thiepval south ward to Ovillers was unshaken, the gap that had been forced in the centre, north of Thiepval, had serious possibilities. Constant messages were received for help from the left company of the 99th Reserve Infantry Regiment in Thiepval as it feared an attack at any moment against its right flank and rear, from the Schwaben Redoubt, which would make its position untenable.

The Schwaben Redoubt was clearly the vital point. General von Soden, therefore, ordered General Auwäter, commanding the 52nd Reserve Infantry Brigade, to retake the Redoubt at all costs and sent forward a battalion of the 8th Bavarian Reserve Infantry Regiment to reinforce him for the purpose.[9]

To give the British no time to consolidate a fresh position, and, at the same time, to deny him as far as possible the advantages of a frontal defence, General Auwäter ordered the counter-attack to develop as soon as possible and to be delivered by three groups concentrically from north-east, east, and south-east. On the right a detachment consisting of three recruit companies, a pioneer company, and two machine-gun companies[10] was to attack from Grandcourt. The centre and left attacks were to be carried out by the battalion of the 8th Bavarian Reserve Infantry Regiment, now moving from Courcelette by the communication trenches, *Staufen Riegel* and *Hessen Weg*, towards the Staufen Redoubt. The orders were issued from 52nd Brigade headquarters at 11 a.m. and General Auwäter waited in feverish anxiety for the beginning of the counter-attack.

It was incomprehensible that the British after capturing the Schwaben Redoubt should continue their advance on the Grandcourt position without first wheeling south behind the Germans holding out in Thiepval and Ovillers. Such a movement was therefore expected at any moment and the consequences might well be disastrous. Both Divisional and Corps headquarters were equally impatient and kept sending urgent messages to press the counterattack, but it was not until 4 p.m. that it began to develop. The delay had been in great measure due to the fact that both the orders for the attack and the final arrangements between the commanders of the attacking groups had had to be communicated by messenger.

Just as General von Soden, commanding the 26th Reserve Division, had marked the Schwaben Redoubt as the key to the German situation between the Ancre and Ovillers, so for British X Corps headquarters Thiepval village appeared the decisive factor in the British situation. The 49th Division, the reserve division of the X Corps, had been ordered, therefore, to launch a frontal attack against the village and this had been attempted early in the afternoon, 2.45 p.m. As soon as its leading brigade—the 146th—was seen to advance from Thiepval Wood, that lay in the British line west of the village, all available batteries of the 26th Reserve Division were turned on the attacking lines, and the left company of

---

9 The 10th Bavarian Infantry Division consisted of the 6th Reserve, 8th Reserve and 16th Infantry Regiments and the 19th and 20th Field Artillery Regiments. The Division had been moved up on the 14th of June to Bapaume behind and as a reserve to, the XIV Reserve Corps.

10 Including No. 2 Machine-Gun Company of the 119th Reserve Infantry Regiment north of the Ancre, which was sent at once to reinforce the recruit battalion in Grandcourt.

the 99th Reserve Infantry Regiment succeeded in checking the assault before it reached the front trench. The defence put up by this company in Thiepval village throughout the day had been remarkable and it was now assisted by a quantity of ammunition and hand-grenades that arrived during the early afternoon along the communication trenches from Courcelette.

Reports from the Schwaben Redoubt which had reached X Corps headquarters showed that the troops holding it were hard pressed and their numbers diminishing rapidly owing to the continuous shelling by German batteries on the north side of the Ancre which enfiladed the main trenches of the work and the line of the Hansa position. Moreover, ammunition was failing owing to the great difficulty of moving from the British original front line across No Man's Land to the Redoubt, the whole of this area being swept by machine-gun fire from Thiepval village as soon as any movement was noticed.

At 4.40 p.m., therefore, a message was sent from X Corps headquarters ordering the 49th Division to place the 146th Brigade at the disposal of the 36th Division for the purpose of rallying the Ulster troops and holding the Schwaben Redoubt at all costs. Two battalions, the order concluded, should suffice "as aeroplanes flying low report very few hostile troops engaged in the counterattack." There was, however, great difficulty in reorganizing the 146th Brigade after the failure of its attack on Thiepval village, and it was not until three hours later, 8 p.m., that two of its battalions were ready to reinforce the Ulster Division. By that time the opportunity that had been open throughout the day of attacking southward from the Schwaben Redoubt behind the Thiepval defences had passed.[11]

The German counter-attack from the Grandcourt line began soon after 4 p.m. On the right the three recruit companies of the 180th Regiment, in extended lines under Major Prager, advanced from Grandcourt village, keeping along the lower slope of the ridge, following the Ancre valley. In this manner they reached the lower part of the Hansa line and thence began to bomb their way up it towards the Schwaben Redoubt. Those Ulstermen who had reached Battery Valley in the morning were either shot down or taken prisoner in their effort to get back. The centre attack, from the Staufen Redoubt, was delivered by three companies of the 8th Bavarian Reserve Regiment led by Major Beyerköhler, but their first effort, advancing in widely extended lines across the open, was frustrated by the British artillery that promptly opened on them. They then decided to move up under cover of the *Hessen Weg*, the main communication trench leading from Courcelette to Thiepval, deploying from it when opposite the south-eastern corner of the Schwaben Redoubt. The left attack, to be delivered by the remaining company of the battalion of the 8th Bavarian Reserve Regiment, was originally intended to move along the *Hessen Weg* and thence deliver an attack against the southern face of the Redoubt. Owing to the change of plan of the central attacking group, all four companies of the Bavarian battalion now joined forces in the Hessen Weg for the attack on the south-eastern corner of the Redoubt.

---

11 During the morning an officer's patrol from the Schwaben Redoubt had moved along the Mouquet switch trench that led from the Redoubt behind Thiepval village to Moquet Farm and reported all clear as far as could be seen.

By 6 p.m. the German pressure on the Schwaben Redoubt was tightening. Some of their troops, who were still holding the front defences about St. Pierre Divion in the Ancre valley, were bombing southward and had already retaken a considerable part of their front trench that had been captured by the Ulster Division during the morning, and were thereby threatening to cut off those British troops holding the Schwaben Redoubt. In the Hansa line the three recruit companies had worked up close to the northern face of the Redoubt, but an attempt to rush it had been driven back with heavy loss. An attempt by the Bavarians to rush its south-eastern corner had also failed. About 7 p.m. fresh attempts were made to assault the British position, but they were again driven off with heavy loss, both Major Prager and Major Beyerköhler being among the casualties. It was now clear to the Germans that the capture of the Redoubt was not possible without an intense artillery bombardment to prepare it for assault, and word was sent back accordingly.

At 9 p.m., soon after sunset, all the guns of the 26th Reserve Division suddenly turned on the Redoubt. From north-east, east, and south-east their shells came hurtling through the air and crashed into the work. The bombardment continued at an intense rate for an hour and then, at 10 p.m. the survivors of the recruit companies on the right and the Bavarian companies on the left moved to the assault. Desperate hand-to-hand fighting ensued in the failing light, but, after half an hour, the Schwaben Redoubt was in German hands. A German diarist describes it as being in a chaotic condition and "strewn with 700 dead of the gallant Ulster Division." A British account of the affair (107th Brigade) states that the senior officers in the Schwaben Redoubt, when they saw themselves counterattacked on all sides, decided that their position was untenable. As both flanks were unsupported, the enemy still holding Thiepval village to the south and the original line astride the Ancre to the north, they ordered the Redoubt to be evacuated in order to avoid being surrounded. In the day's fighting the three Ulster brigades had lost in casualties 5,500 all ranks, a third of their strength.

By midnight on the 1st of July the Thiepval ridge was thus again in German possession. During the night the two remaining battalions of the 8th Bavarian Reserve Regiment were advanced to the Hansa line and the Schwaben Redoubt ready to reinforce the front defences between Thiepval and the Ancre.

On the Front of the British 29th Division

On the front of the British 29th Division opposite Beaumont Hamel, north of the Ancre, the infantry advance had been timed to leave the front trench at the first artillery lift and had thereby given time to the Germans to get out of their dug-outs and man the shell craters. The result of the attack was consequently very similar to that on the front of the 32nd Division[12] opposite Ovillers. At 7.20 a.m., however, ten minutes before the artillery lift, a mine[13] was exploded under Hawthorn Redoubt, a strong work in the German front line on Hawthorn ridge, immediately west of Beaumont village. Two platoons of the 2/Royal Fusiliers, carrying with them four machine guns, at once rushed across No Man's Land to hold the crater, with the idea of getting a footing in the German front position before the main infantry assault. This they succeeded in doing, and, within five minutes of their arrival at the crater, their machine guns were in position on its front lip. The remainder of the Royal Fusiliers came under a heavy machine-gun fire and failed to reach the line

---

12 See Part I in this chapter.
13 With 40,600 lbs. of ammonal.

of the German entanglement though a few got as far as the mine crater. For a similar reason the 1/Lancashire Fusiliers on the left, were unable to pass the line of the German wire, and after losing heavily in their efforts, the survivors took refuge in shell-holes in No Man's Land. The supporting battalions, 1/Dublin Fusiliers and 16/Middlesex, were at first unable to leave the British front trenches owing to the intensity of the fire, and, when at 8 a.m. they finally went forward, they, too, were held up in No. Man's Land, though some of the 16/Middlesex reached the crater. At 9.15 a.m. a further effort was made to capture the front line by sending forward the 88th Brigade, but its two leading battalions, the 1/Newfoundland and 1/Essex, were checked, a few men reaching the crater which seemed to act as a magnet for the advancing lines. The casualties were extremely heavy; of the 750 men of the Newfoundlands, for example, only 40 unwounded returned to the British lines. At 10.5 a.m., on hearing of the failure of these several attacks, the 29th Divisional Commander directed that no more troops should be sent forward until the situation had improved. Such briefly is the British story of the first assault in this sector.

The German 119th Reserve Infantry Regiment held the 2,000 yards of front facing the British 29th Division, in front of Beaumont-Hamel. While the intense bombardment was still in progress, so runs the German account, a tremendous explosion suddenly rent the air, drowning for the moment all the noise of the bombardment. For some seconds the sky was darkened by the heavy clouds of smoke that leapt upwards out of the ground and a rain of stones, chalk and débris fell down on the German position to right and left. The whole of a small salient in the German front line on the Hawthorn ridge was blown into the air with its garrison of some thirty men. The explosion left a giant crater, 60 to 70 yards in diameter and 40 feet deep, in the chalk soil, the ground being white all round and looking like a great patch of snow on the hillside. The adjacent dug-outs were for the most part broken in or their entrances blocked, burying those inside. In this manner the entire 9th Company of the Regiment was put out of action in a few moments. The firing of the mine was regarded by the German regiments to right and left as a signal for the infantry assault, and, although in reality no such meaning was intended, it undoubtedly had the effect of preparing the German defenders north of the Ancre to meet the infantry when a few minutes later they advanced.[14] Wave after wave of men rose from the British front trench and began to move forward as if on parade, their bayonets glistening in the sun. Eight waves in all were seen advancing across the 300 yards of No Man's Land, carrying with them plank bridges and steps for crossing the German trenches, but before the leading wave had reached the line of the German entanglement the German companies to right and left of the mine crater were able to get out in the open and prepare the reception. The 10th and 11th Companies (119th Reserve Infantry Regiment) now poured such a hail of bullets from machine guns and rifles into the advancing lines that they were checked almost immediately and the supporting columns were unable to leave the British front trench. This fire was intensified by cross-fire from a number of machine guns in a work,

---

14 This fact was appreciated afterwards by the 29th Divisional Commander who in his report on the battle stated: "The explosion of the mine warned the enemy of the time of the assault, and better results might have been attained had the mine been fired some time previous to the hour fixed for zero."

the *Bergwerk*, on some rising ground behind Beaumont village, which fired over the heads of the front line defenders.

In the mine crater itself, however, the annihilation of the 9th Company had left a gap in the German line, and a small British detachment by a bold and rapid advance had succeeded in reaching it. Of the four dug-out entrances of this company, only one was not completely blocked by the explosion and from it a few survivors tried to extricate themselves. One of the men was widening the exit whilst on the steps behind him stood Lieut. Mühlbayer, the Company Commander, and others of his command. The British were already in the crater when the leading man came up out of the exit and his skull was promptly smashed in by a British bayonet, the body falling back down the steps on to those below. Sergt. Davidsohn then went up and from the dug-out exit threw a flame bomb in the face of the British sentry. Hand-grenades and stink bombs were sent down in reply, compelling a hasty retreat to the back of the dug-out. A demand to surrender shouted down from the top was not answered for the Germans still hoped help would arrive, and so it did.

Immediately the explosion had occurred, an order was sent to the supports to reinforce the front line and two platoons, one of the 7th Company and one of the 12th Company, hurried forward from the support trench across the open field, followed by the remainder of the two companies by the slower route of the communication, trenches. A British airman flying low threw bombs on the two platoons as they ran forward, but little damage was done. At first an attempt was made to rush the mine crater from the front, but the fire of a British machine gun which was already in a commanding position on the lip of the crater stopped it. The two platoons had lost heavily from this gun when two non-commissioned officers, Hess and Rapp, of the 12th Company succeeded in sniping and killing the men working it. Seeing the situation at the crater, Lieut. Blessing in the support trench of the 10th Company, had quickly collected some bombers, Brose, Fauser, Lutz and Kappelmann, and advanced by way of the front trench towards the mine crater, while Sergeant Moyle with bombers of the 7th and 12th Companies tried to work forward from the other flank. At first these, efforts were of no avail, the bombers being checked by machine-gun and rifle fire from the crater.

After further sniping by selected marksmen, in which more of the British machine gunners were killed, a fresh bomb attack was made from both flanks and the Germans now succeeded in crossing into the crater pit, the British being compelled to withdraw to the farther lip of the crater, beyond which they took up a fresh stand. They left a number of dead-and wounded, including among the latter a subaltern who had shown much gallantry and was taken prisoner. The Germans of the 9th Company still in the dug-out were now free to emerge and they joined forces with their rescuers.

The remnants of the 9th Company were scarcely free of their underground prison before fresh waves of infantry were seen to be advancing from the British trenches. All the batteries behind Beaumont and about Beaumont were fully engaged in assisting the German troops south of the Ancre between Thiepval and Grandcourt, who were hard pressed and in a critical situation owing to the loss of the Schwaben Redoubt. The infantry in front of Beaumont were left, therefore, to help themselves, and the combined fire of the 7th, 9th, 10th and 12th Companies, with their machine guns, was able to check this further attack on the village before it reached the front position, though again a number of men reached the farther lip of the mine crater. A machine gun from a salient in the front trench of the regiment on the right, the 121st Reserve Infantry Regiment, however, was able to enfilade this farther side of the crater and, sweeping it to and fro with fire, soon made it untenable. In a few minutes all those holding it were running back across No Man's Land pursued by bullets, and, by 10.30 a.m., the situation was completely restored and the battle over, so far as this sector was concerned.

The outlook from the German front trench was terrible. The chlorine gas had bleached and eaten away the grass. Khaki forms, dead and wounded, lay in hundreds out in No Man's Land. In the mine crater itself and around its edges lay 200 to 300 British dead and wounded, including men of the Middlesex, Dublin Fusiliers and Newfoundland battalions. Alongside them was also a considerable number of dead of the 7th, 9th and 12th Companies (119th Reserve Infantry Regiment). The front trench here was no longer recognizable and no trace of the former dug-out entrances could be seen. Soon after midday, however, a movement of earth was noticed and out of a hole crawled Lieut. Renz with a few men. The explosion had filled the entrance, but the dug-out itself had stood the shock and after four hours of hard digging they had reached the surface. The losses of the 119th Reserve Regiment during the morning's battle were 101 dead, including 8 officers, and 191 wounded, but it had maintained its position unaided against greatly superior numbers.

On the Front of the British 4th Division

The assaulting battalions of the British 4th Division, attacking north of the 29th Division, were also unable to pass through the German front line except on the front of its left brigade, the 11th, opposite the Quadrilateral (*Heidenkopf*) Redoubt. The left companies of the 1/Rifle Brigade and the right companies of the 8/Royal Warwicks succeeded in storming the German front trench on both sides of this work and advancing beyond it without much loss. Reinforced by the 6/Royal Warwicks and the 1/Somerset Light Infantry, a fresh advance was made towards the German support trench. The position, about 10 a.m., was that the German support trench was held by small parties of the Somerset Light Infantry Rifle Brigade and 6th and 8/Warwicks, while the sector of the German front line that had been broken through was held more strongly by the same units. From this time onwards those troops holding the forward line within the German defences were subjected to heavy bombing attacks on both flanks and down the communication trenches. By 12 noon the majority of them had been pushed back to the German original front line trench. The heavy casualties among carriers who attempted to cross the German artillery barrage in No Man's Land prevented an adequate supply of bombs and trench mortars being sent forward. Efforts made after 11 a.m. by the 2/Lancashire Fusiliers and the 2/West Riding Regiment to reinforce the battalions at the Quadrilateral were unable to make progress beyond the crater. Fighting continued in this area during the afternoon, and, although there was some disorganization owing to the heavy losses in officers, the units continued to hold the line till midnight. By that time the evacuation of all the troops in the crater had been successfully carried out.[15] Now for the German account.

The German 121st Reserve Infantry Regiment between Beaumont and Serre opposed the British 4th Division on an almost equal frontage (2,000 yards). Near Serre and on the Serre— Mailly road a part of the German front line, the *Heidenkopf*, a strong redoubt named after a local commander, formed a pronounced duck-bill salient into No Man's

15 See British 4th Divisional Diary.

Land, a remnant of a former line that lay through Touvent Farm, west of Serre. The Germans had been pushed back closer to Serre but the *Heidenkopf,* named by the British the Quadrilateral Redoubt, had held firm and now formed the salient. It was realized that in the event of a general offensive the work, owing to its prominent position, could now no longer be definitely held, and the Germans, therefore, had undermined it with the idea of blowing it up as soon as the British entered it. On the morning of the 1st of July the *Heidenkopf* was only defended by one machine gun and by a few engineers who were to light the mine-fuze. At the moment of the assault, however, the machine gun jammed after the first few shots and by some error the engineers lit the mine-fuze too soon, with the result that both they and the machine-gun crew were blown up with the Redoubt before the British lines reached it. The effect, moreover, was greater than expected for it blocked up many of the German dug-outs near by, so that the assaulting lines were able to overrun the whole of the position of the 3rd Company, the right company of the 121st Reserve Infantry Regiment that held this sector of the front defences. A few men escaped down a communication trench to the support trench, but the majority of the company were held prisoner by British sentries posted at the dug-out entrances. The leading lines of the attacking troops meanwhile pressed on towards the regimental support trench, but the fire of a German machine gun, hastily placed in position, stopped a part of the advance, the British being compelled to take cover in a communication trench along which they moved. A German lieutenant with a handful of men thereupon piled up a sandbag barricade to block this trench. The barricade was hardly finished before the leading British arrived and threw bombs over it killing the lieutenant. The support trench was now occupied by the British on a narrow frontage and preparations were made to press on to Munich trench, the regimental reserve trench, 300 yards ahead. At this time fresh British lines were seen advancing across the open from the *Heidenkopf* gap, but they, were checked by machine-gun fire both from Munich trench and from the sectors of the front line to right and left of the gap that were still holding out.

For an hour the situation was at a deadlock, until the 3rd Battalion, the reserve battalion of the 121st Reserve Infantry Regiment, occupying this sector of Munich trench, was ordered to deliver a counter-stroke. A company and a bombing section of the neighbouring Regiment, the 169th (52nd Division), was to support it by an attack from the flank, from Serre. At the same time the German batteries behind Serre placed a barrage along the British front trench which effectively prevented the advance of supports to those who had broken through the German front defences.

The ground between the support trench and Munich trench was pitted with shell-craters caused by the British bombardment, and using these as protection the counter-attack of the 3rd Battalion developed rapidly. Working forward from front and flanks the Germans ran from crater to crater gradually forcing back the invaders, most of the fighting being with hand-grenades. The British, the German account admits, defended themselves with remarkable obstinacy and courage, barricading themselves at every step behind sandbags and showing fight to the last. Without supports, however, their supply of bombs and ammunition ran short and they were compelled to withdraw to the Heidenkopf crater by midday. Hand-to-hand fighting in the crater continued throughout the afternoon and it was not until dusk that the Germans succeeded in regaining the line of their front trench. The British survivors in the crater were forced to withdraw across No Man's Land during the night, leaving 200 prisoners and 28 machine guns in German hands. German accounts estimate that at the evacuation of the crater there were 150 German dead in and around it, and about three times that number of British.

Casualties of the British 11th Brigade alone are given in the 4th Divisional Diary as 145 officers and 3,060 other ranks, nearly 50 per cent of the brigade strength before the assault. The casualties of the German 121st Reserve Infantry Regiment during the day's fighting are given in the regimental history as approximately 170 dead and 290 wounded.

The front of the German 26th Reserve Division from the *Heidenkopf* Redoubt southward by Beaumont-Hamel, and across the Ancre to Thiepval and Ovillers was thus by the evening of the 1st of July still intact and unbroken. From the *Heidenkopf* to the Ancre the 121st and 119th Reserve Infantry Regiments, six battalions in all, had succeeded in holding their front without any outside assistance, that is, with their own local reserves, against the attacks of two British divisions, the 4th and 29th, some twenty-eight battalions. In the same way, south of the Ancre, the 99th Reserve and the 180th Infantry Regiments, with the help of one Bavarian battalion, had regained the Schwaben Redoubt and re-established their front position. The defence put up by these regiments during the day must be considered a notable achievement. It showed once again, as during the offensives of 1915 at Neuve Chapelle, Fromelles and Loos, that a gap made in a well-defended front line, small enough to be covered by infantry fire from the flanks, is of doubtful value unless the initial advantage can be followed up in the first rush of the assaulting troops. Once the defenders had re-established their position on the flanks of the gap, they were able to prevent the movement of supports and supplies across No Man's Land to the troops who had broken through, with the result that the latter, though attacked by comparatively small parties of the enemy from front and flanks, were gradually compelled to yield. The belated attempts made in each case to widen the gap by sending in fresh battalions had only resulted in heavy losses.

The 28th Reserve Division holding the line from Ovillers southward by Maricourt to the Somme had, however, given way—but that part of the story must wait for another time.

7

The German Defence of Bernafay and Trônes Woods 2–14 July 1916[1]

Part I

The result of the opening British assault on the 1st of July 1916, between the Somme and the Ancre was not altogether as anticipated. It had been hoped to press the offensive along the Thiepval—Pozières—Longueval ridge from the west, from the front La Boisselle—Thiepval, coming up eventually in a line with the French left about Hardecourt and thereby eliminating the Maricourt salient. The failure to make progress about La Boisselle and Thiepval, or even to capture the German front defences in that sector had, however, led General Haig to doubt the wisdom of continuing with his original scheme. On the other hand, the success of the British XIII and XV Corps, which had overrun the German front defences on a frontage of over three miles along the Montauban ridge, seemed to have prepared the way for an easier approach to the German second line on the Pozières—Longueval ridge, Although there would be considerable delay in transferring guns and supplies to this area, General Haig decided to take advantage of the break in the German line here instead of continuing to press the attack against the unbroken front defences between La Boisselle and Thiepval.

Immediately in front of the new British line along the northern slope of the Montauban ridge was Caterpillar Valley, the bed of a small winding brook rising in Trônes Wood and flowing westward to the Ancre. On the farther side of the brook the ground rises fairly steeply, 150 feet in 1,000 yards, up to the German second line trench that lay on top of the slope between Longueval and Bazentin le Grand. To the right Trônes Wood lay across the head of the valley, the German second line swinging round southwards from Longueval on the high ground beyond the wood, through Guillemont and thence towards Maurepas. It was now General Haig's intention to cross Caterpillar Valley and attack up the northern slope against the German second line on a front Longueval—Bazentin le Grand. Its capture would directly threaten the rear of the Germans still holding out about Ovillers and Thiepval, and thereby lead quickly, he hoped, to the clearing of the entire Pozières ridge.

---

1 The following list of the principal German authorities used for this article may be of interest to any reader wishing to trace further details of the fighting in this sector of the Somme battle front: *Der grosse Krieg*, Vol. 2: Schwarte; *Geschichte des Krieges*, Vol. 3: Stegemann; Bavarian Official History (*Die Bayern im Grossen Kriege*); *Bataille de la Somme; Feld. Art. Regt. Nr. 21*: Jancke; *Feld. Art. Regt. Nr. 57*: Uebe; *Feld. Art. Regt. Nr. 245*: Heydenreich; *Res. Inf. Regt. Nr. 104*: Braun; *Res. Inf. Regt. Nr. 106*: Bamberg; *Inf. Regt. Nr. 153*: Schmidt-Osswald; *Erinnerungsblätter des 178er*; Giesecke; *Inf. Regt. Nr. 182*: Pache.

BERNAFAY AND TRÔNES WOODS 2–14 JULY 1916

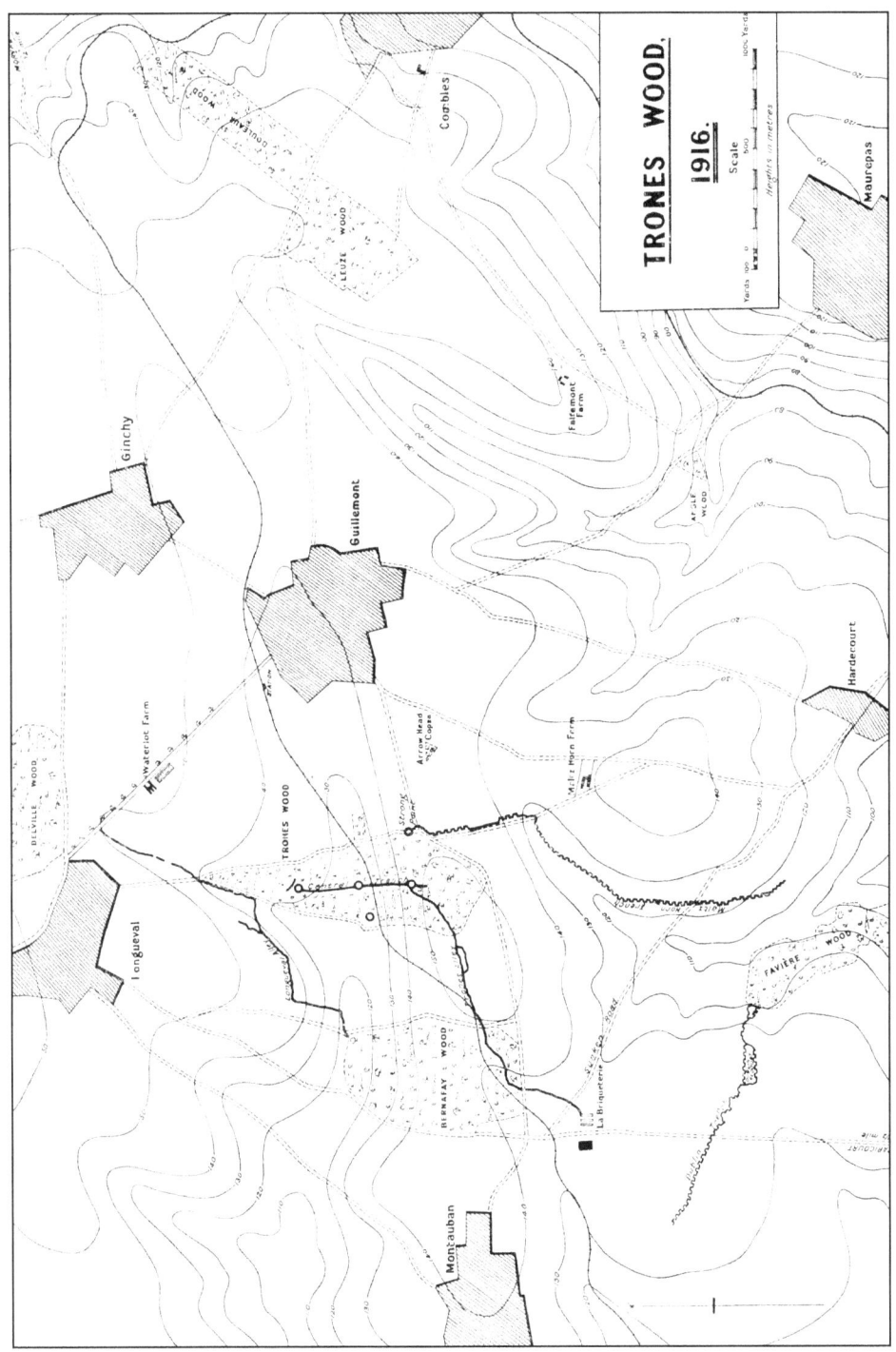

8. Trônes Wood

The attack was to be made up the open grass slope of the chalk downland on a frontage of 300 yards between Trônes Wood on the right and Mametz Wood on the left, both of which covered the length of the slope from the valley almost to the top of the ridge. Large sectors of the attacking troops could be enfiladed from these woods, and General Haig therefore directed General Rawlinson, commanding the Fourth Army, to capture these woods as a preparatory measure to protect the flanks of the main attack.

The few roads leading back southward from the Montauban ridge made very great the difficulties of transport and ammunition supplies. Nevertheless, in spite of the change of plan it was hoped to launch the main attack on the German second line about the 14th of July, and to have captured the woods on the flanks by that date. The capture of Mametz Wood and Contalmaison village on the left flank are described in Chapter 8[2] and it was carried out concurrently with the advance through Bernafay and Trônes Woods on the right.

The German Counter-Attack against the Montauban Salient, 2nd of July

By the afternoon of the 1st of July the remnants of the defenders of the German front trenches on the Montauban ridge, the left of the 28th Reserve Division and the right of the 12th Division, together with the 6th Bavarian Reserve Regiment (10th Bavarian Division), were back in the German second line (*Braune Stellung*) on the front Bazentin le Grand—Longueval—Guillemont, having abandoned a number of battery positions along Caterpillar Valley and in Bernafay and Trônes Woods. Had the British followed up their success at once, both those woods would have been found empty, and little resistance would have been met in the German second line, the only formed unit in the whole of that sector of over two miles being the 16th Bavarian Regiment (10th Bavarian Division) in reserve between Longueval and Flers.

During the evening, however, the opportunity passed, the 12th Reserve Division[3] arriving on the scene in great haste from Bapaume. It was the first of that great stream of German divisions that were to be put in to reinforce the battle front north of the Somme during the following months. It had entrained at Neuville les Cambrai at 9 a.m. (1st of July) as soon as the news of the yielding of the line on the Montauban ridge came through, and from Bapaume it marched south-eastward during the late evening and night to the Combles—Ginchy area. At 6.45 p.m. it came under the 28th Reserve Division and was ordered to advance eastward and to regain a footing on the Montauban ridge about Montauban and Favières Wood (the latter place held by the French). The troops were told that probably parts of the original front trenches were still held by isolated detachments, and that therefore continual reconnaissance would be necessary both to avoid surprise by the enemy and firing into their own troops in front. The advance was to be made with the right, the 51st Reserve Infantry Regiment, past the north of Combles and thence directed by north of Guillemont on the north-east corner of Montauban village; the centre, the 38th Reserve Infantry Regiment, was to attack Favières Wood, and the left, the 23rd Reserve Infantry Regiment, was to advance between Maurepas and Curlu, on the north bank of the Somme. The front lines were to cross the Ginchy—Maurepas road between 7 and 8 p.m., and as soon as the 51st Reserve Infantry Regiment had reached Guillemont,

---

2   See Chapter 8.

3   This Division was taken out of the line at Verdun in the middle of May after losing very heavily (71 per cent of its infantry), and moved into reserve in the Cambrai region at the beginning of June.

the two battalions of the 16th Bavarian Regiment (see above), in position in the second line between Waterlot Farm and Longueval, were to advance with it on its right into Caterpillar Valley, the objective of the 16th Bavarian Regiment being Montauban Alley, between Montauban (exclusive) and the Pommiers Redoubt, that of the 51st Reserve Infantry Regiment being Montauban (inclusive)—La Briqueterie—Dublin Redoubt.

The direction of the attack was thus against the eastern front of the new Montauban salient, and, if successful, would threaten the British hold gained along the Montauban ridge, but there was great delay in getting forward, and it was nearly midnight before the Ginchy—Maurepas road was reached. The British had thus time to get settled in their new position. In the darkness the further advance through Guillemont and past Trônes Wood was slow and difficult, and it was 3 a.m., and light, before the attack came up on either side of Bernafay Wood and approached the British position. North of the wood the leading companies of the 16th Bavarian Regiment moved up from Caterpillar Valley and stumbled against an advanced post of the 17th Manchester in Triangle Point, north of Montauban on the Bazentin le Grand road. This post they rushed and annihilated and about a hundred Bavarians made an entrance into Montauban Alley at that point, astride the road. An S.O.S. message was signalled back from Montauban to the British guns and this sector of the alley was heavily shelled, the majority of the Bavarians quickly withdrawing into the dead ground of Caterpillar Valley and the remainder being subsequently bombed out of the alley. South of the wood the 51st Reserve Infantry Regiment came up against La Briqueterie which was held by a company of the 20th Liverpool. These Germans, however, were completely exhausted, having been on the move since the previous afternoon without food or water, so much so, that as they came forward in close disorganized formation they appeared like a mass of drunken men. A heavy machine-gun and rifle fire was opened on them and they at once fell back into the shelter of Bernafay Wood or back into the dead ground between the wood and Maltz Horn Farm. The attack of the centre and left of the Division was also repulsed by the French at and south of Favières Wood and a number of prisoners taken.

The counter-attack had cost the 12th Reserve Division heavy losses. It had been made on a very wide front; nearly four miles and with the troops in an exhausted condition, and they were now withdrawn into the intermediate position (*Grüne Stellung*), a line of trench, the Maltz Horn Trench, between Trônes Wood and Hardecourt, some 1,000 yards in front of the main second line position, Guillemont—Maurepas.

The British Advance through Bernafay Wood, 3rd of July

During the 2nd of July, a few hours after the failure of the German counter-attack, patrols sent out by the 20th Liverpool (British 30th Division) into Bernafay Wood found that it was not held and brought back about twenty prisoners, men of the 51st Reserve Infantry Regiment who had taken refuge there in the morning and now surrendered without opposition. As a result of the reports of these patrols Bernafay Wood was ordered to be occupied, and at 9 p.m., on the 3rd, the 17th Brigade (6th K.O.S.B.'s on the right and 12th R. Scots on the left) advanced from a front La Briqueterie—Montauban into the wood. By 11.30 p.m. they had reached its eastern edge, having met little opposition, taking some more prisoners still hiding in temporary dug-outs, and also four guns (6th Battery 57th F.A.R.), all that remained of the advanced batteries of the 21st and 57th Field Artillery Regiments; the other guns having been taken back by the Germans the previous night.

The Occupation of Trônes Wood by the 90th Brigade, 8th of July

The capture of La Briqueterie and Bernafay Wood made a still more pronounced salient in the British line, and this was to become the jumping-off place for the further operations. Leaving Bernafay Wood on its northern slope, the Mametz—Montauban ridge continues eastward to Guillemont. On its southern side is a great stretch of open country broken only by the head of a considerable valley that widens out as it falls away southward past Favières Wood to the Somme. Running up the bed of this valley was Maltz Horn Trench that eventually rises on to and crosses the Montauban ridge. On the crest of the high ground on the farther side of the valley stood the ruins of Maltz Horn Farm. The only covered approach from Montauban to this valley was past La Briqueterie and thence by a sunken road.

On the northern slope of Montauban ridge, about half way between Bernafay Wood and Guillemont, is Trônes Wood, the southern edge of which overflows, as it were, the top of the ridge 100 yards or so west of where the Maltz Horn Trench crosses it. The centre of Trônes Wood, traversed by the Montauban—Guillemont railway, lies in the dip across the head of Caterpillar Valley and its northern end rises up reaching to a point towards Longueval. The actual shape of the wood is triangular, the base about 400 yards across on the Montauban ridge, and the length from the base to the apex on the Longueval slope about 1,400 yards. The wood itself was a dense thicket, and owing to its thick undergrowth, uncut for two years, it was all that an equipped man could do to force his way through it, and even then direction was most difficult to keep once inside. A German communication trench, Trônes Alley, ran roughly along the top of the Montauban ridge between Bernafay and Trônes Wood.

The further advance of the British right from Bernafay Wood was delayed owing to the need for support by the French on the right flank, on the high ground, Maltz Horn Farm and Hardecourt knoll, that overlooked the southern end of Trônes Wood. A combined attack was arranged for 8 a.m. on the 7th of July, but on the previous day a German counter-attack retook the northern end of Favières Wood and this delayed the French preparations for twenty-four hours, the attack being postponed till 8 a.m., 8th of July. The British XIII Corps was to occupy the southern end of Trônes Wood and the Maltz Horn Trench as far as Maltz Horn Farm (incl.). On the right the French were to occupy the remainder of Maltz Horn Trench (across Hardecourt knoll) and the general line Maltz Horn Farm (exclusive)—Hardecourt village. After a heavy bombardment of Trônes Wood and Maltz Horn Trench during the early hours the attack was launched. The wood and this trench were at this time held by two to three battalions, composed of companies of 51st and 38th Reserve Infantry Regiments with a few men of the 62nd Regiment (12th Division) that had held the original line before the arrival of the 12th Reserve Division.

In the British sector the assault was delivered by the 2nd Yorkshire Regiment. Moving through Bernafay Wood the companies deployed along its eastern edge and began to advance across the 400 yards of open ground separating it from the southern end of Trônes Wood. On topping the rise of ground between the two woods, however, a heavy machine-gun and rifle fire was opened from a trench at the south-west corner of Trônes Wood and caused heavy loss. Further efforts to get forward were met by the same fire and eventually a withdrawal was ordered to the cover of Bernafay Wood. Efforts were made by bombers to move into the German position by Trônes Alley, a communication trench that lay along the line of advance, but without success.

The French, however, had meanwhile succeeded in capturing Hardecourt knoll and the sector of Maltz Horn Trench there, with the result that their left flank was now exposed to the still unoccupied sector of the trench north of Maltz Horn Farm. Another attack was therefore organized by the British 21st Brigade, and after a heavy bombardment of the trench along the south-western edge of Trônes Wood an attack against it was made by the 2nd Wiltshire at 1 p.m. The bombardment had driven the Germans from the trench and the wood was entered with few casualties. A company of this Battalion had at the same time advanced from La Briqueterie along the sunken road towards Maltz Horn Farm to connect up with the French left. Much of the way was able to be covered in dead ground, and when approaching the German trench in front of the farm the French bombed northward along it, thereby attracting the Germans, and the sector of trench was rushed and occupied, a weak counter-attack from Maltz Horn Farm being repulsed shortly afterwards. A counter-attack on the south part of Trônes Wood from the northern part during the evening had a similar fate.

Maltz Horn Trench lay on the forward slope of the Hardecourt knoll, and the Germans spent the night digging a fresh line of shelter pits in the hard chalk on the reverse slope, about 300 yards beyond. At 5 a.m., on the 9th, the 2nd Royal Scots Fusiliers, who had reinforced a company of the Wiltshires during the night, rushed and occupied Maltz Horn Farm that now lay between the two lines, and the same Battalion bombed the Germans out of the remainder of Maltz Horn Trench as far as Trônes Wood, including the strong point where the Guillemont road enters the wood.

During the night also the 18th Manchester had reinforced the three companies of the 2nd Wiltshire in the southern edge of Trônes Wood, and at 6.40 a.m. (the 9th) the 17th Manchester moved out from Bernafay Wood on either side of the Guillemont light railway against the central and northern part of Trônes Wood. Here, along the western edge of the wood, there was no trench and it was undefended, the 17th Manchester entering it without loss. Central Trench that lay through the middle of the wood, from north to south, connecting three vacated battery positions within it, was rushed, a few Germans there being taken prisoners, and by 8 a.m., after great difficulty in getting through the dense undergrowth, the eastern edge of the wood was reached. From that hour until about 2 p.m. the whole of Trônes Wood was in British possession.

The First German Counter-Attack on Trônes Wood, 9th of July

The German units engaged up to now in this sector of the battlefield had been the battalions of the 51st and 38th Reserve Infantry Regiments (12th Reserve Division) and the remnants of the 62nd Regiment (12th Division) and a few Bavarian detachments. During the 9th, however, the 123rd Division began to arrive in the battle line between Guillemont and the Somme.

The 123rd Division, after a period of rest in Flanders as reserve to the Sixth Army, had entrained on the 5th of July in the area Thorout—Beernem and came by way of Lille and Cambrai to the Second Army zone, detraining during the 6th–7th at Epehy and Gouzeaucourt behind the Somme battle front and 15 miles east of Trônes Wood. It was the intention of the Second Army at this time to employ the division as a whole for a counter-attack on the front Longueval—Hardecourt with similar objectives as those given to the 12th Reserve Division on the 1st of July, but the offensive of the French and British on the 8th against Trônes Wood and Maltz Horn Trench had brought the 12th Reserve Division, which had been seven days in the fighting line, to the end of its tether. On the morning of the 9th two of the three regiments of the 123rd Division, the 182nd and 178th, were therefore rushed up in motor lorries to relieve the survivors and take over the defence of the line, its remaining regiment, the 106th Reserve, moving to Nurlu in reserve.

The 182nd Regiment was the first to be put into the line; the 3rd Battalion reinforced the 11th Reserve Division, hard pressed by the French, about Hem and Clery on the north bank of the Somme, the 1st Battalion relieved the 23rd Infantry Regiment (the left regiment of the 12th Reserve Division) between Maurepas and Hardecourt, also opposite the French, and the 2nd Battalion moved into the Trônes Wood sector opposite the British. The latter, the only battalion of the three which concerns this article, arrived in Morval at 3 a.m., on the 9th, and thence marched towards Ginchy. Here, at 11 a.m., it was placed at the disposal of the 51st Reserve Infantry Regiment (the right regiment of the 12th Reserve Division) whose commander ordered it to attack and retake Trônes Wood, the bombardment to begin at 12.30 p.m. and the infantry assault at 3.30 p.m. (British time).

The bombardment was carried out by all available artillery, that of the 12th Reserve Division and the 3rd Guard Division behind Guillemont and Longueval respectively. Disposed to east, northeast and north of the wood, they were able to concentrate a converging fire on it with such intensity that life within it became insupportable. The 17th Manchester, the Battalion, it will be remembered, which had occupied the eastern edge during the morning, endured this shelling for over an hour, when the battalion commander sent back messages by carrier pigeon asking for artillery fire against the German battery positions to silence them, but the range was too great to be effective, and at 2 p.m. the commander ordered a withdrawal from the wood, along Trônes Alley to Bernafay Wood. The withdrawal of the 17th Manchester uncovered the left and rear of the 18th Manchester, holding the southern end of the wood, and this Battalion was then ordered to withdraw to La Briqueterie. The 2nd Royal Scots Fusiliers, however, continued to hold on to Maltz Horn Trench, though the withdrawal of the Manchesters necessitated the evacuation of the part of the trench by the Guillemont road as far as level with the southern end of Trônes Wood.

In the meantime the 182nd Regiment (2nd Battalion) was moving forward from Ginchy to the assaulting position in the second line trench, the left at Guillemont and the right on the Sugar Factory (Waterlot Farm). This advance was seen by some British aeroplanes flying over Ginchy, and shortly afterwards the artillery laid a barrage along the east side of Guillemont. Two of the companies were unable to get through this, and in order to take their place in the assault the remnants of the 51st Reserve Infantry Regiment in the second line trench were formed up into two composite companies and disposed between the other two companies of the 182nd Regiment that had passed through the barrage. Two companies, one of each Regiment, was to attack the northern part of the wood, north of the railway, and the other two companies the southern part, the whole then pressing through to the western edge.

"At 4 p.m.," so runs an extract from the History of the 182nd Regiment, "came the order to prepare for assault. Our packs were to be left in the trench owing to the difficulty of moving through the wood with them on. That strange and uncomfortable hot and cold feeling down the spine came over us all as we stood up in the trench and tested the hand grenades. At 4.15 the order to advance '*Alles raus*' was shouted along and we clambered out of the trench into the opening muttering '*Walt's Gott*' (God help us), and through the wire entanglement. Spreading out at once into a long firing line we moved on down the open barren slope towards the wood 500 yards away, expecting every moment a burst of machine-gun fire to open from the wood and sweep the line. To our amazement, however, even as we neared the edge of it not a shot was fired at us. The right reached the wood first and disappeared into it, followed by the remainder, all continuing to keep close touch in line. A number of English lay hidden in the dense undergrowth, and some of these as soon as we had passed by them opened fire from behind causing a number of casualties, but they were quickly rounded up or killed. At 5.10 p.m. the western edge of the wood was reached and white light signals were sent up to warn the artillery that now lifted to the eastern edge of Bernafay Wood. Only in the centre of the wood near the railway line was any prolonged resistance met, and here after a stubborn fight at close quarters 40 of the 16th and 17th Manchester Regiment[4] were surrounded and taken prisoners. We then made what cover was possible along the edge of the wood."

The remaining two companies of the Battalion, held back east of Guillemont by the British barrage, now (5.20 p.m.) arrived and strengthened the position, the composite companies of the 51st Reserve Infantry Regiment completely exhausted and with little fight left in them being withdrawn. The right, on the northern side of the wood, gained touch with the 16th Bavarian Regiment about Longueval, and the left was thrown back in touch with the 38th Reserve Infantry Regiment (12th Reserve Division) that still confronted from about Arrow Head Copse southward the 2nd Royal Scots Fusiliers in Maltz Horn Trench.

The Second British Attack on Trônes Wood, 10th of July

At 2.30 p.m. immediately on hearing of the withdrawal of the 17th Manchester from the wood, the 90th Brigade ordered the 16th Manchester, in support south of Montauban, to attack and hold the south edge of Trônes Wood. Forming up in the sunken road (i.e. the slight cutting in the Briqueterie—Hardecourt road) south of the wood, this attack, led by two companies, was delivered at 6.40 p.m., and the Germans who had apparently concentrated their attention on the defence of the western side of the wood, facing Bernafay Wood, were not prepared to meet it, so that although heavily shelled on the way the 16th Manchester were able to reach the southern edge with few casualties, their left in Trônes Alley. Owing to the constant interference by German snipers up trees and by bombers, it was not found possible to hold the actual edge of the wood, and during the night, therefore, a trench was dug and occupied about 150 yards in length parallel to and about 60 yards from the south-western edge. The dense undergrowth of the fallen trees made it impracticable to push on into the wood during the night, but the Battalion was ordered to prepare to advance through it early the following morning (the 10th), and to assist them a company of the 4th South African Regiment (South African Scottish) lent by the 9th Division was sent up at 12.5 a.m. After a preliminary bombardment of the wood the advance began at 4 a.m., companies being broken up into strong patrols of 20 men each of which was to press through the wood as best it could from south to north

---

4 It appears that a few of the 16th Manchester had gone into the wood in the morning to support the 17th Manchester.

in order to clear it. These patrols could only see a few yards to right and left in the dense thicket, and, though some of them met no opposition and reported the wood clear of the enemy, others came up against German entrenched posts and never returned, being overcome or taken prisoner. As an example of the fate of one of these patrols an extract may be given from the diary of a German in the 6th Company (182nd Regiment):

> About 3 a.m. the enemy's artillery increased to drumfire strength and a terrific hail of shells burst upon us, making many gaps in our already thin line of defence. After an hour the artillery lifted and shortly afterwards the English infantry appeared here and there in the wood in strong parties. One of these parties rushed and captured the trench sector of our right company, and we, No, 6 Company, were at once ordered to go to the help of the defence of this gap in the line. As we crept back through the undergrowth a thick branch got caught between a heavy pair of wirecutters and the entrenching tool in my belt, and before I could extricate myself four English rushed at me, caught me and dragged me along with them, joining a party of 20 others. My rifle was taken from me and we went on through the wood, now to the right and now to the left, backwards and forwards. The leader, who spoke German, asked me in what direction the Germans were. I said I didn't know. Then we went to the right and a machine gun fired on us, two of the English falling dead to the ground without a murmur. Then we went to the left and so on, completely lost. The leader then went off alone to the edge of the wood to find his direction, but came back and said he didn't know where we were. At this moment the German artillery fire increased, placing a barrage along the western edge of the wood. The leader asked me if the shells passing over were British or German. I saw my chance of getting nearer my own lines and told them they were British and he believed me, though I knew they came from our own guns behind Guillemont. We turned, therefore, and went towards the sound of the guns, and after some time we came to a large crater which I recognized near the eastern edge of the wood. In this we halted and I was given some bread and cigarettes. Suddenly I heard voices of men of my own company only 25 yards away. While my captors drank from their water bottles and smoked cigarettes I moved to the top of the crater and signalled, and within a few minutes we were surrounded. The British were ordered to hold up their hands and surrender, and they were taken back to Guillemont.

The Second German Counter-Attack on Trônes Wood, 10th of July

At 3 a.m., as soon as the bombardment began, the two companies (182nd Infantry Regiment) holding the western edge of the wood withdrew hurriedly to the eastern edge to escape the shelling, the British guns generally confining their attention to the western side. There they waited for an hour, and at 4 a.m., when the fire slackened, they suddenly saw a number of their own Regiment retiring from the southern part of the wood on Guillemont, followed by other groups at intervals. Soon after, a retreat also began from the northern end and it appeared that the British infantry had entered both ends of the wood. In these circumstances it was impossible to hold the centre, and a withdrawal from the wood was ordered, taking up a position in a number of big shell craters 200 yards to the east of it north of the Guillemont road. Here the companies were to await the enemy and fight a rearguard action, retiring gradually on to the second line. An hour passed and no enemy appeared at the edge of the wood, until at last from the southern flank two groups of British prisoners were seen being led across the open back to Guillemont. This seemed very strange, and patrols were sent forward again into the wood to find out the situation. About 8 a.m. Lieut. Blechschmidt came across from the southern part of the wood and said he was still holding there with 50 men, and had beaten off several British attacks and taken a number of prisoners. He said it would be foolish to abandon the wood yet, and it was decided, therefore, to gather together as many men as possible and to advance through it once more. Some 200 men who had withdrawn to the second line position early in the morning were brought forward again along the railway, and the whole, joining up into a long skirmishing line under Lieut Pache, keeping touch like a linked chain to right and left, advanced into the wood. To quote Lieut. Pache's account in the History of the 182nd Regiment:

> It was hard work in the hot sun forcing our way through the shell-torn undergrowth. Masses of intertwined briars and thorn bushes, great trees with their broken out-spreading branches felled by the bombardment, blocked and encumbered every step, in addition to stumbling into the scores of deep shell holes. Everywhere were dead British and Germans, in one place 5 British in a single heap, clearly all killed by the same shell, bits of equipment and rifles lying about everywhere, and dozens of British packs full of eatables which the men eagerly pounced upon. The line pressed on capturing on the way isolated British parties and individuals who appeared completely lost in the thicket. Crossing Central Trench which runs from north to south through the middle of the wood, we found some men of the 182nd still holding on there and in front of them several Scotsmen in their coloured kilts lay dead (probably South African Scottish). The western edge of the wood was reached and found occupied. Leaving a number of posts along the western edge, the majority of the line were now withdrawn to Central Trench and the prisoners who had been captured in the drive, in all 1 officer and 250 men, were sent back to Guillemont. Central Trench was in a terrible state; tinned foods, razors, letters, brushes, spades, rifles, gas masks, steel helmets, thousands of rounds of ammunition, machine gun ammunition boxes—all in abject confusion, scattered everywhere, and mixed with blood-covered bits of uniform, torn boots and other remnants of shell-battered bodies. For the next four hours comparative quiet, however, reigned in the wood, the British artillery lifting its fire beyond on to the second line position and the village in rear. The men in Central Trench found sufficient tea and food in the British packs to make themselves a good meal. Trônes Wood was once again in German hands.

The British 90th Brigade diary writes on this affair:

> At 5.3o a.m. the Germans counter-attacked, probably coming from the direction of Guillemont, and reoccupied the southern part of the wood, cutting off some patrols of the 16th Manchesters who are missing. Continuous efforts were made during the morning to get into touch with the missing patrols, but they failed owing to the centre of the wood being strongly held by the enemy.

The troops in the line along the western and southern edge of the wood, south of the railway, were now organized into three new companies, called by name after the three commanders; v. Mosch its right on the railway; Pache along the south-western edge of the wood; and Lanzendorf at the southern edge of the wood; also a sandbag block was made and garrisoned in Trônes Alley. North of the railway a composite company of remnants of the 51st Reserve Infantry Regiment was again brought forward from Guillemont and put into the line.

The Third British Attack on Trônes Wood, 11th of July

During the 10th, arrangements had been made for the relief of the British 90th Brigade by the 89th Brigade, which was to renew the efforts to capture Trônes Wood. To assist the relief and to distract the Germans in the wood, a company of the 17th Liverpool from Bernafay Wood was to rush the German post blocking Trônes Alley and hold on there. This was to be preceded by a heavy bombardment on the southern part of the wood, and a few British parties still occupying posts along the southern edge were withdrawn to the trench 60 yards outside it, dug by the 16th Manchester on the night of the 9th–10th (see above). The attack which, according to the History of the 182nd Regiment, came up against the company v. Mosch and the garrison of the advanced hand-grenade post in Trônes Alley, was repulsed with considerable casualties, including the company commander.

Actually during the night of the 10th–11th there were, therefore, no British troops in Trônes Wood, the southern and western edges of which were now held by the three reconstituted companies of the 182nd Regiment and the northern part by a composite company of the 51st Reserve Infantry Regiment. Small posts held the edge of the wood, with the main body at various points along Central Trench in the middle of the wood.

At 11 a.m. the two front battalions of the British 89th Brigade formed up along the sunken road immediately east of La Briqueterie for the renewed attack on the wood. At 3.27 a.m., after 50 minutes' heavy bombardment, the advance began; the 20th Liverpool on the right was to attack the wood south of Trônes Alley and relieve the 2nd R. Scots Fusiliers in Maltz Horn Trench, the 2nd Bedford on the left was to move on that part of the wood between Trônes Alley and the railway, and push through to the eastern edge. It was only just beginning to get light as the attacking companies crossed the open from the sunken road, and they were not observed by the Germans until within 400 yards of the wood. Machine-gun fire was then opened on them from the Trônes Alley-block and many casualties were suffered, this fire also causing much of the attack to be diverted southward, forcing half the Bedfords against the southern edge of the wood, and most of the Liverpools into Maltz Horn Trench. Nevertheless, the wood was entered; two companies of the Bedfords gaining a footing at the southern edge and the remaining two companies at the western edge, south of the railway. The History of the 182nd Regiment describes this attack:

> During the night the bombardment of the wood by the British artillery continued without ceasing, but at about 2.30 a.m. it increased to a great intensity; it became in fact the most fierce and destructive *Trommelfeuer* that had yet been experienced, even surpassing any that the regiment had recently experienced at Verdun. As many as 50 heavy shells a minute burst in the southern part of the wood alone, sending up great masses of earth, trees and scrub. The air pressure of the shell-bursts crushed

one to the ground and took all breath away, the mind and nerves being tortured in a manner indescribable and unforgettable to all that survived it. At times phosphor shells came with the others and burst among us into countless pieces of burning sulphur covering us with flecks of flame and setting fire to some of the trees. This almost intolerable agony continued for a seemingly endless hour, the worst hour the Battalion had yet experienced in the war. At last, about 3.30 a.m., the barrage of such terrible memory moved on beyond the wood, but it had caused us heavy loss, especially in the wood near the railway where a number of small posts of the company v. Mosch had been wiped out leaving a considerable gap in the line of defence. The British infantry attack now developed and broke into the wood at this place, the survivors of the company there, threatened with isolation, retiring through the wood and assembling in the second line at Guillemont. They left exposed the right flank of the two companies, Bache and Lanzendorf, in the southern part of the wood. But at this most critical stage reinforcements arrived.

Part II

The Third German Counter-Attack on Trônes Wood, 11th of July

It will be remembered that of the 123rd Division, brought up on the 9th to the Nurlu District, the 178th and 182nd Regiments had gone into the line to relieve the exhausted 12th Reserve Division; the 178th to Hardecourt opposite Maltz Horn Trench and 182nd on either side of it, two battalions to Hem and Clery on its left and one battalion to Trônes Wood on its right. Its remaining regiment, the 106th Reserve, had been kept back at Nurlu. On the 10th, one of the battalions (the 1st) of the latter had been moved up to east of Ginchy, and, in the early hours of the 11th, two companies were sent forward to the second line at Guillemont. The first half company to arrive, about 100 men, met Capt. v. Mosch and his survivors as they arrived in the second line from Trônes Wood. With this reinforcement Capt. v. Mosch at 5.30 a.m. went forward again and pressing through the wood drove back the Bedfords who had broken through in places to the eastern edge, capturing 200 prisoners. "The right flank of companies Pache and Lanzendorf, threatened with immediate envelopment, was thus saved."

Immediately south of the wood in front of Maltz Horn Trench the 20th Liverpool had gained a footing in the German position now held by a battalion the 178th Regiment. Groups of ten and twenty withdrew to the second line south of Guillemont, but the further advance of the Liverpools was held up by enfilade fire from the south-eastern side of the wood, and, to quote the History of the 178th Regiment,

> ... by the arrival of the battalion adjutant who immediately brought forward again some of these men and organized a counter-attack which not only prevented the gap being extended but also regained a greater part of the lost trench.

Throughout the morning the fighting continued both in the wood and to the south of it, craters and sectors of trenches being taken and retaken, but no further definite progress was made by either side, the Bedfords continuing to hold a small wedge-shaped position into the wood south, of the railway line and a footing in the southern side.

About midday the remainder of the two companies of the 106th Reserve Regiment came forward from Guillemont into the wood and cleared isolated parties of the Bedfords still north of the railway. These retired by way of Longueval Alley to Bernafay Wood. During the evening a counter-attack made on the Bedfords in the southern side of the wood drove them out of it, so the whole wood was again in German hands with the exception of the wedge on the western side, south of the railway, still held by the survivors of two companies ("C" and "D") of the Bedfords. The German hold on the wood at this time was as follows: The western edge north of the railway was held by the composite company of the 51st Reserve Infantry Regiment supported by one company of the 106th Reserve Regiment; south of the railway was the other company of the 106th Reserve Regiment and company v. Mosch (182nd Regiment), the south-western corner with the exception of the Bedford wedge was held by company Pache and the southern side by company Lanzendorf. As before, the edge of the wood was held by small posts with stronger parties in support points in Central Trench.

The battalion (2nd) of the 182nd Regiment which had borne the brunt of the fighting in the wood since the morning of the 9th had by now little fight left in it; the men were so much exhausted that they slept through the heaviest bombardment. The remaining two companies of the 1st Battalion (106th Reserve Regiment), therefore, were ordered forward to Guillemont during the day, and its 2nd Battalion sent up from Morval to the battle-front. Orders were given for the relief of the companies of the 182nd Regiment in the wood, and at the same time to clear the whole of the southern part of it of the enemy. To do this the two remaining companies of the 1st Battalion were to move from Guillemont to the wood and line up in it along the railway, facing south; the advance through the wood to the southern and western edge to begin at 9 p.m. Of the 2nd Battalion one company was to support the left flank of the advance through the wood, two companies were to occupy the second line at Guillemont and the remaining company to remain at Ginchy in reserve. The 178th Regiment opposite Maltz Horn Trench was to assist by attacking with its right that part of the trench south-east of Trônes Wood.

The orders for this attack were found on an officer of the 178th Regiment captured by the French near Hardecourt during afternoon and information was at once (6 p.m.) sent through to British headquarters.

An artillery barrage was immediately placed between Guillemont and Trônes Wood, and the ground east of Guillemont kept under fire. The effect of this is told in the History of the 106th Reserve Regiment:

> The movement of the companies was quickly discovered by the enemy, and from 7 p.m. onwards a heavy artillery fire covered the zone of advance so that the two companies of the 1st Battalion were only able to reach their position of assembly in the wood after much delay and with heavy loss by advancing in small groups or individual rushes from Guillemont. The 2nd Battalion also came under heavy fire in its advance to Guillemont and suffered heavily before it reached the second line position (*Braune Stellung*) there. The 5th Company of this battalion, which was to assist the left flank of the attack, worked forward from Guillemont in small groups, but was unable to reach the eastern edge of Trônes Wood until 11 p.m.

In the meantime, however, at 5 p.m., the order for the relief had reached the companies of the 182nd Regiment in the wood: "Four companies of the 106th Reserve were to push through the wood and pass through us, whereupon we were to retire by sections." The delay in the advance, however, caused some confusion, and, at about 11 p.m., as the companies of the 106th Reserve were forming up for the attack, the survivors of the 182nd were already moving back out of the wood to Guillemont, leaving only a few posts along the southern and western edge. Before the advance of the 106th Reserve from the railway southward through the wood could begin, reports came back of a fresh British attack that had gained a footing in the southern part, and at the same time posts on the western side facing the Bedford wedge sent back for reinforcements. The planned counter-attack was therefore abandoned and the companies sent up instead to strengthen the defence where most needed. Thus the 2nd, 3rd and part of the 5th Companies were sent back to check the advance in the southern part of the wood, the 1st and 4th sent to reinforce the posts on the western side, and the remainder of the 5th held back in reserve near Strong Point on the Guillemont road.

The new British attack referred to was carried out by the 17th Liverpool (89th Brigade). It was intended to occupy the southern edge of the wood before the German counter-attack, referred to in the captured order, could reach it in any strength. At 10.30 p.m. the Battalion in artillery formation, lines of companies in column of groups, advanced from the sunken road, east of La Briqueterie. The trees at the southern edge of the wood stood out against the sky in the failing light and gave the direction. Had the edge of the wood been occupied the Battalion must have suffered heavily but, for reasons already given, the greater part of the defenders had already left and the relieving companies of the 106th Reserve had not yet arrived. The Battalion was able, therefore, to slip into the wood with few casualties except from one of the small posts left behind which was quickly surrounded, and then meeting no organized opposition companies moved through the wood to a line along the south-eastern edge facing Guillemont, the left thrown back into the wood to protect the left flank towards Strong Point. The Liverpools at once wired this line and dug in behind it. About 1 a.m. when the relieving German companies eventually advanced from the railway through the wood towards the southern edge, they were surprised to find wire and organized opposition in the wood itself. One party got hung up in the wire and was disposed of with a Lewis gun; the others fell back and made no further attacks during the night. About midnight the commanding officer of the Liverpools had met the senior officer of the Bedford companies holding the Bedford wedge, and it was decided to dig a trench across the wood joining up the new Liverpool trench with the Bedford wedge. Covering parties were sent out in front of this line taking up concealed positions in the dense undergrowth, and behind them the new line was dug and wired during the 12th.

Meanwhile, the British 90th Brigade and its opponents, the battalion (2nd) of the 182nd Regiment, which had faced and fought each other continuously for three days and nights, were withdrawing out of the battle zone, the 90th Brigade to Bois Celestins and the battalion of the 182nd Regiment to the sheltered valley between Ginchy and Morval. The former had lost during the fighting 33 officers (5 killed, 21 wounded and 7 missing) and 756 other ranks (84 killed, 430 wounded and 242 missing); the German 182nd Regiment gives the approximate losses of its 2nd Battalion during the Trônes Wood fighting as 6 officers (2 killed and 4 wounded) and 560 other ranks (60 killed, 300 wounded, 200 missing).

The Fourth German Counter-Attack, 12th of July

During the 12th orders were given for another effort to clear the British out of the wood. The two remaining companies of the 2nd Battalion 106th Reserve Regiment were to advance at 8.30 p.m. from the second line at Guillemont and to secure the western side of the wood, whereupon the troops in the wood were to assemble along the railway, as on the previous day, and attack southward using flame-throwers (*Flammenwerfer*) to clear the British out of their new position in the southern part. The right of the 178th Regiment was to cooperate by an attack from about Arrow Head Copse against Maltz Horn Trench. The movement of the two companies out of Guillemont was, however, observed by the British artillery, and so heavy was the barrage at once put down between that village and Trônes Wood that the companies were scattered with considerable loss and had to return to the second line trench. The supports (two companies) of the 178th Regiment which had been ordered to move forward to carry out the attack on Maltz Horn Trench, south of the wood, were also so heavily shelled that they were unable to reach their front trench. As a result, the whole attack was again abandoned and the survivors of the two companies (7th and 8th) of the 106th Reserve Regiment were sent up later to Trônes Wood under cover of darkness to reinforce the line there.

The 3rd Battalion of the 106th Reserve Regiment arrived from Nurlu by way of Morval during the night, and, in the early hours of the 13th, moved up into the second line at Guillemont, one company (the 11th) going forward into the wood and reinforcing the posts along the north-western edge, including the northern point of the wood.

The Fourth British Attack on Trônes Wood, 13th of July

On the morning of the 12th, after the failure of the British 89th Brigade to capture the wood, it was decided to put in a fresh division for the undertaking, and, during the night of the 12th–13th, the 30th Division was relieved by the 18th. During the period 8th–13th of July the former Division in the Trônes Wood fighting had lost in casualties 90 officers (21 killed, 61 wounded and 8 missing) and 1,844 other ranks (229 killed, 1,211 wounded and 404 missing).

The offensive on the German second line Longueval—Pozières had already been ordered for 3.20 a.m. on the 14th, and it was considered of the utmost importance that Trônes Wood should be captured by that time in order to secure the right flank of the attack moving up against Longueval, and also to enable guns to be pushed forward on to the northern slope of Caterpillar Valley to support, if possible, a further advance beyond the second line. General Rawlinson, therefore, ordered the XIII Corps to capture Trônes Wood by midnight of the 13th–14th at all costs.

The 18th Division came up on the evening of the 12th, and, during the night 12th–13th, its 55th Brigade took over the trenches, the 7th Buffs to Maltz Horn Trench and the 7th R. West Kent to the southern part of Trônes Wood, with the 7th Queen's and 8th E. Surrey in support. The attack was to be delivered at 7 p.m., the Buffs to hold Maltz Horn Trench and at the same time capture Strong Point on the Guillemont road, the R. West Kent to press through and capture all that part of the wood south of the railway, and the Queen's to attack the northern part of the wood from Longueval Alley. The two latter Battalions were thence to consolidate the entire eastern side of the wood facing Guillemont, placing entrenched posts and machine guns every 100 yards along it.

The R. West Kent suffered losses in crossing the open from the sunken road to the wood, chiefly from artillery fire, but entered the southern part and moved northward passing the new Liverpool—Bedford trench. Soon afterwards, however, its advance was broken by the strong points in the southern part of Central Trench held by the 3rd and 5th Companies (106th Reserve Regiment) and efforts to take them failed with heavy loss. Nevertheless, two of the R. West Kent companies pressed through the wood past these points to the railway line where they remained during the night, but were unable to get word back where they were. To reinforce the 3rd and 5th Companies (106th Reserve Regiment) the 9th Company and a platoon of the 11th Company were sent down Central Trench from the northern part of the wood. The 8th Company continued to hold Strong Point on the Guillemont road, the Buffs being unable to capture it.

The attack of the Queen's from Longueval Alley was met at once by heavy machine-gun and rifle fire from the north-western side of the wood in spite of the fact, as is stated in the History of the 106th Reserve Regiment, that "the German posts along the western edge were smothered with gas shells during the last ten minutes of the bombardment prior to the assault." Most of the attack was checked with heavy loss before reaching the wood, and the parties which succeeded in entering it "were rushed at once by the support of the 11th Company and either driven out again or killed."[5]

Before midnight the 10th Company (106th Reserve Regiment) was sent forward from Guillemont and reinforced with small detachments the posts along the western side of the wood. The Machine Gun Company of the Regiment was also brought up from Morval, two of its sections being sent up to the western edge of the wood, north and south of the railway respectively, and the other two kept back in the second line at Guillemont.

The Fifth British Attack on Trônes Wood and its Capture, 14th of July

By midnight reports which came back to British XIII Corps headquarters as to the situation in the wood were very scanty and unfavourable. The attack by the Queen's on the northern part of the wood had definitely failed and the greater part of the R. West Kent men had disappeared into the middle of the wood, all efforts to reach them or to get word back from them being checked by the Germans still holding the southern part of Central Trench. The XIII Corps commander, Lieut.-General W. N. Congreve, V.C., therefore telephoned to 18th Divisional headquarters and asked how it was intended to secure the right flank of the main attack on the Longueval line due to start at 3.20 a.m. Major-General F. I. Maxse replied that he would relieve the 55th Brigade by the 54th immediately, and that he still hoped to gain possession of the wood before the main attack could be adversely affected. At 12.45 a.m. the operation of capturing the wood was therefore handed over to Brig.-General T. H. Shoubridge, commanding the 54th Brigade.

In view of the need for immediate action, the simplest possible plan of attack was ordered, namely, to advance from the sunken road and to sweep straight through the wood from south to north, establishing a defensive flank along the eastern side, facing Guillemont, as the sweep progressed. It was 4 a.m. and light before the attack, led by the 6th Northants, got under way and casualties were suffered from shell and rifle fire before reaching the southern edge of the wood. Nevertheless, it was entered, and, at 6 a.m., the strong point at the southern end of Central Trench was rushed with the bayonet,

---

5   One platoon of the Queen's, under Lieut. B. C. Haggard, which entered the wood from Longueval Alley did, however, remain in it throughout the night.

the Germans leaving over 50 dead. Other units of the Brigade now came forward into the wood and Colonel F. A. Maxwell, V.C., commanding the 12th Middlesex, took over command in the wood and formed a line of men of different units, including some of the W. Kents who had been there all night, right across it, approximately along the Liverpool—Bedford trench dug two nights previously. This line now advanced northward picking up the R. West Kent companies by the railway and driving ahead of it a number of isolated parties of Germans, most of which left the wood by the east side north of the railway and retired on Guillemont. By 9 a.m. the northern point of the wood had been reached and the wood was clear of the enemy.

The History of the German 106th Reserve Regiment states that:

> The enemy got into the southern corner of the wood and rolled up the defence of South Central Trench, which he attacked from front and rear firing into it with Lewis guns. He then advanced northwards and thereby threatened to envelop the defenders along the western edge of the wood, the left wing, along the southern part of it, being withdrawn to the railway, but suffered heavy loss in doing so. The troops in the northern part of the wood held on till about 9 a.m. when the withdrawal from it was ordered. The survivors of the regiment crossed from the wood to the second line in good order though under a heavy fire and took up a position along it between Guillemont station and the sugar factory (Waterlot Farm). This movement was covered by three machine guns of the two sections of the regimental machine-gun company, all four guns of which had been successfully brought back from the wood. They took up a position immediately east of the wood and kept the eastern edge continually under fire during the withdrawal. Eventually, the crew of two of them were killed by fire from the wood, the other being brought back to Guillemont later in the morning. The enemy did not pursue beyond the eastern edge of the wood.

The Germans Abandon their Efforts to Retake the Wood

During the morning, relying on the capture of Trônes Wood, the main British attack on the German second line, Longueval—Pozières, had been delivered and had successfully entered it in several places. The British 9th Division had entered Longueval village, and during the afternoon the southern corner of Delville wood was occupied,[6] and Waterlot Farm in the second line between that wood and Guillemont was captured. The German 24th Reserve Division, brought from the Champagne to about St. Quentin on the 12th, was marched thence by Hargicourt to the Somme battle-front where it arrived during the 14th, its head, the 107th Reserve Regiment, to Morval. This Regiment had received orders to retake Trônes Wood in order to relieve the British pressure against Longueval, and during the late afternoon its companies had deployed and moved up to Guillemont. Here, however, it was stopped and given counter-orders in view of the British success in Delville Wood and at Waterlot Farm, which threatened Guillemont itself from the north. The Regiment, therefore, was put into the line on the defensive north of Guillemont, making a fresh defensive position from the village northward past the eastern side of Delville wood. The second line position on either side of Guillemont village now became the German front line of defence.

---

6   See Chapter 9.

8

Mametz Wood and Contalmaison

9–10 July 1916[1]

1

In Chapter 6 of this study the stubborn defence put up on the 1st of July, 1916, by the 26th Reserve Division astride the Ancre on a front Serre—Beaumont—Thiepval—Ovillers was described. For a few hours on that day, as a result of the capture of the Schwaben Redoubt by the 36th (Ulster) Division, the Germans had believed imminent the isolation and capture of Thiepval and, with that, the loss of the Thiepval plateau. Time was given, however, for the German counter-attack against the Schwaben Redoubt to develop, and, by the evening of the 2nd of July, the 26th Reserve Division was again established along practically the whole of its original front line trench.

Southward, however, the 28th Reserve Division, the other division of the XIV Reserve Corps, holding the front Ovillers—Fricourt—Montauban, had completely broken, the British capturing the entire Montauban plateau. The 28th Reserve Division was saved from utter annihilation by the timely arrival of units of the 10th Bavarian Division, the only reserve of the XIV Reserve Corps. During the subsequent days the British continued to make gradual progress. On the night of the 2nd/3rd Fricourt village was captured, and on the following day the line was advanced on to the rising ground facing the south-western side of Contalmaison. At the same time, on the right, a position was consolidated along the bed of the Mametz valley, including Caterpillar Wood and Bernafay Wood.

It was the gradual yielding on this part of the front, together with the firm stand of the 26th Reserve Division astride the Ancre and about Thiepval, that now led to the complete alteration of the British plan for the Somme offensive. Sir Douglas Haig decided to abandon his original intention of making his main attack across the Thiepval plateau eastward towards the Bapaume—Péronne road, and instead to attack the Pozières—Ginchy ridge from the south from the line of the Mametz valley, thereby taking advantage of the success already gained there.

This alteration of plan necessitated a considerable amount of administrative work, as it involved the supply of food and ammunition to a far greater force of men and artillery to this sector than had been at first arranged for. By the 8th of July, however, the preparatory orders were issued for the venture, and the 14th of July was given as the date for the beginning of the second phase of the Somme battle, the attack of the Pozières—Ginchy ridge from the south. To give every chance of success the ridge was to be attacked on a comparatively narrow frontage of two miles between Longueval and Bazentin-le-Petit, the German second line which lay in front of those two places being given as the objective. As

---

1 *Das Infanterie-Regiment Nr. 183*: Hase, Dresden, 1922; *Das Infanterie-Regiment Nr. 184*: Soldan, Oldenburg, 1920; *Das Wurttemberg Res. Inf. Reg. Nr. 122 im Weltkrieg*: Mugge, Stuggart, 1922; *Die Schwaben an der Ancre*: Gerster, Heilbronn, 1920.

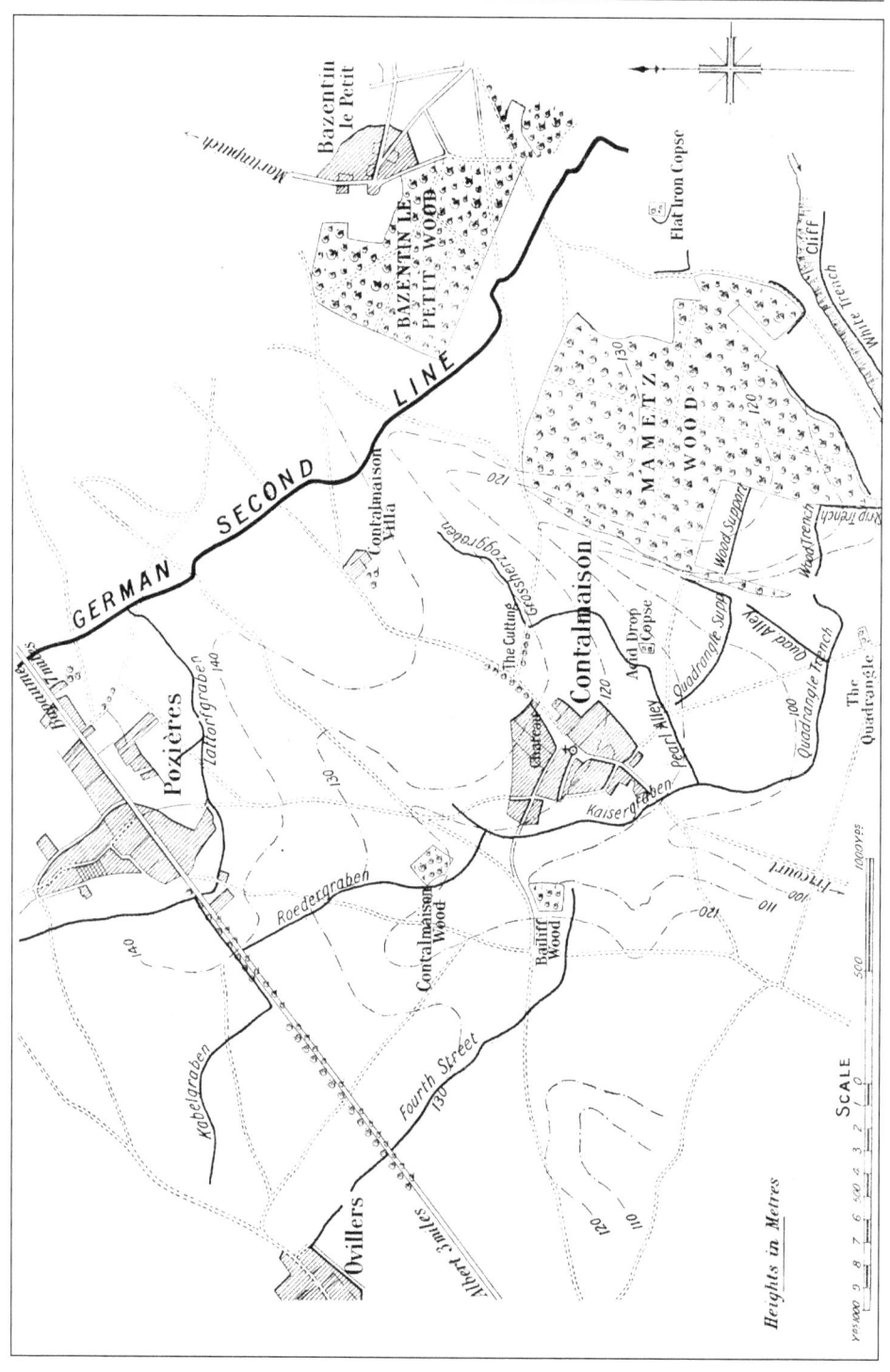

9. Contalmaison, 10 July 1916

a preliminary to the main attack, however, the Fourth Army was instructed to concentrate at once on the capture of Trônes Wood, on the right flank, and of Mametz Wood and Contalmaison on the left. Unless these localities were in British possession it was felt that the flanks of the main attack on the 14th of July would be insecure.

In accordance with these instructions orders were issued by the Fourth Army on the 8th of July for an attack on Mametz Wood and Contalmaison by the 38th, 17th and 23rd Divisions, to begin the following day, the 9th.

2

In the meantime the German 3rd Guard Division had been hurried forward from Valenciennes, and it relieved the remnants of the 28th Reserve Division and the 10th Bavarian Division, its right on the Bapaume—Albert road, south of Ovillers,[2] and its left east of Flat Iron Copse, including the whole of Mametz Wood.

The German original second line position lay along the southern side of the Pozières—Ginchy ridge, but after the capture of the front line on the 1st of July the Germans continued to hold various intermediary positions across the southern spurs of the ridge that reach out into the Mametz—Montauban valley. The keystone of the position taken up by the 3rd Guard Division was the Kaisergraben that lay across the Contalmaison spur protecting Contalmaison village. This trench had been constructed some months previously and was fairly complete, well wired in front and with good dug-outs some twenty feet deep into the hard chalk soil. On the right the Kaisergraben was connected with Ovillers by Fourth Street (Quergraben III) and its left joined on to Mametz Wood by Wood Trench.[3]

On the night of the 4th/5th July the British (52nd Brigade, 17th Division) captured the sector of the Kaisergraben between the Contalmaison—Fricourt road and Wood Trench, and named it Quadrangle Trench, also a part of Wood Trench, though about fifty yards of the latter, nearest the Wood, was still held by the Germans. On the night of the 6th/7th a party of the 10th Lancashire Fusiliers (52nd Brigade), pushing on again from Quadrangle Trench, had entered the southern end of Contalmaison village, but they were not supported, and at daylight the Germans counterattacked and forced them back to Quadrangle Trench. That part of the Kaisergraben in front of the western edge of Contalmaison, north of the Contalmaison—Fricourt road, was still in German hands.

On the 7th July the 3rd Guard Division was in its turn relieved by the 183rd Infantry Division from about Cambrai, consisting of the 122nd Reserve, the 183rd and 184th Infantry Regiments. On the march up the greater part of the 184th Regiment was diverted from Le Sars to assist the neighbouring division which was heavily engaged and hard pressed in Trônes Wood. Only two regiments were thus left to relieve the 3rd Guard Division. These reached the German second line about Pozières and Bazentin-le-Petit during the night 6th/7th. The trenches here had been badly battered by the British artillery during the preceding days and a large number of the dug-outs had been blocked. In the circumstances little protection could be obtained, and as it was already garrisoned by the supports of the 3rd Guard Division, a large number of the new arrivals had to lie out in the open. During the morning the trench was continually shelled and the casualties were consequently heavy, the 3rd Battalion, 122nd Reserve Infantry Regiment in particular, losing 5 officers and 220 other ranks. The ground about Pozières, Contalmaison and Mametz Wood was also

---

2   See map.
3   See map.

continually under British shell fire, Contalmaison village itself, says the German account, being frequently hidden in a cloud of black smoke, great fountains of débris rising up above it at times as the heaviest shells fell among the ruins.

The relief was carried out during the night of the 7th/8th. The 183rd Infantry Regiment took over from the 9th Grenadiers between Ovillers and Contalmaison (exclusive), and 122nd Reserve Infantry Regiment from the 163rd Infantry Regiment between Contalmaison (inclusive) and the south-western corner of Mametz Wood. The other regiment of the 3rd Guard Division, the Lehr Regiment,[4] holding the southern edge of Mametz Wood and about Flat Iron Copse, was not relieved.

The German dispositions on the evening of the 9th between Ovillers and Mametz Wood were therefore as follows: The 2nd and 3rd Battalions of the 183rd Infantry Regiment were in the Kabel and Roedergraben with the 1st Battalion in reserve in Pozières. Of the 122nd Reserve Infantry Regiment the 1st Battalion (Nos. 1, 2, 3 and 4 Companies) held Contalmaison village and the Kaisergraben to west of it, with battalion headquarters at the Chateau. The 3rd Battalion held Quadrangle Support (Nos. 10, 11 and 12 Companies) and Wood Support (No 9 Company), with battalion headquarters in the Wood. The 2nd Battalion of the regiment was in reserve in the German second line behind Contalmaison Villa, but during the 9th the 9th Company in Wood Support and part of Wood Trench lost 50 per cent of its strength in casualties during a British bombardment of Mametz Wood, and the 5th Company was sent from the 2nd Battalion to reinforce it. The 8th Company was also sent forward into Mametz Wood as a closer support for the 3rd Battalion, but half of this company was subsequently sent across to Contalmaison to reinforce the 1st Battalion there. This left only the 6th and 7th Companies in reserve in the second line position.

The Lehr Regiment held the southern edge of Mametz Wood with its 2nd Battalion, while the 1st Battalion occupied the trenches about Flat Iron Copse, and the 3rd Battalion was in reserve about Bazentin-le-Petit.

3

There were delays in the preparation of the British 38th, 17th and 23rd Divisions for the offensive against Mametz Wood and Contalmaison that had been ordered to begin on the 9th of July, and an attack by the 17th Division, in the centre, against Contalmaison was all that materialized on that day. This was delivered by the 50th and 51st Brigades from Quadrangle Trench northward, against Quadrangle Support at 11.20 p.m. under cover of the darkness. On the right the 50th Brigade was checked almost at once by machine-gun and rifle fire and had to return to its trenches, but on the left the 51st Brigade was temporarily successful. The 8th South Staffords and the 7th Lincolns carried the western end of Quadrangle Support and advanced between it and Contalmaison village. The 11th Company, 122nd Reserve Infantry Regiment, was almost entirely obliterated, but Lieutenant Irion, the senior German officer in Quadrangle Support, was able to form a stop at the western end of the trench with sandbags and a machine gun and thus prevent the capture of the trench itself. Parties of the Lincolns and South Staffords, however, pressed on astride Pearl Alley to about Acid Drop Copse. Here they halted, finding both their flanks unsupported. Meanwhile the attack of the 50th Brigade had been definitely

---

4   The Lehr infantry battalion of the Guard Corps was in peacetime, as its name implies, an instructional unit which was attached to the 1st Guard Infantry Brigade. On mobilization the battalion was expanded into a normal regiment of three battalions and formed part of the 3rd Guard Division.

held up by the German 10th and 12th Companies, and the Lincolns and South Staffords were ordered to withdraw to Quadrangle Trench before daylight to avoid being cut off. A machine gun and its crew near Acid Drop Copse appear not to have received this order and remained in position. They were to do useful work later on.

By daylight (the 10th) the situation had not materially changed except for the arrival of the 6th Company, 122d Reserve Infantry Regiment sent forward from the second line position (2nd Battalion) to reinforce Quadrangle Support. The march of this company during the night up to the front line is of interest if only to show that the Germans also had their troubles. The company commander, Lieutenant Köstlin, a civil engineer in times of peace, gives full details in his report. The order to reinforce the 3rd Battalion about Mametz Wood reached him during the afternoon of the 9th. At dusk he marched his company from the second line position about Bazentin back to the ammunition depôt at Martinpuich, to fill up with ammunition and hand-grenades and to have a square meal from the battalion field-kitchen cart. Their dinner was interrupted by a shell which so much frightened the horse that it bolted at a gallop, food, kitchen and all into the darkness. It was after midnight before the ammunition had been issued and the company left Martinpuich with its two machine guns. The night was very dark, and although two guides had been sent from the 3rd Battalion to lead the way, Lieutenant Köstlin preferred to march across the open by compass. At first the companies marched in file, but the crossing of the many trenches and shell holes between Martinpuich and Bazentin in the dark soon made the column very extended, and much time was lost in halts for closing up. After crossing the second line position at Bazentin, therefore, he formed the company into column of sections in file, and this method of advance proved much simpler and quicker. But from now onward the ground they had to cross was constantly shelled. Every few minutes shrapnel burst somewhere among the column and many casualties were suffered. Since Mametz Wood had been a special target of the British artillery for some days, and was a very easy place to get lost in at night, he decided to move across the open between the wood and Contalmaison village, following roughly the line of the Grossherzogsgraben (Pearl Alley), formerly a communication trench leading from the second line up to Quadrangle Trench, and then reach the wood from Quadrangle Support. Soon after crossing the Bazentin—Contalmaison road the two guides said they thought the front line was close at hand, so he halted the company and told the guides to go on and see, and to ask where his company was wanted. It was about 2.30 a.m. and there was a faint glimmer of the dawn.

"After some twenty minutes," he writes, "the guides returned saying the trench was straight ahead with the 10th, 11th and 12th Companies, and that reinforcements were badly needed there. The company therefore moved on at once, but after a few yards a machine gun suddenly opened fire close by from the rising ground on the right. Fortunately it was not yet light enough for the gun to take accurate aim and the bullets passed over our heads. For a moment, however, there was a great confusion, some lay down, some ran back and some forward. I shouted 'Double march, into the trench in front,' and hurried on, believing the company to be with me. But the trench was further than I thought, some 300 yards, and on reaching it I found that only thirty had arrived out of the whole company."

Later, he heard that in the confusion his order had not been heard and the men believing themselves up against an enemy's position had gone back to the second line about Bazentin or remained in shell holes on the way. Lieutenant Irion, who met him on his arrival at the trench, said that the British had broken through the western end of the trench during the night, and this undoubtedly accounted for the machine gun.[5] Lieutenant Irion also said that since midnight no communication had been possible to battalion headquarters, Major von Zeppelin, in Mametz Wood, whose last instructions were that companies were to act independently and not to await orders from him. The three companies in the trench, Nos. 10, 11 and 12, had lost very heavily during the past twenty-four hours, and the total now holding it, including the new arrivals, was 6 officers and 160 other ranks. Lieutenant Köstlin, being the senior officer present, took over command of the trench.

4

The attack of the 38th (Welsh) Division on the right against Mametz Wood had been postponed till 4.15 a.m. (the 10th). The bombardment of the southern part of the wood began at 3.30 a.m. The Germans had found the wood difficult to put in a state of defence. It consisted chiefly of fair-sized oak, beech and alder trees averaging 30 to 40 feet high, and beneath was a thick and in places almost impenetrable tangle of undergrowth, briar, bramble and saplings. The bombardment which had destroyed many of the trees, uprooting them or slashing them to pieces, had made the wood still more impassable. Except for a few machine guns in shelter pits here and there along the ridges and in small clearings, the Germans had, therefore, left the wood itself alone, confining their attention to a line of trench along the southern edge, with support lines in the open ground on both sides half-way up it, Wood Trench (Tote Stellung) and Wood Support (Weissgraben) on the west and a line of trench about Flat Iron Copse on the east.

The operation by the 38th Division on the morning of the 10th took the form of a direct assault against the southern edge of the wood, held by the 2nd Battalion Lehr Infantry Regiment. At both corners of the southern end a narrow strip of wood reaches out some 200 yards towards the bed of the Mametz valley in which the Welsh infantry had assembled overnight for the assault. The final bombardment was very heavy and accurate, and the right and left of the assaulting brigades, 114th and 113th respectively, advancing behind a smoke screen, were able to secure the trenches at the end of the two strips of wood on the flanks before the Germans could get out of their dug-outs. The centre of the attack, the inner flanks of the two brigades, was held up, as the companies had a great distance of open ground to cover, giving the Germans time to get into a firing position to meet them. The assault here lost heavily and wavered, the lines lying out in the open for about an hour, taking cover in folds of the ground as best they could. Gradually, however, the troops worked along the strips of wood on both flanks into the wood itself, and the remnants of the 2nd Battalion Lehr Regiment either retired or were surrounded. By 6 a.m. the whole of the southern edge of the wood was occupied and the advance continued northwards through it, units moving generally by companies in single file with patrols in front. Here and there machine-gun posts were encountered, but their field of fire in the dense undergrowth was very limited and they were soon put out of action with bombs. Beyond that no serious opposition was met in the wood itself. Nevertheless, progress was slow, and it was late in the morning before the ride across the centre of the wood was reached. The fifty yards of Wood Trench still held by the 5th and 9th Companies (122nd Reserve Infantry Regiment) was outflanked from the wood and evacuated, the Germans

---

5   This was probably that of the South Staffords left near Acid Drop Copse a few hours before. According to the German account it received a direct hit from a British shell during a bombardment of the village later in the day, and all its crew were killed outright.

running back under a heavy fire to Wood Support, where they held on obstinately. On the eastern side of the wood the 3rd Lehr Battalion about Flat Iron Copse gave incessant trouble. As soon as the Welshmen had advanced up the wood beyond the level of their trench a number of men would run into the wood and fire into them from behind, causing a temporary panic and loss, and then would withdraw to their trench again. With both flanks held the advance through the wood now lost its drive. Units were considerably intermingled and the line was reorganized along the line of the central ride, where it remained till about 4.30 p.m.

5

It is clear that had the night attack of the 50th Brigade (17th Division) succeeded in capturing Quadrangle Support, the position of the two German companies (5th and 9th) holding out in Wood Support would have been untenable, and the 38th and 17th Divisions could now have swept on without opposition to the Contalmaison—Bazentin road. Already at 8.30 a.m., with a view to cooperation in this manner between the two divisions, the 50th Brigade had been ordered to take every step to secure Quadrangle Support and to be prepared to advance northward as soon as the 38th Division came up on its right. Since the Brigade had failed to cross the 200 yards of open ground between the opposing trenches under cover of darkness, it was not, however, considered practicable in daylight, and instead, an attempt was made to take it by bombing. A communication trench, Quadrangle Alley, led up from Quadrangle Trench to the eastern end of Quadrangle Support, and it was hoped that a detachment of bombers would be able to get along the Alley into Quadrangle Support trench and bomb their way up it, thereby preparing the way for an infantry assault. To this end the battalion bombers of the 7th East Yorks moved along Quadrangle Alley. Within 20 yards of the German trench, however, the Alley had been blocked and filled in by the Germans, and, according to the battalion (7th East Yorks) diarist, the first three men who attempted to rush across were immediately shot down. Although a great effort was made, the bombers found it impossible to get across to Quadrangle Support.

The report of Lieutenant Köstlin gives the German version of this effort, and explains how Quadrangle Support held out. His trench lay aslant the slope of Shrapnel Valley, and was sheltered from artillery observation by a shoulder of the Contalmaison spur along which lay Quadrangle Trench and the British line.

"During the morning," writes Lieutenant Köstlin, "the British made further efforts to reach our trench by the sap (Quadrangle Alley) that came within 20 yards of our own left. My sentries, however, noticed steel helmets moving about above ground-level at the sap-head and kept it under careful watch. Each time the men began to climb up out of the sap-head and run forward at us with bombs, the sentries gave the alarm, and we were able to greet them with a heavy fire at point-blank range. Then others crowded at the sap-head and repeated the effort, but with equal failure, and by midday a heap of British dead and wounded lay about the sap-head. Each time they had been checked one of my men in particular ran forward across the open and threw bombs into the saphead and returned unhurt. The last time, however, about midday, he was shot before he could get back."

From Lieutenant Köstlin's position in Quadrangle Support he was also able to watch the progress of the fighting in Mametz Wood on the opposite slope of Shrapnel Valley. He saw to his astonishment the sudden retirement of the remnants of the 5th and 9th

Companies from Wood Trench to Wood Support for no apparent reason, the actual advance of the 38th (Welsh) Division through the wood itself not being visible to him. An hour later, about midday, a sentry drew his attention to the edge of Mametz Wood, about 400 yards to his left rear, where he thought he saw a man in khaki.

> I looked through my glasses. I looked again, it was incredible. But there he was, an Englishman in khaki and steel helmet, standing bolt upright, regardless of cover as usual, near a long, bare tree trunk. Looking more carefully, I saw others among the trees near by. They must have broken through and come past our left flank under cover of the trees in the bed of the valley, and that explained the sudden withdrawal of the 5th and 9th Companies. I ordered fire to be opened on the patrol at the wood edge, and the men moved away into the cover.[6] It did not alter the fact, however, that Mametz Wood was now probably in British possession, threatening our line of retreat to Bazentin.
>
> But the surprises of the day were not at an end. Whilst still searching with my glasses, there suddenly appeared in the big open clearing in Mametz Wood, across which was Wood Support Trench (Weissgraben), lines of skirmishers who advanced across the open directly against Wood Support. From that trench came no sound, it seemed that both the 5th and 9th Companies had vanished into space. Nevertheless, from our trench the advancing lines offered an excellent target, as we were in a position to enfilade them at a range of 600 yards. I scarcely needed to give the order. My men had already seen the target, and a rapid fire opened almost at once. Every rifle was at work, the officers picking up rifles and joining in, until soon all the rifle barrels were red hot. Not a single Englishman seemed to reach Wood Support trench, and a large number lay dead and wounded about the open clearing.[7] From the firing in the wood it was evident that we had only held up the left flank guard of the main force advancing through the wood itself.
>
> Our ammunition was getting short, and we scraped together all we could find in the trench and the dug-outs and from the dead and wounded. Shortly afterwards a line of skirmishers suddenly appeared from a fold in the ground near the line of tall trees in the valley and advanced against the left of our trench. We were only just in time to stop them, the first extended line being shot down within a few yards of us. Already the second line was moving forward, and this was dealt with in the same way.[8] Fortunately, our old enemy in the sap-head had remained quiet after the lesson

---

6   This was probably a patrol of the 6th Dorsets. The battalion diary states: "2nd Lieut. C—led a patrol up the belt of trees running from the west end of Wood Trench to Wood Support. The patrol was fired on, and Lieut. C—and one man were wounded."

7   At 10 a.m. the 6th Dorsets were ordered to "push two or three platoons from Wood Trench to Wood Support and occupy it if possible, if not already occupied by the 'Welsh Division." The 50th Infantry Brigade diary states that "the attack on Wood Support came under a heavy machine-gun fire in the open and failed because the troops of the 38th Division had moved away into the Wood and failed to cooperate."

8   This probably refers to an attack by the 7th E. Yorks. The battalion diary states: "At midday orders were received from the brigade to do all that was possible to cooperate with the advance in Mametz Wood. I, therefore, reorganized companies in Quadrangle Alley, preparing 'C' and 'D' Companies to attack across the open up the valley. I waited until I considered conditions favourable, and this moment arrived when I saw British troops on the right and in the Wood, and some actually on the fringe of the Wood in rear of Wood Support. ... Lieut. C—and his men were almost immediately subjected to machine-gun fire,

we had given him in the morning. An attack from there at this moment might well have been fatal for us.

In the meantime the Welsh Division had continued its advance from the central ride northward through Mametz Wood to within 50 yards or so of the northern edge, where they established themselves for the night, having lost 2,390 all ranks during the fighting. The remnants of the 5th and 9th Companies in Wood Support trench had been either killed or taken prisoner. The battalion (3rd) commander, Major von Zeppelin, whose headquarters had been in the wood, was mortally wounded by shrapnel on leaving it.

6

Since the 17th Division had failed to take Contalmaison from the south on the night of the 9th/10th, the 23rd Division was now ordered to take it from the west, from the direction of La Boisselle. For this purpose the 69th Brigade, on the morning of the 10th, was ordered to pass through the front brigades of the division and attack Contalmaison village at 4.20 p.m., keeping south of the La Boisselle—Contalmaison road. The assaulting battalions of the brigade, the 8th Yorks on the right and the 9th Yorks on the left, had 1,500 yards, nearly a mile, of open rolling down to cross in daylight before reaching their objective.

The Germans were still holding the village with the 1st Battalion (Nos. 1, 2, 3 and 4 Companies) of the 122nd Reserve Infantry Regiment, with battalion headquarters at the chateau, but the losses had already reduced the battalion strength to less than 600 all ranks. Odd detachments had been sent forward to reinforce the garrison, but were far from adequate to fill the gaps. Moreover, the casualties were ever increasing for the British III Corps artillery was doing its work well, and Contalmaison, shelled for two days and nights, was now a heap of rubble. The beginning of the renewed bombardment at 3.20 p.m. seems to have been the final factor that broke the staying power of the defenders. A number, estimated by British observers at 200, ran back towards Bazentin and Pozières, anywhere out of the village, the others taking refuge in any of the deep dug-outs still open either in the Kaisergraben (that part of Quadrangle Trench west of Contalmaison village) or in the village itself. Two restless days and sleepless nights, constant alarms, constant shelling and fighting and repairing trenches and dug-outs, had completely exhausted them, so that when the alarm was given at 4.50 p.m., at the conclusion of the bombardment, it had little effect. According to the regimental diary only 1 officer and 15 men of the two right companies (Nos. 3 and 4) appeared above ground, and these occupied some ruins at the western end of the village, but the air was so full of smoke and the dust of crumbling ruins that the advance of the British could scarcely be seen.

At first the 8th and 9th Yorks were consequently able to carry out their long advance with little loss, the right, the inner flank, of the 9th Yorks directing and marching on the church, almost unrecognizable and invisible in the centre of the village. Crossing a depression within 500 yards of the village, the extended lines came under an accurate fire from the German batteries and suffered considerably, nevertheless, by 5.20 p.m., they were

and this officer was killed in the attempt. 'D' Company, under Capt. H—, advancing across the open in extended order in two lines also came under heavy fire, Capt. H— being killed. Upon launching this attack I sent down orderlies to bring up the other two companies, 'A' and 'B,' in support, but did not consider myself justified in committing them to the same attempt. The attack was attempted with great determination, and if it could have been accomplished at that time I am confident we should have done it."

approaching the Kaisergraben. Masses of wire entanglement and wreckage that formed an obstacle in front of it was soon crossed and the trench entered without opposition. The 9th Yorks went straight ahead into the village, odd Germans here and there among the ruins being killed or taken prisoner. On reaching the main street the 9th Yorks wheeled left-handed, northward, and halted along the northern end of the village, their objective.

The 8th Yorks had to pay more dearly in the last part of their advance, as they crossed the 50 yards between the Kaisergraben and a garden hedge bordering the houses of the village. This was probably due to the action of the 1 officer and 15 men mentioned above who had taken up a position among the ruins at the western edge of the village and now opened a sudden burst of fire that swept the lines of the 8th Yorks, just when victory seemed in their grasp. The 8th Yorks lost 4 officers and over 100 other ranks in a few moments, but this did not suffice to check the assault and, pressing on without delay, the village was entered. They now joined hands with the 9th Yorks and a general line was taken up round the northern and eastern edges of the village, including the château at the north-eastern corner. At this latter place the battalion commander (1st Battalion 122nd Reserve Infantry Regiment) in charge of the Contalmaison garrison was taken prisoner. In all, the 69th Brigade claims to have captured 8 German officers and 160 unwounded men, in addition to some 100 wounded lying in the dug-outs, also 6 machine guns and a quantity of ammunition. The total casualties of the 69th Brigade itself during the day and the following night were 39 officers and 816 other ranks.

No. 2 Company holding the south-eastern edge of the village was now taken in rear, and a counter-attack made by it against the road junction, south of the church, was driven off by the 8th Yorks. The company fell back by Pearl Alley, a small party holding on to the Cutting until nightfall.

The situation of the remnants of Nos. 6, 10, 11 and 12 Companies still holding out in Quadrangle Support soon became very precarious and their commander, Lieutenant Köstlin, seems to have been well aware of the fact. "His men," he writes, "were quite exhausted and so thirsty that they drank the yellow muddy water out of the trench for want of better." He saw that his only chance of escape was to hold on till dark, although, surrounded on three sides, he thought they would all inevitably be taken prisoners. The evening hours dragged on interminably and still no attack was made. He writes:

> It seemed, indeed that the enemy did not consider an attack worthwhile, as finally we should have to fall like ripe fruit into his hands. At one moment there was a ray of hope, when we heard a heavy machine-gun and rifle fire open from our second line position on the northern edge of Mametz Wood. It might, we thought, be a counterattack which would drive the British back through the wood. Immediately afterwards, however, a heavy bombardment by the British artillery opened on the second line position and the ground between it and the wood, great black and green clouds rising up from the northern side of Mametz Wood amid tremendous explosions. The infantry fire from our supposed counter-attack suddenly died away and with it our last hope of escape. At dusk, however, the British still made no attack on us from the front nor, as far as we could see, made any attempt to move behind us, either

from Contalmaison or from Mametz Wood. In consultation with the other officers we decided to make a dash for safety as soon as it was dark. To do this, a number of selected men were told off to run forward to the enemy's trench, throw hand-grenades into it as if an attack was about to take place, and under cover of this feint withdraw the whole of our force to the second line position, making our way the best we could, keeping Mametz Wood well on our right. After dark the ground behind our trench was being continually shelled, but about midnight this fire ceased and we decided to rush for it. The plan worked successfully, and although a number of men were wounded by shells and stray bullets we succeeded, a total of 5 officers and 120 men, in reaching the barbed wire entanglement in front of the second line position at 1.30 a.m. Here we were greeted by a machine gun which suddenly opened from the trench, but throwing ourselves on the ground and shouting we soon convinced the gunner of his error, and luckily with no cost to ourselves.

7

The 183rd Regiment, in the Roedergraben, north of Contalmaison, had made two attempts to get forward to Fourth Street (Quergraben III). The first was made the night after its arrival, the 8th–9th, and timed for midnight,[9] but owing to the heavy rain of the previous days the communication trenches were so filled with mud and water that there were great delays in forming up in the assaulting position, so that it was 3 a.m., and daylight, before units were in their places. The deployment was seen by the British observers (34th Division) south of Ovillers, and the development of the attack was prevented by artillery and machine-gun fire. The second attempt was made on the 9th, when, at 11.45 a.m., Divisional (183rd) Headquarters again ordered Quergraben III to be captured, the attack to begin at 1.30 p.m. after half an hour's artillery preparation. Before the orders could be written out the regimental commander, Colonel Schultze, was severely wounded, and it was some time before the next senior officer to take his place could be found. As a result the infantry attack was not delivered until 3.30 p.m., long after the conclusion of the bombardment, and it only succeeded in reaching some scraps of trenches half-way between the Roedergraben and Fourth Street. On the afternoon of the 10th, the regiment was ordered to make a renewed attack on Fourth Street, beginning at 5 p.m. This met a simultaneous attack of the British 111th and 112th Brigades (34th Division) which had been ordered to cooperate with the attack of the 69th Brigade on their right against Contalmaison. The 34th Divisional diary states that:

> … the 111th Brigade was driven back to Fourth Street after an encounter with the enemy in which the brigade had heavy casualties, estimated at 8 officers and 350 other ranks, but took 100 prisoners. The 112th Brigade was also forced to retire, the enemy following up to within 50 yards of our trench. The 11th Royal Warwicks then advanced upon them and got in with the bayonet. It appears that these forward movements of our brigades forestalled the enemy, and that he was himself contemplating an attack.

The diary of the 183rd Regiment attributes the failure of its attack to the situation on its left in Contalmaison village, which had been entered by the British at 6 p.m., and who thereupon began to open fire against the left flank and rear of the regiment about the

---

9 All times given are Greenwich times.

Roedergraben. At 8 p.m. an order arrived: "Contalmaison is still held by us with a weak force, but may have to be abandoned at any moment. This will expose the left flank of the 183rd Infantry Regiment." The regiment, therefore, was ordered to withdraw to the Kabel and Latorff trenches and hold Pozières at all costs.

8

By dawn, on the 11th, the Germans had taken up their fresh positions.

On the right the 183rd Regiment had withdrawn to the line of the Kabel and Latorff trenches around Pozières. The losses of the regiment had been heavy, nearly 1,000 all ranks.

In the centre the remnants of the 122nd Reserve Infantry Regiment had withdrawn into and behind the German second line between Pozières and Bazentin-le-Petit, leaving machine-gun posts in front, along the northern edge of Mametz Wood and towards Contalmaison. On the 9th its three battalions had lost 13 officers and 217 other ranks, and, on the 10th, 17 officers and 964 other ranks.

On the left the Lehr Regiment continued to hold the line about Flat Iron Copse and eastward.

9

Summing up the battle the German historians praise the defence of Contalmaison as a very creditable performance by the German units concerned. The historian of the 183rd Infantry Regiment writes that the regiment was at that time at the zenith of its efficiency, having many of its pre-war regular officers and non-commissioned officers and a majority of young, able-bodied men who had undergone a whole winter of strenuous training. But the odds, he says, were too heavy against them—three British divisions (roughly thirty-six battalions) attacking concentrically against nine German battalions (183rd, 122nd Reserve and Lehr Infantry Regiments). The same writer describes the British infantry as determined and full of go, but as lacking in intelligent tactical work and showing no skill in making use of the successes they gained. Still more, however, he attributes the German difficulties to the great preponderance of strength of the British artillery, even greater than that of the infantry. The comparatively few German batteries available were quite incapable of dealing with the mass of British guns and howitzers arrayed against them and were consequently unable to give much assistance to their infantry in the defence. Further, he adds, the British artillery shot very accurately and picked up their targets quickly and well, their observation being undoubtedly much assisted by having command of the air, the loss of which, after the 1st of July, being a great disadvantage to the German batteries. The historian of the 122nd Reserve Infantry Regiment sums up the battle from a similar point of view. He maintains that his regiment had done all that could be expected of it, and that it was owing to the stubbornness with which it had held its ground that the British had had to deploy such a mass of infantry, expend such a great number of lives, and waste such a vast quantity of ammunition and so much valuable time in order to capture an intermediary position held by a comparatively small force.

9

Delville Wood

14–19 July 1916[1]

After the first assault by the British and French forces between the Somme and the Ancre on the 1st of July, 1916, the continuous fighting and heavy pressure against the German defence had led to such a confusion of units and commands as fresh reinforcements arrived that in the middle of the month a complete reorganization took place. The battle area was divided by the enemy into permanent corps sectors. The corps commander and staff, the heavy artillery and supply services remained unchanged in these sectors, but the corps itself ceased to act on the battle front as a fighting unit. It formed a framework into which the constantly changing fighting divisions and brigades were brought, played their part and were taken out again. The work of the permanent corps staff was to direct their several efforts and to support and feed them. This method solved to a great extent the problem of command in such a mixed mass of units and also ensured a continuity of policy throughout the varying phases of the battle. As a system it was the model on which the Germans worked to the end of the war.

Thus in the middle of July the battle front between the Somme and the Ancre was organized into three corps-sectors: Group Gossler (VI Reserve Corps) with the 11th Reserve Division, 123rd Division and 24th Reserve Division from the Somme to Hardecourt; Group Sixt von Armin (IV Corps) with the 10th Bavarian Division, 7th Division and 8th Division from Hardecourt to Pozières (Albert—Péronne road) and Group Stein (XIV Corps) with the 26th Reserve Division, 52nd Division and and Guard Reserve Division from Pozières across the Ancre to Gommecourt.[2]

The British attack on the 14th of July against the four-miles front of the German second line position (*Braune Stellung*) Longueval—Bazentin—Pozières was thus met by the centre group, General Sixt von Armin. Elements of the 10th Bavarian Division held the front Guillemont—Delville Wood—Longueval—Bazentin le Grand, and the 7th Division from that village to Pozières. The 8th Division was in reserve south of Bapaume.

The British units engaged were the XIII, XV and III Corps. This chapter only deals with the right attack, that made by the XIII Corps. After capturing the German second line on both sides of Longueval village the task of the XIII Corps was to establish a

---

1 The following list of books used for this article may be of interest to any reader wishing to follow up details of the fighting at this period in Longueval and Delville Wood: *Der Grosse Krieg*, Vol. 2: Schwarte; *Geschichte des Krieges*, Vol. 3: Stegemann; *Bavarian Official History* (*Die Bayern im Grossen Kriege*); *Bataille de la Somme*: Palat; *Feld. Art. Regt. Nr. 18*: Lipinsky; *Feld. Art. Regt. Nr. 57*: Uebe; *Leib. Grenadier Regt. Nr. 8*: Schöning; *Grenadier Regt. Nr. 12*: Schönfeldt; *Inf. Regt. Nr. 52*: Reymann; *Inf. Regt. Nr. 153*: Schmidt; *Inf. Regt. Nr. 182*: Pache.

2 There were also two groups facing the French offensive south of the Somme: Group Quast (IX Corps) and a XVII Corps Group. Towards the end of the month all these groups were placed under the command of General von Gallwitz, called away from Verdun to take over the direction of the defence on the Somme.

10. Delville Wood, July 1916

strong defensive flank about the village. There the German front turned southward by Troves Wood, facing Guillemont and across the head of Caterpillar Valley, so it was of the utmost importance both for the success of this attack, and for the preparation of subsequent attacks, that the right flank at Longueval should be consolidated and held as a corner buttress of the new line.

The village of Longueval, in the midst of the German defensive system, lay on the high ground of the Ginchy—Pozières ridge and consisted of a cluster of cottages at the junction of four roads. The market place was at the cross-roads and the cottages straggled for a few hundred yards along three of the roads; one leading northward to Flers, another eastward to Ginchy, and the third southward down the slope of the ridge to Montauban. Immediately north-east of the village and almost overshadowing it was Delville Wood, a thick tangle of trees, chiefly oak and birch, and dense hazel undergrowth. It was triangular-shaped, occupying the whole area between the Flers and Ginchy roads for some 700 yards out of the village, with an irregular eastern face of about 1,200 yards, and offered, therefore, a covered approach into Longueval village. In the circumstances it was considered essential to occupy Delville Wood as well as the village, if the latter was to be satisfactorily defended.

The Fighting in Longueval

The 9th Division, the right division of the XIII Corps, was responsible for the assault on Longueval, and at dawn on the 14th of July its two leading brigades, the 26th and 27th, after a most ably conducted approach march of over 1,000 yards under cover of darkness up the slope from Caterpillar Valley, successfully carried the German position at daybreak and entered the village. There, however, the resistance of the second battalion, 16th Bavarian Regiment, was very obstinate, and during the morning the attack was definitely checked about the market place and on the roads leading east and west through the centre of the village. On the left, however, the first battalion, 16th Bavarian Regiment, holding the area between Longueval and Bazentin le Grand, was overrun and surrounded,[3] the British pressing on towards High Wood. In view of this success, the South African Brigade, in reserve about Montauban, the remaining brigade of the 9th Division, was ordered to send forward one battalion to assist in carrying Longueval.

Advancing in eight lines of sections in file across the mile of open grassland up the slope from Caterpillar Valley, this, the 1st South African Regiment, reached the German original trenches south of the village with little loss, and reinforced the 26th and 27th Brigades near the market place about 2p.m. From here they were told to advance on either side of North Street, the road leading to Flers, and to clear the cottages along it as well as the orchards and gardens between the street and the wood.

Meanwhile, however, the second battalion, 16th Bavarian Regiment, had been reinforced by a battalion of the 26th Infantry Regiment. This battalion, which had been hurriedly sent across from 7th Divisional reserve, now took up a position in Longueval and along the southern edge of Delville Wood. In face of this reinforcement the advance

---

3   The resistance of the third battalion of this Regiment between Bazentin le Grand and Bazentin le Petit was also broken after eight hours' fighting and the position captured. The Bavarian official history states that all three battalions of this Regiment were practically annihilated. They had been in the line for fourteen days, having been sent up to occupy the-second line position in support on the 1st of July, and when, on the 15th of July, the men still remaining were assembled, the losses were found to be 72 officers and 2,559 other ranks.

of the 1st South African Regiment proved a difficult task. A number of German machine guns had been hidden among the ruins of the houses and along the edge of the wood. Many of the cellars of these cottages were connected by subterranean passages, and, after three or four of them had been cleared by our troops, parties of Germans suddenly emerged from a cottage in rear and fired into the back of the attacking parties. For these reasons each attempt to get forward was checked, and, by nightfall, the 1st South African Regiment was occupying a frontage of 500 yards, its left on North Street 50 yards north of the market place, and its right on Prince's Street, a track leading from the market place eastward through the centre of Delville Wood. On its left was the 27th Brigade, west of North Street, and during the night the 5th Cameron Highlanders (26th Brigade) came up on the right. and began to entrench along the line of Buchanan Street, a grassy ride in the wood leading at right angles to Prince's Street to the southern edge.

Capture of Delville Wood, 15th of July

The reports received from the front line during the afternoon of the 14th led to the belief that the capture of Longueval was imminent, and General Lukin, commanding the South African Brigade, was ordered, therefore, to be in readiness to move forward to capture Delville Wood. For this purpose he was to employ the whole of his Brigade, less the 1st Regiment, already sent forward to assist the 27th Brigade in the village. The hour of attack was given as 5 p.m. and then altered to 7 p.m. and later to 7.30 p.m., these changes being due to conflicting reports as to the situation in Longueval and the belief that the capture of the whole of the village was a necessary prelude to launching the attack on Delville Wood. During the evening, however, at a conference with General W. T. Furse, the divisional commander, it was decided that the attack should be postponed till 5 a.m. the next morning, the 15th.

General Lukin's final orders for the attack on Delville Wood by the remainder of the South African Brigade were issued at 9 p.m. that evening, the 14th. The 2nd and 3rd Regiments, with the 4th in support, were to move forward under cover of darkness to Longueval, the whole of which it was hoped would be captured before their arrival. They were then to deploy along the western edge of the wood and to move through it, taking up a position along its further perimeter, facing north, east and south-east.

The brigade was clear of Montauban village by 2.30 a.m., the Brigade headquarters being established in an old German dug-out in the north-west corner of the village.

The three regiments, under Colonel W. E. Tanner, moved in open order astride the Montauban road up the hill leading to Longueval, the 3rd Regiment in front followed closely by the 2nd, and with the 4th in rear. The German original trenches south of Longueval, where the Montauban road enters the village, were reached as it was beginning to get light and the troops took shelter in them, while Colonel Tanner went forward with Colonel E. F. Thackeray, commanding the 3rd Regiment, to find out the situation in Longueval. From battalion commanders of the 26th Brigade he learned that the northern part of the village was still in German possession, and that although the south-west corner of the wood, bounded by Prince's Street and Buchanan Street, was held by companies of the 1st South African Regiment and of the 5th Cameron Highlanders, the situation in the remainder of the wood was obscure. In view of these facts Colonel Tanner decided that an attack on the wood from the west as originally intended was impracticable, and he decided to clear the wood in sections, attacking first that part of it south of Prince's

Street from the front of Buchanan Street. Having established a front along the southern side of Prince's Street, an attack could then be delivered northward from Prince's Street to the northern and north-eastern perimeter of the wood. A guide from the 5th Cameron Highlanders led the 3rd South African Regiment successfully to the line of Buchanan Street, making use of the German original trenches and communication trenches which offered a covered approach the greater part of the way. The line of Buchanan Street was reached about 6 a.m. on the 15th.

The early hours had been cloudy with a light mist, but as the sun rose the clouds and mist dispersed, the prelude to a hot and cloudless day. At first the attack of the 3rd Regiment moved swiftly and little resistance was met, the chief delay being the thick undergrowth and mass of broken trees felled by the bombardment of the previous days. Patrols out in front took prisoner 3 officers and 135 other ranks who, attacked from the rear from the wood, were taken by surprise in their dug-outs in and along the southern edge. By 7 a.m. all that part of the wood south of Prince's Street had been occupied by the 3rd Regiment, supported by a company of the 2nd Regiment which followed close behind. Colonel Tanner now sent the remaining three companies of the 2nd Regiment to occupy the line of Prince's Street from which they were to move northward through the remainder of the wood, forming a defensive flank on the left about the line of the grassy ride known as the Strand, which abutted on the uncaptured northern part of Longueval village. By midday the whole of the wood was in British hands with the exception of the north-west corner, west of the Strand.

Efforts to advance beyond the perimeter of the wood met with no success since the German 8th Division, IV Corps reserve, had moved forward into the battle zone during the night from Bapaume, and its leading units were now assembling in the intermediary line of trenches[4] between the northern edge of the wood and the villages of Flers and Ginchy. The German batteries were already beginning to bombard the wood, and it was clear that it would soon become a dangerous shell-trap. General Lukin's intention was, therefore, to thin out the troops in the wood leaving it to be held by a number of machine-gun posts along the perimeter, eight between Flers road and Prince's Street, where the situation was difficult owing to the probability of a counter-attack from Flers, and two between Prince's Street and Ginchy road where a good command of the ground could be obtained for some 1,000 yards in front as far as the villages of Ginchy and Guillemont. This plan, however, was frustrated before it could be carried out, owing to a series of counter-attacks delivered during the afternoon from the German intermediary position against the perimeter of the wood. As there had not been time to construct machine-gun emplacements in the hard chalk soil, all available rifles were required to check the German attacks. Thus at 3 p.m. one was delivered from the east from astride the Ginchy road, and at 4:30 p.m. and 6.30 p.m. further efforts were made from the direction of the Flers road, but all these were driven back before the enemy reached the edge of the wood.

The casualties of the South Africans had been heavy during the day, chiefly from shell fire, and the two companies, "C" and "D" of the 1st South African Regiment that had been in support south of Longueval village, and two companies of the 4th South African Regiment, were sent up to reinforce the front line. By nightfall, consequently, the perimeter of the wood, a frontage in all of 1,800 yards, was being held by twelve companies much reduced in strength. The 3rd Regiment held the southern part of the wood, south

---

4   See map.

of Prince's Street, and the 2nd Regiment the northern part with one company of the 4th Regiment in close support to each. "C" and "D" Companies of the 1st Regiment formed the left defensive flank along the line of the Strand facing west, their left in touch with "A" and "B" Companies of the same Regiment which were still in position along Prince's Street, between Buchanan Street and the market place of Longueval. The remaining two companies of the 4th Regiment had been sent to assist the 26th Brigade to capture Waterlot Farm, 500 yards to the south-west on the Longueval—Guillemont road. Colonel Tanner's headquarters was established in the wood at the junction of Buchanan Street with Prince's Street.

Consolidation of the Position, 16th-17th of July

About sunset the activity of the German batteries increased and continued through the night. The orders to the South African Brigade were to hold the wood at all costs in order to give time for the preparations for a further offensive towards Guillemont village and High Wood, on either side of the Delville Wood salient. Their position around the perimeter of the wood, therefore, was to be entrenched and strengthened. This was no easy task, as the hard chalk and the tangled roots of the trees made digging a tough proposition. The work was carried on throughout the night and by the morning, Sunday, the 16th, a certain amount of cover had been obtained.

At 2.35 a.m. General Lukin received orders from divisional headquarters to cooperate with the 27th Brigade, on the left, in a further effort to clear the Germans from the northern part of Longueval village and the north-western corner of the wood. The 11th Royal Scots (27th Brigade) were to capture the remainder of the village, while "A" and "B" Companies of the 1st Regiment, which, it will be remembered, were holding Prince's Street between the village and Buchanan Street, were to clear the north-western corner of the wood, joining hands with the Royal Scots on the Flers road. The British and German troops were so close to one another in this sector that a preparatory artillery bombardment was not considered practicable, and it was decided to bombard the Germans with trench mortars before the attack. The infantry assault was delivered at 10 a.m. but every effort to advance was immediately checked by the enemy's heavy machine-gun and rifle fire, both from the northern part of the village and from a strong stone-built redoubt at the edge of the wood.

The weather was again very warm and the enemy kept up a constant bombardment of Delville Wood and the British communications behind Longueval, covering the whole battle zone with dust and smoke. The supply of much needed water, food and ammunition to the troops in the front line, therefore, was very difficult, most of it having to be sent forward by carriers. That afternoon General Lukin went forward to Longueval and impressed on the battalion commanders the importance of holding the wood at all costs, as the safety of the right wing of the new front depended on it. That evening orders were given for another attempt to clear the village and the north-eastern corner of the wood by an attack at dawn the following morning, the 17th. This attack, however, met with a similar fate as that of Sunday morning and further diminished the ranks of the 1st South African Regiment, which tried to assist by attacking westward from the Strand.

The remainder of the day passed comparatively peacefully, but it was a lull before the storm, and at dusk the German batteries again began to shell the wood from all three sides, north, east and south-east. During the evening Colonel Tanner was wounded and

Colonel Thackeray, commanding the 3rd Regiment, succeeded him in command of the troops in the wood.

The German Counter-Attack, 18th of July

During the night the German bombardment on Longueval and Delville Wood increased and became intense. For long periods the flashes of the explosions turned night into day and the wood became an inferno, justifying its nickname of Devil's Wood. At times, according to estimates, as many as 400 shells a minute were falling into it. The village itself was in flames and the wood was enveloped in the dark smoke of the bursting shells: the noise of the explosions, of falling debris and of crashing trees was almost overpowering. To complete these miserable conditions, a heavy rain which had begun to fall on the previous day continued, turning the shell craters into mud-holes and drenching the battle zone. This devastation went on throughout the morning and afternoon of the 18th until, at 3.15 p.m., the German infantry advanced against the wood and the village from east, north and north-east. The first crisis of the fight for Delville Wood now began.

The enemy's attack from the east was made by the 107th Reserve Infantry Regiment astride the Ginchy road, and failed. It is not clear from the records whether this was intended as part of the main attack, but in any case it had little chance of success. The trenches of the 3rd South African Regiment along the eastern edge of the wood were well sited, and had an almost uninterrupted command of the flat grassland in front as far as Ginchy. The advancing lines suffered heavily from the outset, and after a short distance seemed to melt away. No further attempt was made here to get forward beyond the intermediate line.

The principal attack was that made from the north and north-east by the 8th Division supported by the 5th Division,[5] about 9 battalions (6,000 men) in all actually taking part in the operation against Delville Wood and Longueval village. From the north the 153rd Regiment was to advance from the intermediate line south of Flers and drive the British out of Delville Wood, regaining the German second line position along the southern edge. The leading battalion was to occupy that part of the original second line trench south of the wood on the Longueval—Guillemont road as far as Waterlot Farm, the second battalion to occupy the southern edge of the wood, and the third a line along Prince's Street in the middle of the wood. The advance was assisted by the sunken stretch of the Flers road through a cutting 150 yards north of the wood, and here the leading lines formed up for the assault. The attack came up against the trenches of the 2nd South African Regiment, along the northern edge of the wood. These had been severely handled by the bombardment, and a quantity of gas shells put a number of men temporarily out of action. Three most exhausting days and nights with little rest had had their effect on the

---

5   Reports from the German front during the evening of the 14th gave an exaggerated impression of the British success at Bazentin le Grand and had led to the belief that the German line had broken. Orders were, therefore, sent to the 5th Division, assembling near St. Quentin from Lorraine, to move up at once into the IV Corps zone: "The enemy has broken through between Longueval and Pozières and is advancing on Bapaume." During the night the Division left in great haste by forced marches and in motor lorries for Vendelles, east of Péronne, and thence marched in two columns with advanced cavalry patrols and infantry advanced guards on Rocquigny and Bapaume. While still on the march these precautionary measures were dropped as a report came through that the British attack had been brought to a standstill. The Division halted south-east of Bapaume, where it remained during the 16th and 17th in support to the 8th Division.

defence, and here and there the Germans, after much loss, were able to gain a footing in the wood. The arrival of the successive lines of companies from the Flers road gradually forced the South Africans back into the wood, many of the machine-gun posts and trench garrisons being killed outright and others captured by the enemy. Some escaped back into the undergrowth, and a few of these found their way to Colonel Thackeray's headquarters at the junction of Prince's and Buchanan Streets. Here, with the assistance of 150 men of the 1st South African Regiment, a defensive position had been organized commanding the rides and facing north and east in order to hold the south-western corner of the wood.

After capturing the northern edge of the wood the Germans moved forward towards the southern edge, a distance of nearly 1,000 yards. On crossing Prince's Street the leading lines of the 153rd Regiment came under a heavy machine-gun fire from Colonel Thackeray's party near Buchanan Street, but continued under cover of the undergrowth to the southern edge. On emerging into the open from here towards Waterlot Farm they were exposed to such a heavy fire from Longueval, and also to artillery fire from the Montauban ridge, that they had to withdraw to the wood again having suffered extremely heavy losses. All 15 officers of the leading battalion had been put out of action, including the battalion commander who was severely wounded and the four company commanders who were killed. The second and third battalions of the Regiment had also gone into the wood, but their losses were so heavy[6] that they were unable to make headway beyond Prince's Street.

A message was now sent back for reinforcements, and at dusk (about 9 p.m.) the second battalion of the 52nd Infantry Regiment (5th Division), sent forward previously from about Barastre (south-east of Bapaume) to Gueudecourt and Flers, advanced on Delville Wood. The regimental diary tells its story:

> The second battalion moved out of Flers towards Delville Wood in successive lines as steadily as if on the parade ground. No. 5 Company in the front line, Nos. 6 and 7 in the second, and No. 8 in the third. The British artillery barrage lay along the entire northern edge of the wood and this was only passed through with the heaviest loss, including 4 officers. Parts of Nos. 5 and 6 Companies pressed straight through the wood to the southern edge, and a number of isolated British parties in the wood were taken prisoner. Touch however was not obtained with the 153rd Regiment and a number of British machine guns in the south-western corner of the wood, reinforced from Longueval village, kept up a constant fire against the rear of the companies along the southern edge, so much so that these front troops had to be withdrawn into the interior of the wood to a position immediately south of the big ride that traverses it from west to east. In the tangle of the wood in the growing darkness direction and touch were difficult to maintain. Lieut. Hering and a platoon of No. 6 Company suddenly found themselves surrounded by the enemy, but he himself shot down more than a dozen of the British, and breaking through their line with his men rejoined his company. The battalion spent the night in a state of indescribable confusion in the dense undergrowth of the wood, its right flank in the south-western part, its centre about the big east-west ride, and its left in the south-east portion. Odd parties of the enemy were moving about in the wood throughout

---

6   The History of the German 153rd Regiment gives the losses of its three battalions during this action as 38 officers and 1,300 men.

the night trying to regain their units, so that continual alarms and rifle fire resulted. During the night touch was gained with the scattered remnants of the 153 Regiment.

Simultaneously with the assault on Delville Wood, a German attack had been delivered against Longueval village from the north-west by the 26th Infantry Regiment, supported by the third battalion of the 52nd Regiment (5th Division). This had succeeded in driving back the British 27th Brigade through the village to the market place and the roads to east and west of it, but here the attack was checked after very severe fighting and many critical moments.

By nightfall the Germans were thus in possession of the greater part of Longueval village and the wood, with the exception of the eastern side and the south-west corner, and though they made a further attack from north and east against the south-west corner, Prince's and Buchanan Streets, they were repulsed by Colonel Thackeray's force with heavy loss. The 3rd South African Regiment along the eastern side of the wood had in the meantime suffered severe losses from artillery fire, and a number of men, seeing the danger of being cut off by the German advance through the wood behind them, had broken back to Buchanan Street. The greater part of the survivors, however, still held out along the eastern edge where the night was full of incident. Accounts from both sides are available of the events that followed on this portion of the front. The South African account states that only "B" Company of the regiment (3rd South African Regiment) was now left to defend this end of the wood, and that it had made its position as strong as possible in the circumstances. During the night 18 men of the 2nd South African Regiment, who had been taken prisoner and disarmed in the afternoon, managed to escape in the darkness and joined up with "B" Company. A number of Germans, 30 in all, groping at different times through the wood came on the South African trenches unexpectedly and were captured. At daybreak the danger from inside the wood was apparent and, the trench had to be defended by manning alternate bays facing opposite directions, so as to protect front and rear of the position. Ammunition, however, was by this time getting short, and, by 8 a.m., after repelling various attempts by the Germans to rush the position, only about five rounds per man were left. By 9 a.m. this had been expended and the garrison, 3 officers and 150 other ranks, surrendered.

The German account (52nd Regimental History) states:

> At 4.30 a.m.[7] the first battalion that had been moved up to the Sunken road near Flers the previous evening (10 p.m.) was placed at the disposal of Colonel Könemann, commanding the 153rd Regiment and the troops in Delville Wood. At daybreak two companies (Nos. 1 and 2) were moved up into the wood and directed through the dense thicket towards the eastern edge until close up to the British position which had been located there during the night. They were not seen until the last moment and the British opened fire but, without replying, the two companies rushed forward with the bayonet and overran the position in one assault, capturing 5 officers and 195 other ranks of the 3rd South African Regiment, also a number of machine guns. They also released 1 officer and 16 men of the 153rd Infantry Regiment who had been captured by the British during the night.

---

7 German time. British time one hour earlier.

About midday, the 19th, the remaining two companies (Nos. 3 and 4) of the first battalion, 52nd Regiment, were sent up from Flers to reinforce the troops in Delville Wood and to press on and occupy the southern edge. They succeeded in advancing 300 yards into the wood, but were then checked by constant fire along the rides from Longueval and the south-west corner of the wood. In the afternoon, however, a more or less connected front was established. The left of the 26th Infantry Regiment, with the third battalion of the 52nd Regiment, held the northern part of Longueval village, the remnants of the 153rd Regiment, with the second battalion and half the first battalion of the 52nd Regiment, held the north-western and centre parts of Delville Wood in an "S"-shaped position facing Prince's Street and Buchanan Street. The remaining half of the, first battalion 52nd Regiment (Nos. 1 and 2 Companies) still held the eastern end of the wood, its left in touch with the 107th Reserve Infantry Regiment in the intermediate line at a point 100 yards south of the Longueval—Ginchy road.

During the morning of the 19th, the British 76th Brigade (3rd Division) had arrived to assist in holding Longueval and Delville Wood, relieving the survivors of the South African Brigade. When this Brigade went into action on the 14th of July it had numbered 121 officers and 3,032 other ranks. When the roll was taken on the 21st of July in Happy Valley (Bray-sur-Somme) there were present 29 officers and 751 other ranks.[8] Nevertheless, the Brigade had succeeded in holding the corner buttress of the new line and thereby enabled the preparations for the next big push towards Flers and Guillemont to be made unmolested.

This brought to a conclusion the first stage of the fight for Delville Wood.

---

8   The casualties were:
    1st Regiment 558 all ranks
    2nd Regiment 482 all ranks
    3rd Regiment 771 all ranks
    4th Regiment 509 all ranks
    These figures include 23 officers killed, 7 died of wounds, 47 wounded and 15 taken prisoner or missing.

10

The Somme

15 September 1916[1]

The British offensive on the 15th of September, 1916, marked the beginning of the third phase of the long-drawn-out fighting on the Somme in that year. The attack on the 14th of July and subsequent minor actions had brought the British line near to the top of the Bazentin ridge. Sir Douglas Haig now intended to cross the ridge and occupy a position on its northern slope that fell away gradually to the upper reaches of the Ancre. A success here would, he hoped, force the Germans to evacuate the strongly entrenched Thiepval end of the ridge farther west, thereby loosening their hold altogether on the Somme uplands.

The III Corps of the British Fourth Army which was to carry out the main attack was faced by Bavarian troops. The 3rd Bavarian Division occupied the front line from Martinpuich to High Wood, and the 4th Bavarian Division from High Wood to Delville Wood. These, forming the II Bavarian Corps, had arrived from Lille at the end of August. The country from Delville Wood eastward to south of Ginchy was held by the 5th Bavarian Division, part of the III Bavarian Corps, that had come from Lens and only been in the line about ten days. The troops in reserve were also new to the ground. The 50th Reserve Division, in rear of the 3rd Bavarian Division, had recently arrived from the Armentières sector; while the 6th Bavarian Division, in reserve to the 4th and 5th Bavarian Divisions, did not complete its arrival from the Argonne till the day of the battle.

There were, therefore, about five German divisions opposed to the nine British divisions which delivered the offensive on the Martinpuich—Ginchy line. The German position consisted roughly of three main trench systems. The front line, the Foureaux Riegel (Switch Trench) consisted of a series of trenches approximately 500 yards in front of the British line. It lay along the south side of the top of the long Bazentin ridge. A 1000 yards beyond, and on the farther side of the ridge in front of the village of Flers, was the second system known as Flers Riegel (Flers Trench). Some 1500 yards beyond again, between Flers and Gueudecourt and in front of Lesboeufs and Morval, was the third system, the Gallwitz Riegel (Gird Trench).

The bombardment opened on the 12th of September. The weather, except for occasional heavy showers, was fine throughout the three days of its duration. Caterpillar-armoured cars (tanks) were used by the British for the first time to support the infantry advance. Forty-seven of these strange-looking machines were allotted to the Fourth Army for the

---

1 References are: *Die Bayern im Grossen Kriege, 1914–18* (Munich, 1923); *Das K.B.5 Infanterie Regiment* (Munich, 1929); *Das K.B.6 Infanterie Regiment* (Kallmünz, 1919); *Das K.B.7 Infanterie Regiment* (Munich, 1922); *Das K.B.10 Infanterie Regiment* (Munich, 1925); *Das K.B.11 Infanterie Regiment* (Munich, 1921); *Das K.B.14 Infanterie Regiment* (Munich, 1931); *Das K.B.19 Infanterie Regiment* (Munich, 1930); *Das K.B.21 Infanterie Regiment* (Munich, 1929).

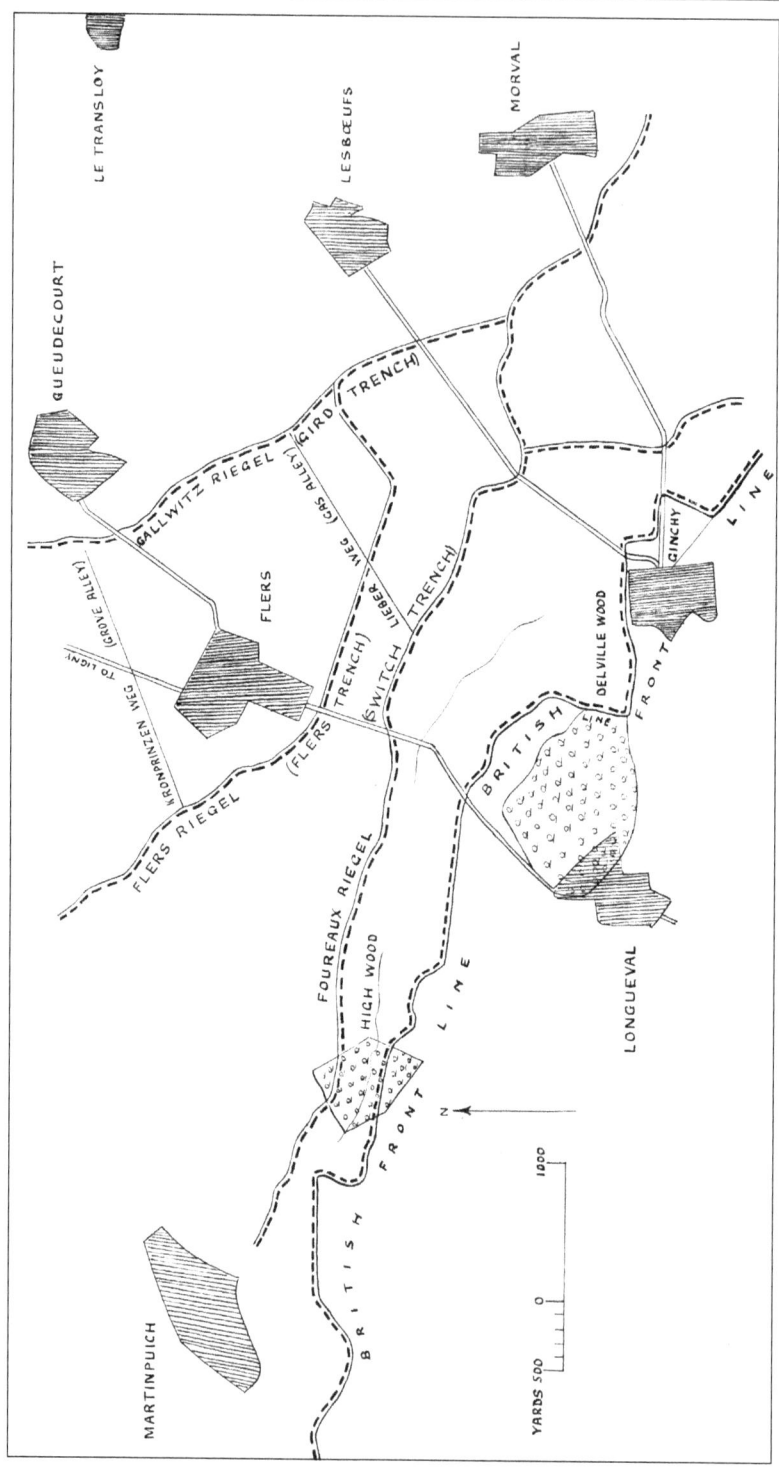

11. The Somme, 15 September 1916

purpose, but seventeen broke down or were ditched in shell holes before reaching the front line, and the majority of the remainder arrived too late to take an effective part in the battle. Those, however, that got into the thick of the fighting did some admirable work, terrifying the Germans wherever they went. During the bombardment period German observers had noticed preparations for an offensive about High Wood, Delville Wood and Girichy, and German aeroplanes had sighted the tanks, reporting them as "heavily armoured cars." Nevertheless, no special preparations were made to meet the attack, and the actual hour of assault remained a secret.

On the 13th, to avoid unnecessary loss from the bombardment, the garrison of the front trench system was limited to one man for every 2 yards of front with a strong complement of machine guns, an average of three groups each of three guns on each battalion front. Every man had with him three days' food supply and two large flask-bottles of water. The bombardment increased during the day and continued throughout the following night. A German battalion (21st Bavarian Infantry Regiment) marching up into the second line under cover of darkness found Morval like this:

> The ruins of a village suddenly appeared ghostlike out of the darkness; jagged edges of roofless houses, walls split from top to bottom, great beams thrown from their sockets and burnt out, all in utter confusion. The bursts of heavy shells in continuous flashes throw a red flickering light over the whole scene of devastation, and a perpetual rain of pieces of shell and chips of stones seemed to be falling on it. The street itself was difficult to see. We trod over a mass of broken rubble, bricks, tiles, iron gutters, split beams, tree trunks, and a litter of kitchen and household utensils, with here and there large gaping shell craters.

5th Bavarian Division

On the 14th, the bombardment increased to almost drum-fire intensity. The loss of men and the destruction of the front trench system was very severe, and most of the telephone connections with the rear systems were cut. The night of the 14th was quieter, but, in the early hours of the 15th, the shelling became more intense than ever, a large proportion of gas shell being added. It had been a clear moonlight night, but towards daybreak a thick mist rose and the quantity of gas shell and smoke made visibility very difficult. About 6 a.m. the Bavarians (21st Bavarian Regiment) near Ginchy was surprised to see three clumsy vehicles rolling out of the Mist towards them, picking their way through the shell holes in No Man's Land. At first, owing to the blue-and-red crosses on their sides, the Bavarians thought that they must be stretcher lorries. The two flapped portholes in front made them look like prehistoric monsters paddling slowly, and with great difficulty, towards them.

> Suddenly machine-gun and rifle fire opened from them into the trenches, and it was then realized this was the new tank of which rumour had already spoken. In the face of a mass of bullets the cars came close to the trench parapet, kept up a continuous machine-gun fire along the trench for several minutes and then turned back to their own lines again. One was knocked out by a direct hit from a shell and was abandoned by its crew in No Man's Land.

At 6.30 a.m., zero hour, the British troops clambered out of their trenches on the whole front of attack and moved forward at a steady pace through the clouds of smoke and mist that now covered the battle zone. An artillery barrage preceded the infantry, which was to lift 50 yards every minute until the second trench system was reached. The German artillery was very feeble in its support of the defending infantry. A wounded officer (14th Bavarian Regiment) going back through Flers to Gueudecourt passed some German batteries:

> The gunners were all in their dug-outs and knew nothing of the attack as all telephone communication had broken down, and owing to the mist and smoke they had not seen the flares from the front trenches asking for artillery support.

This misunderstanding caused a very general failure of the German artillery support and accounts in no small measure for the ease with which many of the British battalions advanced.

In most parts of the line the German infantry were thus left to deal with the attack single-handed. Their trenches had by now been battered to pieces:

> The front system, Foureaux Riegel, was almost impossible to locate as it had been reduced to a mass of shell craters where the surviving defenders still held on. The greater part of the second line, the Flers Riegel, had been broken in and few of the dug-out entrances were passable, though here and there occasional lengths of trench still existed. With no communications and under such conditions a methodical defence with any prospect of success against this mass-attack was out of the question.

The greater part of the advancing infantry reached and captured Switch Trench, the first system, without difficulty, although in a few places a stout resistance was given. For example, the diary of the 21st Bavarian Regiment, in the sector of the 5th Bavarian Division, south of Ginchy, says:

> Crouching in shell craters and shelter pits the men awaited the oncoming infantry. The artillery barrage moved on past us and then, in front, five or six lines of infantry (British 6th Division, XIV Corps) stood up and advanced towards us. Cold-blooded fellows! and yet how many of them against one of us. We could now see their steel helmets, their fixed bayonets and even the bag on their left side containing hand grenades. Quickly a hail of bullets from the line of shell holes, from machine guns and rifles poured into their ranks making large gaps. The Tommies couldn't stand up against it, they began to waver and then lay down, trying to get forward in small groups. Some reached bombing distance. A particularly daring party entered a piece of broken trench, but they had come to the wrong place as they were met by the champion hand-grenade thrower of the regiment, a stonemason of Passau, who promptly killed several and others were shot down as they ran back. At 9 a.m. the attack was still held up in front of the regiment and hundreds of dead and wounded English were strewn over the ground in front.

This opposition to the British 6th Division affected the advance of the divisions on either side, the 56th on the right and the Guards on the left. The advance of the greater part of the Guards Division was, however, successful. It came up against the 7th Bavarian Regiment astride the Ginchy—Lesboeufs road:

> The dense lines of skirmishers were followed by groups in column and behind again were two tanks. Twenty or thirty aeroplanes circled over low down, firing into us with machine guns. We had little support from our artillery and our rifle and machine-gun fire was inadequate to prevent this mass of men overwhelming our front position, hemming in the defenders on all sides. They then advanced to the second line and by 11 a.m. it was in their possession. The 2nd Battalion with remnants of the 1st and 3rd, which were able to get back to it, now prepared to hold the third line, the Gallwitz Riegel, but the attack had spent itself and did not follow up.

The left of the Guards Division on reaching the second line captured two battalion staffs of the 14th Bavarian Regiment which was holding the line on the right of the 7th:

> On the approach of the British, flares were sent up for artillery support, but had no effect. As the attacking waves were now close to us, the adjutant set fire to all the books, maps, diaries, etc., in the dug-out. A shell then blocked the entrance and a few moments later, about 6.50 a.m., the trench garrison appears to have surrendered. We heard loud laughter and excited talk at the entrance of the dug-out and then several bombs were thrown down among us putting out the lights by their explosion. The dug-out was now filled with a cloud of dust, smoke, the stench of powder and the groans of wounded, but still above us outside under the blue sky the joking and jubilation continued. Shortly afterwards the entrance was opened and we were taken prisoners. On our way back through the mass of troops opposed to us we were searched to the skin by undisciplined soldiers of the London Guards (sic) and robbed of anything of value.

4th Bavarian Division

On the front of the 4th Bavarian Division the attack by the XV British Corps opened well. The front troops of the 9th and 5th Bavarian Regiments, holding the Switch line in front of Delville Wood, were overwhelmed, and the 18th Bavarian Regiment, on their right up to and including High Wood, was driven from its position:

> From 5.30 a.m. the bombardment had become increasingly intense on all the positions in front of Flers and on the village itself. After half an hour wave after wave of the enemy (N.Z. Division, XV Corps) from the High Wood—Delville Wood line appeared out of the mist and smoke in front of the 18th Bavarian Regiment. The devastating barrage of artillery fire moved on, and then the lines rushed forward into Switch Trench where they overcame all resistance. Here the leading waves of the attack halted whilst others behind came up and passed through towards the second position, the Flers Riegel. On their way they were met by a desperate resistance from the support trench of the Switch position with fire and hand grenades, but the overwhelming mass of the attack soon smothered it. The arrival of tanks on the scene

had the most shattering effect on the men. They felt quite powerless against these monsters which crawled along the top of the trench enfilading it with continuous machine-gun fire, and closely followed by small parties of infantry who threw hand grenades on the survivors.

Wounded of the 18th Bavarian Regiment brought back the first news of the British attack to the supports, units of the 5th Bavarian Regiment, in Flers trench:

> Every effort was made to obtain artillery support, but evidently the red flares could not be seen owing to the mist, and none of the pigeons or messenger orderlies appear to have reached their destination owing to the heavy shell fire the enemy's guns maintained on the rear lines.

By 7 a.m. the whole of the Switch trench system had been captured and the crest of the long Bazentin ridge was at last in British hands. The mist was fast clearing and there was every promise of a fine day. The attacking infantry now overlooked a wide expanse of fresh country, a succession of wooded slopes falling gradually away to the north, with green fields and unshattered villages in the middle distance. Their next objective was the Flers Riegel, the second German line. Here some companies of the 5th Bavarian Regiment, among others, were in position:

> In front of us the English [New Zealand and 1st Divisions] were held up. They had been moving at right angles to the Longueval—Flers road and were now taking cover among the shell craters in front of the Flers position. Suddenly a tank appeared coming along the road. It moved on relentlessly in spite of all our fire until astride the trench itself which it proceeded to rake from end to end with machine-gun fire-causing heavy loss. It then crossed to another sector of trench and treated it in the same manner. From there it went on towards Flers, and passed out at the northern exit of the village. Thence it took the road to Ligny, but was eventually put out of action by a direct hit from our artillery.

The appearance of the attack had, however, sufficed to overcome the opposition and the British now cleared the Flers Riegel in this sector and Flers itself was occupied.

British aeroplanes had taken an effective part in the capture of the Flers defences. According to the diary of the 14th Bavarian Regiment:

> … the men suffered much from aeroplanes which fired along sectors of trench and shell cratered positions with machine guns from a height of 300 to 400 feet, causing heavy losses.

Soon after 9 a.m. the regimental staff of the 14th Bavarian Regiment from its battle headquarters in the Gallwitz Riegel, the German third line, could see the British about 1,000 yards in front. They were advancing out of Flers village on either side of the Gueudecourt road and, behind Flers, supports were continually coming forward in small groups from the direction of Delville Wood into Flers Trench. The remnants of the regiment, which had rallied in the Gallwitz Riegel, now—

prepared a very hot reception for the English as they came down the slope from Flers. The regiment commander himself stood on the firestep with a rifle to fire with his men, and the machine-gun commander personally handled one of the guns. Inspired by this the men regained their spirits and the repeated efforts of the English to reach the trench failed. Gradually the drive behind the attack seemed to wane and the lines of skirmishers took shelter in craters and lengths of communication trenches.

At 12.30 p.m., in front of Gueudecourt, the reserve (3rd) battalion of this regiment arrived from Le Transloy, crossing the open in small groups to reinforce the Gallwitz Riegel position. At the same time on its right battalions of the 5th Bavarian and 5th Bavarian Reserve Regiments came up into position astride the Ligny—Flers road. The 4th Bavarian divisional orders at this time were to hold the Gallwitz Riegel at all costs. The constant flow of supports coming from the direction of Delville Wood into Flers were kept under fire.

3rd Bavarian Division
On the front of the 3rd Bavarian Division the attack by the British III Corps also made headway. Martinpuich itself, held by the 17th Bavarian Regiment, was captured. The 23rd Bavarian Regiment after stubborn resistance which caused the British 47th Division heavy losses was driven from High wood and its position between High Wood and Martinpuich, but rallied north and east of the village.

The German Counter-Attack
On the front of the 4th and 5th Bavarian Divisions, units from the 6th Bavarian Division in reserve were sent up during the morning from Le Transloy, Barastre and Caudry, reinforcing the Gallwitz Riegel from 1 p.m. onwards. At 2.30 p.m. the 4th Division ordered a counter-attack to be made, supported by the right of the 5th Division, for the recapture of Flers and Flers trench. This counterattack was a very disconnected affair, as so many of the units concerned had only just reached the line with no knowledge of the situation. Battalions of the 5th Bavarian and of the 5th Bavarian Reserve Regiments attacking west of the Gueudecourt—Flers road drove the advanced British infantry back on Piers, inflicting heavy loss on them, and retaking a park of engineering material and a Bavarian battery of field guns which had fallen into British hands.

At 4.30 p.m. two British tanks appeared in Flers, with the assistance of which the enemy appeared to be about to begin another attack, but they were both smashed up by the German artillery, and the attack did not develop. The Germans now occupied an old communication trench, the *Kronprinzen Weg* (afterwards Grove Alley), 400 yards north of Flers, where they were reinforced by machine guns of the 18th Bavarian Regiment and also by companies of the 9th and 10th Bavarian Regiment. This position, facing Flers, they continued to hold during the night.

On the right, astride the Ligny—Flers road, two battalions of the 10th Bavarian Regiment attacked at 5.10 p.m. They were met by heavy machine-gun and rifle fire from the north-west corner of Flers village, which killed a number of officers and men and broke up the attack. One battalion withdrew to the Gallwitz Riegel, the other continuing the line in the Kronprinzen Weg.

To the east of Piers the counter-attack did not develop till later. At 6.30 p.m. units of the 10th, 11th and 14th Bavarian Regiments advanced from the Gallwitz Riegel line. They were met by heavy fire but succeeded in advancing some 500 yards, recapturing an advanced field gun undamaged, which they turned on the enemy and fired all the ammunition left with it. By 10.30 p.m. this attack had reached within 50 yards of Flers trench, taking up a position for the night among the shell craters astride the communication-trench *Leiber Weg* (Gas Alley), as they were unable to enter Flers Trench itself.

Farther south, in the sector of the 5th Bavarian Division, the—

> ... remnants of the 7th Bavarian Regiment counter-attacked from the Gallwitz Riegel in front of Lesboeufs and drove back the enemy (Guards Division) who was entrenching in front of the Flers line. They were, however, unable to push them beyond Flers Trench and entrenched for the night in front of it.

The British had continued throughout the day their efforts to dislodge the 21st Bavarian Regiment that had withstood the first assault of the 6th Division south of Ginchy:

> Between 6 and 7 p.m. the British artillery fire increased to a deafening intensity. The light of the setting sun was almost completely obliterated by the mass of dust and dirt, smoke and fumes thrown up and filling the atmosphere. Dug-outs were blown in and large stretches of the position seemed to have no one left alive to defend them. At 8 p.m. it quietened down and we expected the infantry assault, but it never materialized. This wild day of battle gradually died away until only an occasional white flare through the darkness marked the battle zone.

On the front of the 3rd Bavarian Division, battalions of the 50th Reserve Division had moved up from reserve during the day and counter-attacked at 5.30 p.m. This reinforcement together with the remnants of the 23rd Bavarian Regiment, reached and occupied a new line only a few hundred yards behind their original front between High Wood and Martinpuich, while the village itself remained in British hands.

The great expectations of the day's fighting had not been altogether achieved by the British. Sir Douglas Haig had intended to capture the villages of Gueudecourt, Lesboeufs and Morval, but no portion even of the Gallwitz Riegel that lay in front of those villages had been reached. On the following day, the 16th, the British divisions were ordered to continue the attack, and reached the objectives given the previous day:

"But night," as the diary of the 21st Bavarian Regiment rightly says, "is the friend of the defender. It bound the enemy's eyes which in daylight could see everything on these level uplands. Every advantage was taken of darkness to improve the rough defence line that had been taken up, getting into touch with units to right and left, and bringing up food and water."

This was successfully done, and little further progress was made by the British the following day. The Germans then established themselves in the new line.

In conclusion must be mentioned a criticism of the battle by members of the two battalion staffs captured early in the day, as related above, which is in the diary of the 14th Bavarian Regiment:

When we came behind the British lines and saw the immense mass of material and supplies that the British had at their disposal compared with our own meagre resources we thought that our poor Germany could have little chance against all this wealth and luxury in the way of armament, food and equipment. We were sure of one thing, however, that if the situation had been reversed we should not have stopped at any second or third line lightly held by a few battalions, but should have pushed straight on through and finished the war.

11

The Capture of Thiepval

26 September 1916[1]

The capture of the Bazentin ridge east of the Albert—Bapaume road by the British Fourth Army on the 15th of September, 1916,[2] and the further progress made by it on the 25th of September, prepared the way for the attack on the western end of the ridge, which included the Thiepval salient.

Sir Douglas Haig decided to deliver an offensive against it at once before the enemy had time to recover. The first objective consisted of the whole of the crest of the ridge, that is all that part of it west of the Albert—Bapaume road on a frontage of 3,000 yards between Courcelette and Thiepval. Every detail of the attack had been worked out and practised behind the lines by the troops concerned. The 2nd and 1st Divisions of the Canadian Corps were to carry out the right of the attack between Courcelette and the Zollern redoubt, the 11th and 18th Divisions of the II Corps the left of the attack between the Zollern redoubt and Thiepval (inclusive).

The troops for the assault moved up into the line during the night 25th–26th, and the actual advance began at 12.35 p.m. on the 26th. There had been a spasmodic though severe bombardment of the German position and rear defences during the previous four days, but, on the morning of the attack, it quietened down until zero hour when an intensive barrage was laid along the whole German front line. An average of 250 yards separated the opposing front trenches: the barrage remained long enough for the advancing infantry to come close up to it and then lifted in front of them.

After some rain during the night the morning was bright and sunny.

The German Defence

The offensive came as no surprise to the Germans. Already, on the 22nd of September, First Army orders announced that all information pointed to an offensive by the British against the Thiepval—Courcelette sector in the immediate future. The defence of the sector was in the hands of the German 7th, 8th and part of the 26th Reserve Divisions. The first line of defence lay around the northern front of Courcelette and thence westward past Mouquet Farm, itself in No Man's Land, to the southern side of Thiepval, the ruins of the village being about 300 yards behind the line. Beyond its south-western edge the front line turned sharp to the north towards St. Pierre Divion where it crossed the Ancre. At an average distance of 1,000 yards behind this front line lay the Staufen Riegel, and

---

1 References are: *Das Infanterie Regiment 26* (Stalling, Oldenburg, 1925-29); *Das Infanterie Regiment 66 im Weltkriege* (Kolk, Berlin, 1930); *Das Infanterie Regiment 72 im Weltkriege* (Stalling, Oldenburg, 1930); *Das Infanterie Regiment 153* (Stalling, Oldenburg, 1927); *Das Infanterie Regiment 165 im Weltkriege* (Stalling, Oldenburg, 1927); *Das Wurttembergischer Infanterie Regiment 180* (Belsersche Verlagsbuchandlung, Stuttgart, 1921).
2 *Army Quarterly*, July 1933.

THE CAPTURE OF THIEPVAL

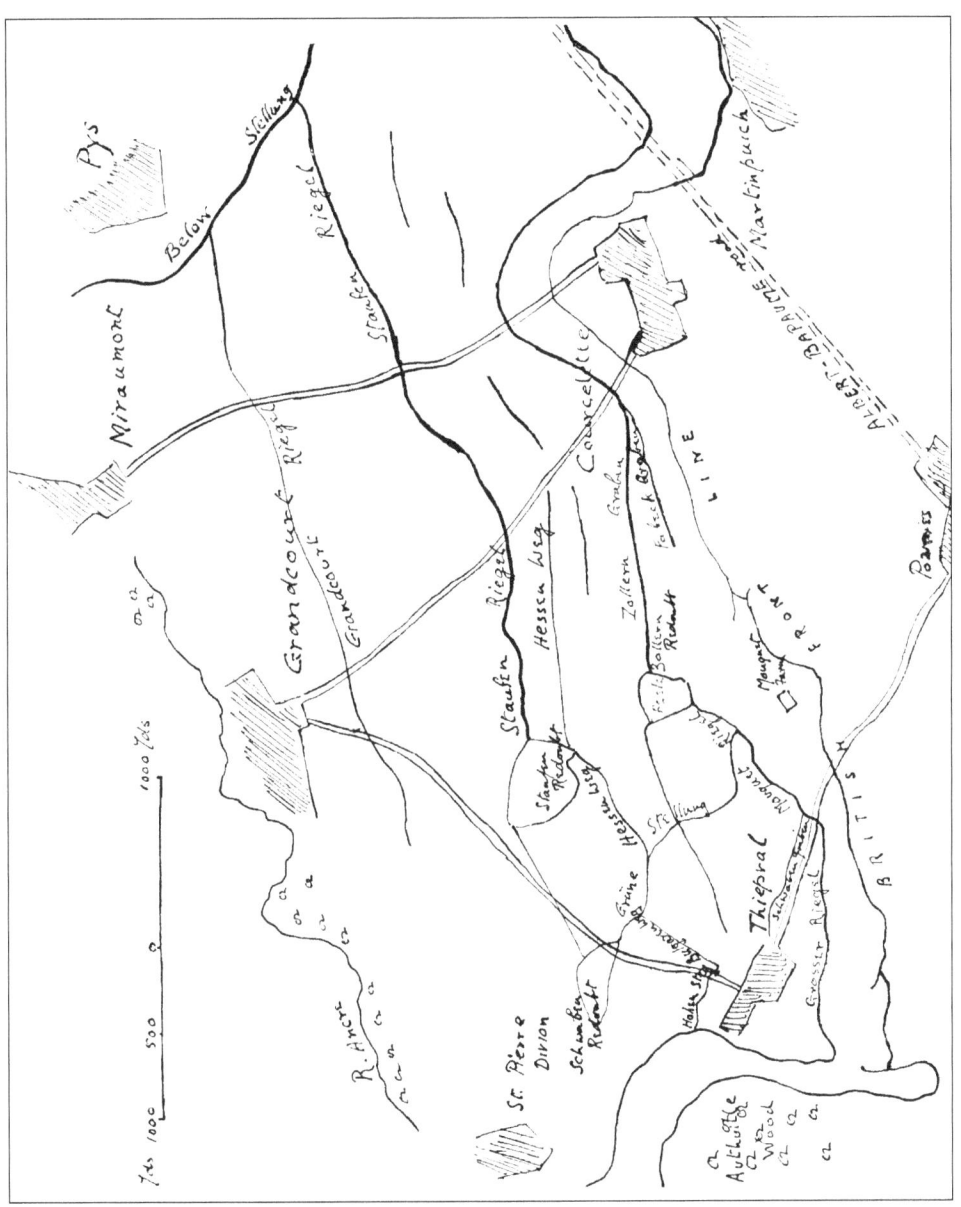

12. Thiepval, 26 September 1916

behind again at approximately the same distance lay the Grandcourt Riegel. These were the three main lines of defence. They included also three fortified trench systems: the Schwaben, Zollern and Staufen (named "Stuff" by the English tongue) redoubts.

7th Reserve Division

The attack by the 2nd and 1st Canadian Divisions, the right of the offensive, was met by the 393rd, 72nd and 26th Regiments, of which each had one battalion in the front line, one in support, and one in reserve. The front trenches of the 393rd Regiment, immediately west of the Albert—Bapaume road, were taken by the Canadians in the first rush. The front battalion of the 72nd Regiment, however, in the centre facing the northern front of Courcelette, held its ground. The front defences of the 26th Regiment were taken, but not without considerable loss to the Canadians. This was due to the unsuspected occupation by a company of the 26th Regiment of a section of old trench, Fabeck Graben, in No Man's Land, one that was missed out by the bombardment as it was believed empty. The advance was met by massed fire from this trench and the Canadians fell in great numbers soon after crossing the parapet. Fabeck trench, however, was soon outflanked by the waves of attack on either side, and its capture with fifty surviving Germans about 12.55 p.m., is graphically described in the history of the 48th Canadian Highlanders. This delay had not stopped the attack on either flank, which swept on over the Zollern Graben, overrunning it so rapidly that only one message, to say that the English were attacking and asking for an artillery barrage, got back from it to the headquarters of the 26th Regiment. After that there was complete silence. The whole of the front battalion of the regiment was in fact either killed or taken prisoner, scarcely a man getting back to the Staufen Riegel.

The situation about 1.30 p.m. was that the 72nd Regiment in the centre still held out, but the withdrawal or capture of the front troops of the 393rd and 26th Regiments on either flank left it in an unpleasant position. This was remedied by two companies of the supporting battalion with machine guns which took up a position facing south-west along a sunken part of the Courcelette—Miraumont road, south of the Staufen Riegel. The fire from this support saved the right flank of the position, and also was largely responsible for the failure of the Canadian attack to capture the Staufen Riegel. On the left flank the remainder of the supporting battalion joined up with the withdrawn flank of the 393rd Regiment and enabled it to hold its ground.

At dusk the British artillery again bombarded the front of the 72nd Regiment until its sector of the Zollern Graben was little else than a mass of shell craters. During intervals of the bombardment aeroplanes flew along the position about 150 feet up and swept it with machine-gun fire. In spite of this the Canadian attack that followed was again repulsed with heavy loss. As soon as darkness set in two companies of the battalion in reserve arrived to strengthen the front line, and a further Canadian attack at midnight was driven back.

Meanwhile, the situation on the front of the 26th Regiment had been extremely critical. The Canadians on either side of the Fabeck trench had pushed on towards the Staufen Riegel, regardless of the check in the centre. In this way the defences of the Zollern Graben and the eastern end of the Hessen Weg in rear were outflanked on both sides and fell an easy prey when, eventually, after the capture of the Fabeck trench the centre came up into line again. So it was that not only the front battalion, but also the greater part of the supporting battalion of the 26th Regiment were annihilated, only a few detachments of the latter getting back to the Staufen Riegel. As half (two companies) of the reserve battalion had already been sent forward to assist the 72nd Regiment on the left, there were now only two companies and the survivors from the Zollern and Hessen trenches to defend the 1,700 yards of the Staufen Riegel for which the regiment was responsible. The Canadians, if they could have got through this second line of defence at this period of the battle, might have walked on down the northern side of the ridge across the Grandcourt Riegel to the Ancre with little opposition. That they were unable to do this was chiefly due, says the regimental history, to the commander of the two companies. At 3.50 he sent a message to regimental headquarters in Pys that the British infantry had reached the ridge in front of the Staufen Riegel, but that the position would be held. From his post at the junction of the trench with the Courcelette—Miraumont road he handled the small force at his disposal so ably that the Canadians were effectively checked throughout the afternoon. Only on the extreme right, where the Staufen Riegel is crossed by the Courcelette-Grandcourt road, did they succeed in entering it on a frontage of about 200 yards. Here the Germans on either side made a barricade in the trench and held it.

About 5 p.m. reinforcements from Pys began to arrive. It was now hoped to deliver a counter-attack from the Staufen Riegel to enable the 72nd Regiment to hold on to the front trenches of the Zollern Graben in front of Courcelette. Captain Vethacke, commanding the battle sector of the 26th Regiment, reported, however, that the situation could not be restored by a counter-attack on a small scale.

> The front line of the regiment has been completely overrun and the breakthrough is on a bigger scale than at first imagined. In my opinion it is perhaps possible with the weak force now available to maintain our hold on the Staufen Riegel, but even for that I need all the reinforcements received and more. To retake the lost sectors of the Hessen and Zollern Graben would need a strong force of fresh troops, whereas mine have been for nine days lying out mostly in shell-holes without cover and under constant fire. A counter-attack with such troops would not only fail to achieve its object, but might also lead to the loss of the Staufen Riegel.

In view of this report on the situation, which was passed on through the 7th Division to Army headquarters, the divisional commander ordered at 9 p.m. that "the Division by orders from Army headquarters will withdraw to and hold the Staufen Riegel and the Below Stellung. The movement is to begin at 2 a.m." This meant that the 22nd Regiment was to continue to hold the Staufen Riegel, reinforcements from the 14th Brigade in reserve being sent up to it during the night: the units of the 72nd Regiment, which had held out so well in the Zollern Graben throughout the afternoon and evening, were to be brought back, one battalion to occupy the Staufen Riegel from the Miraumont—Courcelette road to its junction with the Below Stellung and the other the adjacent part of the Below Stellung (so heavy had been their casualties that their companies had to be amalgamated, two into one): the 393rd Regiment was to be brought back to the Below position, west of the Albert—Bapaume road, in touch with the 72nd Regiment.

8th Division

The German 8th Division was responsible for the front defences from the Zollern Redoubt (inclusive) to Thiepval (exclusive). The 93rd Regiment held the Zollern Redoubt and part of the Zollern trench to east of it, with supports in the Hessen Weg and Staufen Riegel.

The 165th Regiment continued the line westward from the Zollern Redoubt along the Mouquet Riegel to the Thiepval—Pozières road, with one company holding Mouquet Farm as an advanced post in No Man's Land. Its supports were in the Grüne Stellung, Hessen Weg and Staufen Riegel. The 153rd Regiment held the Grosser Riegel from the Pozières road to the eastern borders of Thiepval village, with supports in the Schwaben and Hessen trenches.

It is clear from the German accounts that the main break in this sector of the line was caused by the appearance of three British tanks on the front of the 153rd Regiment on the outskirts of Thiepval village. The history of this regiment stated that after ploughing over the shell craters they came up to the German trenches, terrifying the defenders, especially when it was discovered that no amount of hand-grenades or machine-gun fire had any effect on them. The waves of the attacking infantry followed the tanks and overcame all opposition, the whole garrison of this sector of the Grosser Riegel and Schwaben trench (one and a half battalions) being overwhelmed, hardly any escaping. The defence was made more difficult by the dust and smoke caused by the artillery barrage which, owing to the stillness of the day, hung over the battlefield like a dense mist during the afternoon and sheltered the advancing infantry, most of whom, the account adds, were drunk. Whatever their condition, the attack was not brought to a standstill till it reached the Hessen Weg defended by the two reserve companies of the regiment.

This breakthrough by the British 11th Division (II Corps) had a disastrous effect on the defence to right and left. The defenders of Thiepval village found themselves suddenly threatened from the flank and rear with results to be described later, whilst on the left the front line companies of the 165th Regiment saw their right flank hopelessly in the air. Their initial resistance to the assault of the right of the British 11th Division that swept in successive waves past Mouquet Farm against the Mouquet Riegel was thus overcome, the survivors falling back along the Grüne Stellung. The garrison of the farm itself (6th Company), surrounded on all sides, held out in the deep fortified cellars of the building until 6 p.m., when they, one officer and fifty-five other ranks, surrendered.

The front companies of the 93rd Regiment in the Zollern redoubt and east of it, held their ground. Their records state that their own artillery put up a very accurate barrage 150 yards in front of them, and this, together with their own machine-gun and rifle fire, held up every effort of the enemy to get forward. A British battery, which unlimbered in full view a thousand yards south-west of the Zollern redoubt, was put out of action by their machine-gun fire, the gunners running off. At 3 p.m., after a further bombardment of the front line, the British again attacked, eight to ten waves of infantry advancing across No Man's Land, but these were again repulsed by machine-gun and rifle fire. About this time, however, the effect of the advance of the 1st Canadian Division, which had overwhelmed the 26th Regiment on the left, could no longer be withstood. The infantry of the 1st Canadian and 11th Divisions began to work round behind both flanks, one of the company commanders was killed, the only two serviceable machine guns left were put out of action and ammunition was getting scarce, so the survivors withdrew as best they could to the Hessen Weg. During the night the divisional commander ordered that the Staufen Riegel was to be made the front line of defence, though any advance positions still occupied were to continue to be held.

By the early hours of the 27th, the new line had been successfully established. The pioneer company of the 93rd Regiment dug and occupied a fire trench connecting the

Hessen Weg with the Staufen Riegel, at the junction of the latter, with the Grandcourt—Courcelette road, thereby gaining direct touch with the right of the 7th Division. From here the 8th Division's new front lay along the whole length of the Hessen Weg, in front of the redoubt to the Grüne Stellung. The defences of the redoubt were manned by the pioneer company of the 153rd Regiment. The reserve companies were moved back to the Grandcourt Riegel.

The Germans had, thus had to evacuate the whole of their front line between Thiepval and Courcelette, a frontage of nearly two miles, including the Zollern Graben, Mouquet Riegel, the Grosser Riegel, the Zollern redoubt and the southern part of the Grüne Stellung. The utter destruction of the German trenches by the British bombardment is stressed by all the German accounts. For example, a messenger of the 165th Regiment, returning to the Hessen Weg just before the attack, could not find his company until at length, discovering one of his officers, asked where the company was. "You've just walked over them," was the reply. The dug-outs, with over seventy officers and men, had been completely smashed in and blocked beyond help. The further story of this messenger, his company officer and the remaining twenty men of his company is a good instance of the great privations that so often had to be endured during the ghastly progress of the Somme battle. They moved along till they came to two empty dug-outs, and these they entered, as the artillery bombardment was still intense. After a pause the look-out in the trench above shouted down "Here they are." Emerging from the dug-out, they lined the trench and saw the British infantry coming towards them at the double.

> We were obviously powerless against the mass of men now advancing on us, and if we had attempted to escape across the open, we should have been shot down like rabbits. Some asked that we should surrender, but one of the sergeants opened fire, and so we all did the same, It was, however, quite useless, and soon the enemy was all round us, so we ran back down into the dug-out. The sergeant who opened fire was the last to come and was killed by a bullet in the head as he entered. Immediately afterwards several hand-grenades were thrown down into the dug-out, but, as we were all pressed into the farthest corner, the splinters only hit a wounded man on the floor. We expected the Tommies to come down at any moment, but nothing happened. The first wave of the attack must have gone on to the next position, and we could hear more troops coming into the trench above. Two English stood on the top step, but didn't come down. Hours passed with always the hope of a counter-attack and our release. The suffocating fumes left by the explosions of the hand-grenades still filled the dug-out, the atmosphere was appalling and our thirst almost unbearable. We decided to leave the dug-out as soon as it was dark and run for it, making for Grandcourt. Shortly after making this decision, our own artillery opened fire preparatory, we hoped, to a counter-attack, but suddenly there was a violent explosion, the whole dug-out seemed to crack and sway, and then utter darkness. A direct hit had struck the entrance and we were buried alive. For ten minutes, no one spoke a word, we sat crouched together, fourteen of us, in a corner. The night which followed was beyond description. The atmosphere became worse, my head ached to bursting-point. We tore pieces of chalk from the walls to cool our foreheads. Some of the men drank their own urine. One man wanted to shoot himself, but his rifle was taken from him. It was decided that we must hold out now till daybreak, as if

the English found us in the dark we should certainly be killed. All night long the officer was asked the time, as he had an electric torch. It seemed an eternity. At last, at 6.30 a.m., we could stand it no longer. We kept hammering on the top step and shouting till we were heard. English voices now replied, and one of us who could speak English called out asking for help. Sounds of spades and axes hacking at the entrance put fresh life into us. We tore at the earth with our hands, pulling it away from the steps. The noises from outside became clearer until at last a small shaft of light burst through into the dug-out. Soon the opening was large enough for us to crawl out, one after the other. Two Canadian soldiers stood at the entrance with rifles at the ready. There was a patch of grass on the edge of the trench with the early morning dew still wet on it, and this we licked like animals to cool our tongues. This appeared to arouse the sympathy of the Tommies, and they gave us each a drink from their bottles. Never in my life shall I forget this most precious, priceless drink. We heard that one man had been taken prisoner the previous evening from the other dug-out, the others having been killed by the hand-grenades thrown down. We were then taken back across the battlefield, which was strewn with corpses, through the English gun positions back to the prison camp.

26th Reserve Division

The sharp salient, or nose position as the Germans called it, around Thiepval and the village itself, was occupied by the 180th Württemberg Regiment and part of the 77th Reserve Regiment. The Schwaben Redoubt and the front defences north-west of the village as far as St. Pierre Divion were held by the 66th Regiment. The supports and reserves of these regiments were in the Schwaben trench, Grüne Stellung and western end of the Staufen Riegel.

The British attack came as no surprise, for, as the records of the 180th Regiment state, new assembly trenches had been seen in the process of construction in the British lines south of Thiepval for some days beforehand.

The leading wave of infantry of the British 18th Division was, states the same history, annihilated before it reached the barbed wire. The second, a still denser one, also fell back with heavy losses, unable to face the machine-gun and rifle fire poured into it. Suddenly, from Authuille Wood an armoured tank appeared and moved towards the German lines, followed closely by a third wave of infantry. Picking up the stragglers of the first two waves, this new attack reached close up to the German position. For a short time it seemed that it, too, would be repulsed, but at this moment the breakthrough east of the village, as described already in the 8th Division defence, began to take effect. The three front companies of the 77th Reserve Regiment on the left were killed or captured almost to a man. Almost immediately afterwards the front companies of the 180th Regiment occupying the southern and western faces of the "Nose," found themselves being bombed with hand-grenades by troops moving behind their trench, advancing westward through the ruins of Thiepval. The occupation of the eastern outskirts of Thiepval at the outset of the battle had, in fact, enabled the British to advance against both the southern and western defences of the village from the rear. Some even reached the Bulgaren Weg, almost completely cutting off the troops in Thiepval, but barricades were rapidly constructed across the trenches there, and the German supporting companies prevented any further advance westward across the open.

Within half an hour of the beginning of the assault, British troops had also reached the Grüne Stellung, and thirty or forty of them pushed on across the open beyond the Hessen Weg, but these were met and driven back by a supporting company of the 180th Regiment. Of the garrison of the Thiepval defences, both the 180th and 77th Reserve Regiments suffered heavily, some companies losing 75 per cent of their establishment. The whole of Thiepval village was evacuated and a new line of defence taken up astride the Thiepval—Grandcourt road, the remnants of the 77th Reserve Regiment occupying the Hohen Steg, in touch with the 66th Regiment in the front defences south of St. Pierre Divion, and those of the 180th Regiment holding the Bulgaren Weg up to its junction with the Grüne Stellung. Here, reinforced by a company of the 66th Regiment from the garrison of the Schwaben Redoubt, they were in touch with the right of the 8th Division, and this position they maintained throughout the night.

Summary

The success of the offensive was, therefore, according to German accounts, due principally to the breakthrough in two places, on the front of the 26th Regiment north-west of Courcelette and on the front of the 153rd and 77th Reserve Regiments immediately east of Thiepval. In the former case, as sufficient reserves were not available for a counter-attack to force back the Canadians, the whole of the 7th Division front had to be withdrawn to the Staufen Riegel and Below Stellung. In the latter case, the breakthrough by the 11th British Division enabled the whole of the Thiepval defences to be taken in flank and rear, resulting in the capture of the village and the greater part of its garrison.

During the following days the battle continued in a desultory fashion. The British pushed forward their line north of Thiepval up to the Staufen and Schwaben Redoubts by continual hand-grenade fighting, but the German garrisons still held the redoubts. With the exception of this extreme western end of the Bazentin ridge, and that part of it near Scilly Saillisel, the whole length of its crest line was now in British possession. With it, they had gained direct observation over the upper reaches of the valley of the Ancre and over the spurs and valleys held by the Germans on the northern bank of the river.

12

In Front of Beaumont-Hamel

13 November 1916

The fighting during September and October 1916, by the British Fourth Army south of the Ancre, in continuation of the long-protracted campaign on the Somme, had given it a firm foothold on the western end of the Thiepval ridge. The commanding position thus obtained prepared the way for the offensive north of the Ancre that was to drive the Germans from their strong defences in front of Beaucourt, Beaumont-Hamel and Serre. The preparatory artillery bombardment began in the early days of November, and the infantry assault was delivered soon after daybreak on the 12th. It was carried out by the 63rd, 51st and 2nd Divisions. The 63rd Division on the right was completely successful, overran the German front defence system and reached its objectives up both sides of the Ancre valley. On the left the 2nd Division, between Beaumont-Hamel and Serre, had a very different fate: the German defence was broken through in places, but nowhere on a sufficiently wide front to make a serious gap, so that by nightfall those who had got through had either to retire or be taken prisoner, and the German front line was restored intact. The 51st Division, in the centre, narrowly escaped a similar catastrophe owing to the stubborn defence put up by a battalion of the German 62nd Regiment in the Beaumont-Hamel salient. The right of the Division was held up there, but the left succeeded in pushing through on a wide front into Beaumont village. Nevertheless, to quote the divisional diary: "Between 10 a.m. and noon the situation was very critical as the Germans were still holding out in the salient." It was feared that they might be strong enough to cut off those of the Division who had passed on through into Beaumont. But the success of the 63rd Division on the right, advancing up the Ancre valley on Beaucourt and threatening the rear of these Germans holding out in the salient, decided the day. No reinforcements could be sent up to help them, so that, during the afternoon, they were surrounded and the 51st Division was able to move on to its objectives.

The history of the German 62nd Regiment has been recently published.[1] It includes an account of the defence of the Beaumont salient on this occasion, written by an officer of the unit concerned, and of which the following is a summary.

The Battalion was in rest billets in Cambrai in the early days of November 1916. Its barrack-room was a church. The pews had been removed, most of them finding their way to the cook-house fire. The altar itself was generally hung about with washing. Marmalade tins, bread and other food lay where once had stood the chalice. A side altar famed for its

---

1 *Das Infanterie-Regiment 62 im Kriege 1914–1918*. Reymann. Sporn, Zeulenroda.

IN FRONT OF BEAUMONT-HAMEL 133

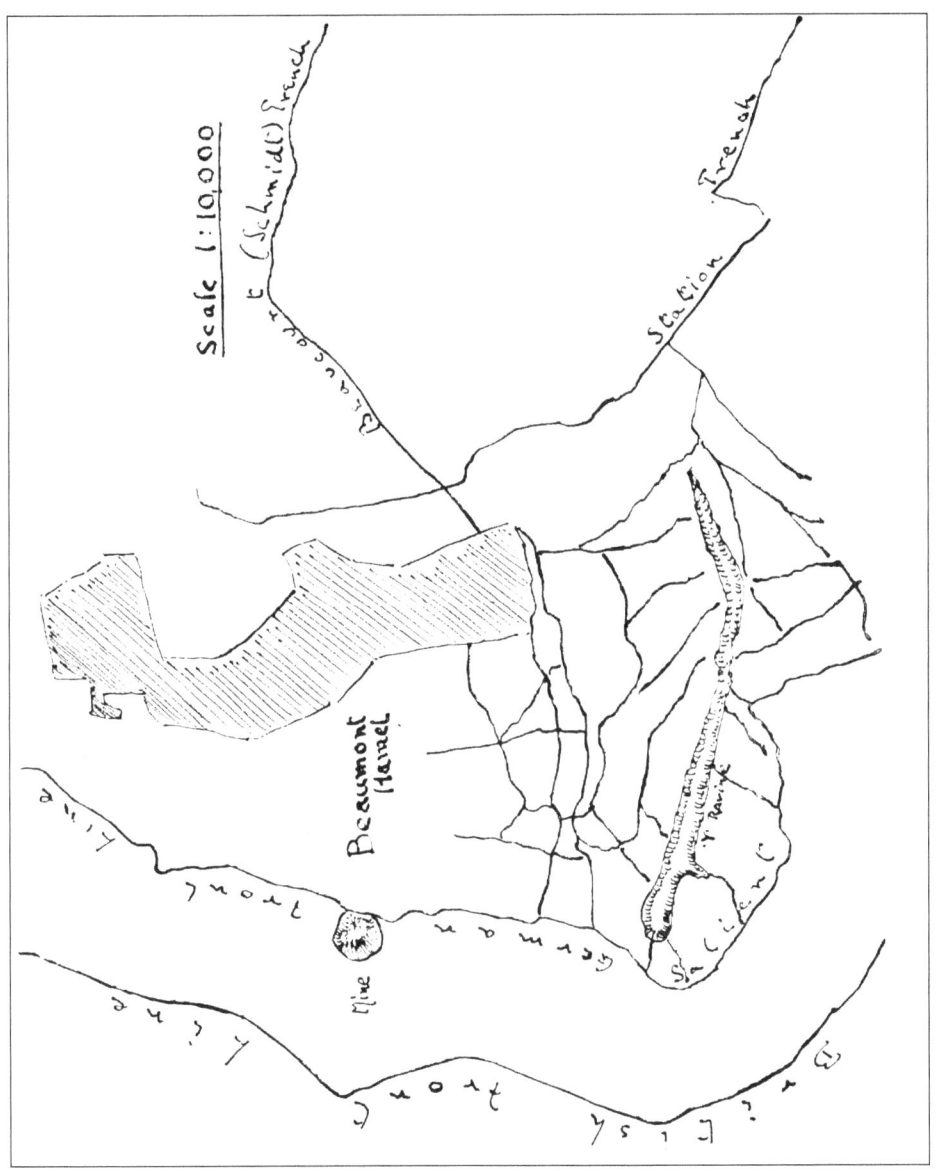

13. Beaumont Hamel, 13 November 1916

miraculous healing-powers served as a dining-table and the prayer-stools had been moved to the middle of the chancel for writing-desks, clothes-racks and rifle-stands.

Meanwhile, the noise of artillery fire in the west had become daily more persistent, the roar of the heavy guns more constant. The older men knew that that foretold the imminence of an offensive and that they would probably soon be sent into the thick of it. And so it happened. Marching orders arrived. Everything unessential was packed up and left behind, valuables and spare money were sent home and one fine morning the Battalion formed up outside the church and marched away from it forever. That night was spent in Ervillers, and as the men moved on westward the following day towards the sound of the guns the reality of the approaching battle became evident. Before leaving Ervillers another long column of troops in battle-order with steel helmets had marched through the village, also westward bound. Ammunition wagons hurtled along at the gallop, covering the infantry with mud. Wounded with blood-soaked bandages and smothered with dirt passed the column continuously. Gradually these signs and portents began to damp the laughter and joking in the ranks, the men's thoughts ruminating rather on their own fate.

That evening the Battalion came into the danger-zone and the rest of the march was carried out in artillery formation with intervals between companies and platoons. Along the left side of the road men were hard at work building dug-outs into the bank and laying telephone cables along it. Occasional shells burst to right and left as darkness closed in on the column which was now enwrapped in utter silence. The monotonous tramp, tramp, tramp of many feet in unison and the rattle of equipment was all that could be heard of it as it passed on into the night. The farther they went the more frequently came the shells. At times shrapnel would burst just above them. There would be a shout, an involuntary scattering to the sides of the road, only after a moment to reform and move on again. Eventually Miraumont was reached. The road here was torn up by the shelling, the craters filled with the recent rain, and as the houses were under shell-fire the troops hurried through the row of ruins and battered streets as quickly as possible.

Beyond the village they turned right-handed, and after plodding on for a while longer through the clinging, chalky mud they reached the crest of the Thiepval ridge. As they crossed it a wondrous sight almost staggered them, for now ahead and beneath them lay the whole stretch of the battle-line from Thiepval northward across the Ancre valley to Beaumont-Hamel, Serre and beyond. The whole length of the western horizon seemed ablaze. Accentuated by the darkness of the night, showers of Very lights turned into brilliant white illuminations as they descended to earth. Red and yellow star-shells and rockets mingled in the firework display, while the orchestra of the artillery, with the occasional humming of machine guns, played incessantly.

For many of the men this was the first entry into the battle-zone and their exclamation of amazement at the spectacle that now confronted them broke the long silence of the march. So much engrossed were some of them in the scene that they forgot to watch their steps, and walking on like "Johnny-head-in-airs" blundered into the rain-filled shell-holes and had an unwelcome cold bath. Eventually, following a field rail-track, they moved down the slope of the ridge into the Ancre valley and crossing the river at Beaucourt entered the long rambling communication-trench, Schmidt Alley, or, as the English later named it, Beaucourt trench. The men were now tired out. Their feet moved automatically and led them on, following each other like sheep, up into the thick of the battle-line. In the early hours of the morning, almost without knowing it, they arrived in the front line trench, the salient west of Beaumont-Hamel and literally stumbled down the steps of the dug-outs, collapsing on to the floor into a deep sleep. The Würtemburg troops whom they were relieving stared at them incredulously, as if they had been strange animals from another world.

The dug-outs were deep and well made, the chalk out of which they were dug forming strong walls needing no further support. The mattresses of the wire beds were alive with fleas, but otherwise the conditions were as comfortable as the conditions permitted. Several of the dug-outs were connected by tunnels, so that if the exit of one was blocked those within could get out by another. From one of the dug-outs a tunnel led forward under the trench with an exit in the barbed-wire entanglement where a machine gun was posted behind a concrete shelter. There was an adequate supply of ammunition and also of bombs, but the latter were of old and various types, and although a large quantity of the new pattern hand-grenades were on the way up they never reached the front line owing to the constant artillery fire that made their transport along the communication trenches too risky. There was a great scarcity of machine guns, but the few available were in good positions with an excellent field of fire.

The front trench itself was still in fair condition, but, with the continuation of the bombardment, it needed constant hard work to keep it free to pass along the length of it. This was especially the case in the salient where much of the trench could be enfiladed by the British guns which took full advantage of the fact. Great sandbag-traverses had been erected every ten yards or so across it to isolate the effect of shell-fire, but these were frequently broken down by high-explosive and their repair was no light task. The wire entanglement was already much broken, in one sector a length of it had been blown sky-high landing on a barren tree-top, where it long remained. The field of fire from the trench was good, and some dead ground in front was commanded by machine guns on the flank.

The German air force on the Somme at this period of the war was no match for the British, being both outnumbered and outpaced. Scarcely a single German aeroplane appeared in the Beaumont-Hamel neighbourhood during the period of the bombardment, except on one morning, much to the astonishment of the German infantry, twenty-seven machines suddenly arrived flying towards the British lines. But they had scarcely crossed before they were attacked by faster British aeroplanes, one German was shot down, his opponent swooping down after him like an eagle after its quarry, and the remainder hastily withdrew. The great disadvantage of this complete loss of air-power was daily demonstrated. For example, a quantity of heavy mine-throwers were brought up close to the British front line to bomb the German trenches. The Germans located their exact position in a certain sunken road and could hear the trolleys rolling up each night along a light railway with ammunition for them. A German battery was told off to deal with them, but at the first shot British aeroplanes came cruising over the lines and before long the whole battery was put out of action. The communication between the British machines and the artillery was remarkable. They were flying over the German trenches and back-zones all day long and if a shot was fired at one of them that particular trench sector would be given an extra dose of shelling shortly afterwards. The astonishing accuracy with which the communication trenches were bombarded was ascribed by the Germans to the same cause, the heavy shells plumping right into the trench each successive shot along it, and in spite of continuous work to keep it open, it was a hopeless task. The arrival of food was interrupted and became scarce in the front line, many men living on dry bread alone.

Candles ran out and the front dug-outs were in darkness except for home-made candles of margarine, called "Hindenburg lamps."

During the days immediately preceding the offensive, the rain was continuous. The mud in the trench began literally to flow down the steps of the dug-outs. The men's clothes were soaked, and no drying arrangements were possible. The stitchings of their boots were rotted with the constant mud and damp, few men having a pair fit to wear. Some were so chilled in consequence that they could scarcely speak.

Throughout the 17th of November the British artillery concentrated on the German front line. All through the day the Germans expected the British infantry to assault at any moment. The foul air in the dug-outs pressed like a dead-weight on their heads as they lay awaiting the attack, awaiting their chance of revenge for all these days of misery. By nightfall the trench had been rendered impassable, and altogether in a lamentable condition beyond hope of repair. An officer going the rounds found little else than a succession of shell-craters, so much so that he lost his way and wandered out into No Man's Land, not discovering his mistake till challenged by one of his own sentries. Many of the dug-out entrances were blown in and others only kept open by constant spade work. The bursts of the high-explosives shook the ceilings and walls, and lumps of chalk and soil kept tumbling down. Gas-shells were also used during this day and a number of men, who did not put on their masks soon enough, died of the effects, including the officer commanding the machine-gun company. The ghastly sufferings of these men, who could not be got back owing to the state of the communication trenches, added to the appalling conditions existing during these anxious hours in the front line.

Early in the night, however, the bombardment suddenly ceased completely. The rain, too, had stopped during the afternoon, and as the night drew on utter peace reigned once more. The moon high in the heavens covered the scene of devastation with a bright silver radiance, the stars shone out as if from a summer sky. The ecstasy with which the German account describes the wondrous beauty of this particular night is doubtless due in part to the contrast with it of the horror of the preceding ones, but the fact remains that not a shell, not a rifle-shot, not even a Very light appears to have been fired to disturb those hours of darkness, and the men were able to get some sleep. As dawn broke they were roused and formed up on the steps of the dug-out, which had become almost a routine as each morning of late the British had made a great noise and much-ado in their trenches as if about to attack. Now, however, the complete quiet of the night hours continued. As the moon set a mist formed over No Man's Land gradually thickening with the first lights of dawn.

The German sentries stared blindly towards the British lines; they could neither see nor hear anything, and reported all quiet. At this moment three large sacks of letters and parcels arrived in the trench, the absence of shelling during the night having enabled them to be brought up, also food and ammunition. The state of tension in the dug-outs was released and the post greeted joyously, the first for many days. The officers and many of the men were, however, very uneasy at the strange stillness outside—What could it mean? In their anxiety some went up, letters in hand, to peer into the dense mist when, of a sudden, one of the sentries, famed for his keen senses, rushed up and said he heard noises in front. They listened and heard a repeated muffled thumping, not the thumping of picks in the trenches nor that of patrols repairing the entanglements, but decidedly the of a mass of feet in the heavy plodding mud.[2]

Almost simultaneously other sentries reported the same noise and the news spread like a flash to right and left. The men left their letters and their food, grasped their rifles, prepared their hand-grenades and assembled in readiness packed on the dugout steps. Now, it was thought, was the moment for those machine guns on the right to open fire and sweep the stretch of dead ground in front. The thought was scarcely expressed before a mighty, deafening explosion shook the whole trench and a gigantic pillar of fire and smoke, magnified by the mist, leapt high in the air. An underground mine had been fired under the trench on the right, including the machine guns in question, and at the same moment shrapnel shell burst along the whole length of the position together with a mass of *minenwerfer* bombs. The sentries jumped back under cover. They realized that this was the final barrage and that the enemy's infantry would be advancing immediately behind.

After a moment of extreme suspense, a loud shout from the sentry in the advanced machine-gun sap in the entanglement was heard above the din. "They're coming." Almost at once a hand-grenade hurtled over the parapet and burst in the trench. They were close up already, and as the Germans rushed out from the dug-outs to right and left to line the position, each threw a hand-grenade over the parapet to cover himself while he got onto the fire-step and opened fire, a method that had became part of a regular drill for meeting an attack. Simultaneously all the machine guns on the front sent a stream of bullets into the mist and swept the assaulting troops. The machine-gun and rifle fire from the German lines at this opening stage of the battle is described by a German officer as terrific. Whether on account of this or not,[3] the enemy did not arrive together in extended lines as was their usual method, but scattered groups appeared through the mist at intervals, even solitary individuals wandered casually up smoking cigarettes and with their rifles slung over the shoulder. One was already in the trench when the Germans rushed out from the dug-outs and he was promptly taken prisoner.

Red and white rockets were sent up as a signal to the artillery to open fire on the British position, but it was soon apparent that owing to the dense mist they could never be seen. The remainder of the rockets were therefore thrown out at intervals into No Man's Land to light up the shadowy forms of the enemy advancing across it and make them an easier target. The few enemy who entered the trench were captured and disarmed, a mass of dead and wounded lay in front, some shot so close that they tumbled over the parapet into the trench, and the remainder retired back into the mist.

For over two hours the attacks continued. The rifle-barrels of the defenders were so hot that they could scarcely hold them, and their arms exhausted with so much firing.[4]

2 No Man's Land had been churned up into a morass by the bombardment, and the shell-holes and craters filled with water. The men floundered about ankle-deep in the mud, many being bogged up to their waists. Small wonder then that the Germans heard them.

3 The 6th Black Watch and 7th Gordon Highlanders who were assaulting this sector of the Beaumont salient came into the barrage. This broke up and delayed the initial impetus of their attack and accounts perhaps for their haphazard and piecemeal arrival at the German position. The 51st divisional diary adds that they "were also held up by machine-gun fire from the high ground south of the 'Y' ravine, and the German garrison in the salient was thus enabled to man the front trench and beat off our attacks at this point. This position he maintained for several hours and rendered communication with the forward troops that had swept on extremely difficult."

4 The 51st divisional diary says: "By 7.50 a.m. casualties had been heavy and the reserves of the 153rd Brigade had been used up to cope with the situation in the salient where a large number of the enemy,

Gradually, however, the flow of men across No Man's Land against the salient began to slacken and then to cease altogether. The defenders were now in high spirits. The pride and joy of victory, for such it seemed to them, filled every breast, shone out from every face. The terrible privations of the past days and nights were forgotten. All the discipline, self-control and hard work were at last being rewarded. In spite of the enemy's complete command of the air, his apparently limitless supply of guns and shell, and the great superiority of numbers with which he had attacked, he had failed. The Germans felt that they had accomplished almost a miracle. Their triumphant elation was shared by a gnawing hunger and thoughts of the interrupted meal still awaiting them in the dug-outs. They asked their officers' permission to go down, but no sooner were the words spoken than loud, long-continued hurrahs came through the mist from the direction of Beaumont, well behind them.

The shouts were definite and distinct, containing all the enthusiasm of men advancing to victory. It must be the reserves, thought the Germans in the salient. But what could they be cheering at, back behind Beaumont? After a while a long procession of German troops appeared dimly in the mist—reinforcements, no doubt. Many of the men jumped up on the parapet and waved to them. But the column turned away to a flank and as it pushed on into the mist again the Germans were astounded to see English troops in front, behind and on either side of them. Those who noticed the column thought they must have seen a phantom procession; it was incredible.

Soon afterwards the mist lifted slightly, and away to the right line after line of the enemy could be seen advancing without opposition across the trench formerly held by No. 1 Company. It was now realized for the first time that the enemy had broken through the front defences. There was no further thought of the food in the dug-outs. As the attacks from the front had now ceased the men got out of the trench and lined up facing right, firing standing or kneeling against the lines of enemy crossing their right flank. This fire enfiladed the advance, causing heavy casualties. Isolated parties turned and walked straight towards them as if ignorant of the fact that they were Germans, and paid the penalty.[5] Before long, however, a machine gun opened fire from the left rear, from about the support position, and compelled the Germans to get back under cover. They thought at first that it might be reinforcements, that the reserves had at last pushed back those of the enemy who had broken through and were now gradually working forward, not knowing which parts of the line were still held. Another machine gun from the right, where the British had made the gap, also began to enfilade the trench and the casualties rapidly mounted up. We are given a picture of how the best non-commissioned officer in the company, a forester by trade and a crack rifle-shot, met his end. He kept firing continuously at the British passing on the right, a smile lit up his lean, bronzed features as each bullet found its mark. A wounded Englishman (or perhaps Scotsman) lying near at the bottom of the

---

estimated at three or four hundred, were offering a stout resistance. On this report two companies of the 4th Gordon Highlanders were sent up from divisional reserve and placed at the disposal of the 153rd Brigade. At 8.40 a.m., as the situation had not yet been cleared up, a further two companies of the 4th Gordons were placed at the brigadier's disposal. The lack of news from the forward troops in Beaumont-Hamel was found later to be due to their runners being shot by the party of the enemy still holding out in the salient."

5 The 51st divisional diary states: "Patrols were sent out to find out the strength of the Germans in the salient. After a time they returned with the information that it was still strongly held and that the Germans could he seen through the mist standing up ready to fire at any one who approached."

trench whom the Germans had regarded as a corpse, now raised himself, picked up his rifle and shot the forester dead, thereby signing his own death-warrant.

The situation was becoming increasingly critical when suddenly a single figure approached through the mist from behind. A runner with a message perhaps? No, it was an officer. Strange, an officer by himself. The Germans called out to stop him going too far to the right into the hands of the enemy there. He came up to the trench. He was disarmed. They could not believe their own ears when he told them he was a prisoner and was bound for France, that the enemy were in occupation of the support and reserve positions and had captured Beaumont. He himself had been captured, he said, behind the third line, the reserve position.

The Germans in the salient were now in desperate straits. They were running short of ammunition, and, if this latest report were true, it would be quite useless to attempt to retire. The surviving officers discussed the situation, and decided that it was madness to go on resisting until all were killed. If the British were already holding the second and third lines behind, they would be giving up their lives for no useful purpose; they would be of more service to Germany in the future alive than as a heap of rotting bones on French soil. Scarcely had this decision been arrived at than a strong force of British bombers advanced along the trench throwing hand-grenades and rushing from crater to crater. The Germans lay down their rifles and surrendered to them.[6]

Thus ended the fight for the salient, and that afternoon the British troops were able to push their line forward on the whole front between Beaumont-Hamel and the Ancre to their allotted objective.

---

6 The 51st divisional diary says: "At 12.40 p.m. the enemy, 103 in all, the salient surrendered to two bombing parties of the Black Watch who had effected an entrance into their trench from the western end of the 'Y' ravine."

13
Battle of Arras
9 April 1917[1]

The Hindenburg Position, the materialization of the elastic defence-in-depth, was the German answer to the great strides made by the British and French Governments in the mass-production of munitions in 1915 and 1916. Those strides can be best appreciated by figures. At Festubert, for example, in May 1915, only 26,000 shells were available to prepare the British assault on a frontage of three miles. At Loos, five months later, 233,000 shells prepared the assault on a frontage of six miles, but even that quantity did not suffice to flatten out the German front trench system; only where it was supplemented by cylinder gas did the infantry succeed in breaking into the position, and where it failed the German garrison mostly held the line: By the following summer the munition production had so greatly increased that the British artillery was able to batter the German front defence system on the Somme uplands with 1,508,000 shells on a fourteen-mile front preparatory to the infantry assault on the 1st of July, 1916, over twelve times the weight of metal per mile of frontage used at Festubert. This succeeded in demolishing wide sectors of the German trench lines except for the deepest mined dug-outs; but, sheltered in these deep caverns, a large percentage of the garrison survived to meet and check the assault.

Before the conclusion of the Somme battles General Ludendorff realized, that the *Materialschlacht* was about to enter a new phase. He foresaw that in the immediate future the mass-production of munitions would enable his opponents on the Western Front to batter or to neutralize not only a trench system 400–600 yards in depth but an entire zone back to effective range of the field batteries, a depth averaging 1,500 to 2,000 yards. His new text book, issued on the 1st of December, 1916, made provision to hold that zone, doomed to become a wilderness of shell-holes, only lightly by a mobile or elastic defence, and to concentrate the bulk of the defence forces close behind it, ready to make an immediate counter-attack. These troops would be fresh, whereas the attackers would be exhausted after crossing the crater-field of their own creation, and the defending artillery would be in closer support. But in the first two tests by battle of this new German doctrine, at Verdun on the 15th of December, 1916, and at Arras on the 9th of April, 1917, its fundamental requirement, the presence of the bulk of the defence forces close behind the second line was neglected, and the whole machinery of the doctrine broke down accordingly.

---

[1] References are the German official monograph, *Die Osterschlacht bei Arras, 1917*, Reichsarchiv, Berlin, 1929; *Mein Kriegstagebuch*, Kronprinz Rupprecht von Bayern, Munich, 1929; and the histories of the German infantry and artillery regiments concerned. Also the French and British Official Histories; the histories of the British divisions and regiments concerned; and the Canadian Official Historian's "Canada on Vimy Ridge," published in the *Canada Year Book*, 1936.

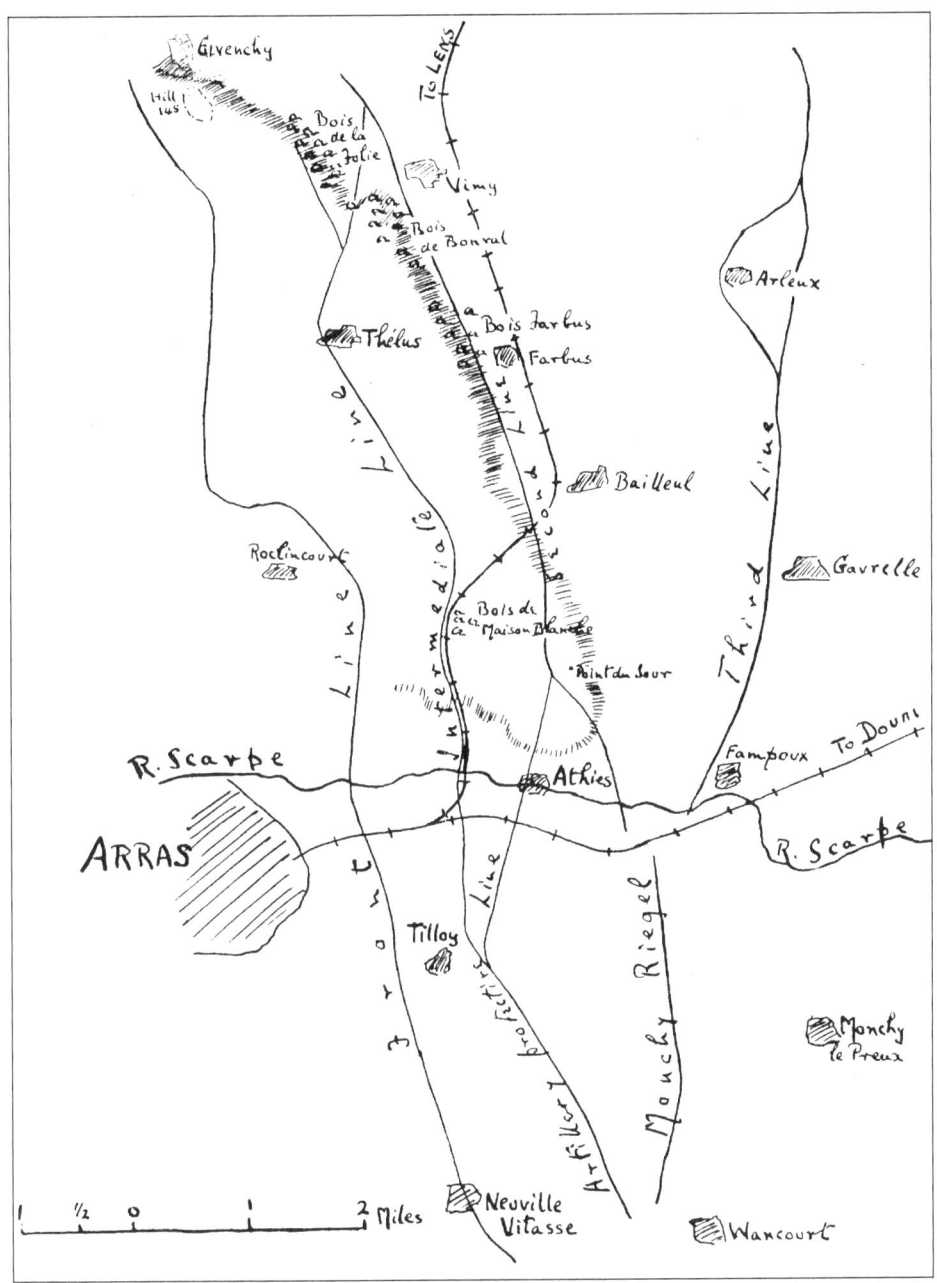

14. German position in the Arras Battle, 9 April 1917

1

The French counter-offensive on a six-mile (11,000 yards) frontage near Verdun on the 15th of December, 1916, was delivered under the direction of General Nivelle by four fresh divisions, with the four divisions in position following as a second line of attack,[2] supported by 827 guns. More than ever it was a case of *"l'artillerie conquiert, l'infanterie occupe."* The artillery preparation lasted for six days before the assault, and had been worked out in minutest detail during the four previous weeks. The final preparatory bombardment, directed by aeroplanes, battered every trench, every dug-out entrance, and every observation post in the German battle-zone and every battery position behind it. At 10.30 a.m. on the day of the assault, in weather overcast but clear, the infantry advanced. The troops were preceded by a double creeping barrage, one of shrapnel 70 yards in front and one of high explosive 150 yards in front, and simultaneously a barrage of shrapnel was laid along the second line at the back of the battle-zone, to cut off the retreat of the front garrison survivors and to stop reinforcements. In addition, every known dug-out entrance was kept under shell-fire until the infantry was close upon it. To cover the infantry assault in this manner and for the preparatory bombardment over a million (1,169,000) shells had been allotted, approximately double the proportionate quantity used to prepare and cover the opening British assault on the Somme nearly six months before (1st of July) 1916). So it was that the period, already foreseen by General Ludendorff, had arrived when the mass production of munitions enabled the neutralization not only of a trench system but of an entire battle-zone.

The five German divisions, supported by 533 guns of all calibres, defending this battle area, 2,500 yards in depth, had two-thirds of their strength in the battle-zone and one-third back in rest billets six to ten miles away.[3] But the deep dug-outs, in which the front garrison was sheltering, proved to be man-traps out of which only a few of the defenders escaped before either the entrances were blown in or the French infantry had reached them. Out of a total strength of 21,000 these five front divisions lost 13,500 in casualties during the battle (15th–16th), of which about 9,000 were prisoners.

The reserve battalions of the front regiments (i.e. the third part of the front divisions in rest billets) did not reach the battlefield till the evening of the 15th. The two *Eingreif*-divisions, although ordered forward on the evening of the 14th in anticipation of the attack, at mid-day on the 15th were still 14 miles from the battlefield, and their leading regiments did not reach it till early on the 16th. Both they and the reserve battalions were too late to make an immediate counter-attack, the French having already consolidated for defence the captured positions. The entire battle-zone and most of its garrison were therefore lost. The necessity, expressly laid down by General Ludendorff in his textbook, issued a fortnight previously, for bringing up the reserve formations close behind the battle-zone had been neglected, and the two commanders responsible, of the Fifth Army (General von Lochow) and of the XIV Reserve Corps (General von Zwehl), were dismissed the following day.

---

2 In all 56 battalions with 10 of the 48 battalions in position took part in the assault, the remainder being in the second line of attack.

3 Two of these divisions were already weak, about 3,000 each strong instead of the normal 7,000. There were in all 29 battalions, approximately two-thirds of the infantry strength, in or near the battle-zone.

2

Although the two outstanding reasons for the collapse of the German defence on this occasion, the deep dug-outs in the front trench system and the absence of reserves for the immediate counter-attack, were stressed in a pamphlet issued by O.H.L. shortly afterwards (25th of December, 1916), both mistakes were repeated almost identically on a larger scale at the battle of Arras-Vimy, four months later.

The Arras battlefield extended for nearly eleven miles astride the Scarpe (see Map). The seven-mile sector north of the river, to Givenchy, comprised mainly the Vimy Ridge position, which lay on a long forward slope with a steep escarpment behind it. This position had been constructed during 1915 on rigid defence principles with accommodation for the bulk of the front garrison in deep-mined dug-outs in the front trench system (1st and 2nd trenches), and very few dug-outs in the rearward lines. The supporting batteries lay either along the upper edge of the woods which cover the escarpment or about the open ground at its foot, chiefly behind the Lens–Arras railway embankment; their fire-direction was entirely dependent on reports from observers along the crest of the Ridge. The four-mile sector south of the Scarpe to beyond Neuville Vitasse consisted mainly of the new Hindenburg Line to which the front garrison had swung back in the middle of February. That, too, had been constructed on rigid defence principles with deep-mined or in places concrete dug-outs for the bulk of the garrison in the front trench system, and was here sited near the top of a long reverse slope which lent itself to be built up in depth behind.[4] The batteries were in the wide and mostly shelterless depressions behind the artillery protective line and among the ruins of Athies in the Scarpe valley; their observers were back in the Monchy Riegel with good observation over the long reverse slope of the infantry position.

During December and January a programme of reconstruction and training, emphasized in all the regimental histories concerned, was drawn up for the garrison on the principles of the new elastic defence in depth, laid down in General Ludendorff's text-book of the 1st of December, 1916. This meant the creation of a deep fortified zone which was to be defended by a mobile defence, instead of the former rigid defence of a front trench system. The programme was also influenced by the supplementary pamphlet issued by General Ludendorff nearly a month later, 25th of December, 1916, on the "Experience of the Recent Fighting at Verdun (15th of December, 1916)"[5] which gave as one of the first lessons of that "serious and regrettable reverse" that the front part of the new fortified zone was to be held lightly, par like an outpost zone. "The front trench cannot be held too thinly," it said, and suggested as a suitable garrison "one man to every 6 yards, or one shallow dug-out (of concrete and steel girders) to accommodate a group (1 non-commissioned officer and 12 men) every 55 yards or double group every 110 yards," which was equivalent to making the front trench into a line of strong sentry posts; it also insisted that as deep-mined dug-outs in the front trench system are man-traps they should only be used in the rearward lines. It emphasized that "depth is essential," and, for that

---

[4] The lie of the ground in this Tilloy–Neuville Vitasse sector did not favour building up a battle-zone in depth in front of the existing line, as had been done in the First Army sector, south of Quéant, neither would it have been practicable owing to the nearness of the enemy.

[5] A captured copy of this pamphlet was printed (2,000 copies) by British G.H.Q. on the 28th of February, 1917. A copy of General Ludendorff's text-book was not captured until April, 1917, but this Verdun pamphlet showed the tendency of the new defensive battle, the defence of a deep zone rather than of a trench line.

reason, the rearward portion of the fortified zone will consist of a system of strong points and machine-gun nests." On that network of fortified localities the mobile defence of the zone by counter-attacks was to be based.

The programme of reconstruction, therefore, demanded primarily the construction of concrete shelters (*Mannschafts-Eisen-Beton-Unterstände*) in the front trench system to replace the deep-mined dug-outs, the excavation of an extra number of deep dug-outs in the back (intermediate and second) lines for distributing the garrison in depth, and the building of a number of fortified localities and concrete machine-gun emplacements in the intervening ground. If Sixth Army headquarters had been as far-seeing as the First Army, on its left, which already in February was reshaping its sector of the Hindenburg Line into a Hindenburg Position, the main line of resistance would have been brought back from the front trench system to the intermediate line, north of the Scarpe, and to the artillery protective line, south of the river; there is, however, no indication of any such suggestion in the Sixth Army sector.

Although the Arras offensive was foreseen as early as mid-February,[6] this programme remained, in its essentials, a paper one, and various reasons are given. The Crown Prince Rupprecht of Bavaria, commanding the Northern Group of Armies, writes in his diary that it was "due to shortage of labour that the position, built on obsolete principles, was not reconstructed in time." Some of the regimental histories say that it was owing to the very wintry conditions of that early spring which prevented the concrete setting, others that it was feared to thin the front garrison as British raiding parties might notice the change and alter their plan of attack accordingly, and another reason given is that the careful watch kept by the British aeroplanes enabled all new work in this chalk-covered district to be easily spotted by photograph and to be shelled to destruction immediately. Probably all these reasons contributed to the result that, when the British and Canadian artillery bombardment opened in the latter part of March,[7] defence in depth by the German garrison had not been achieved—neither of men nor of machine guns nor of fortified localities. Of the five or six fortified localities in each battalion sector, few were in fact where most required—in the rearward part of the battle-zone; most were in the forward part of the battle-zone, often extemporized out of existing dug-outs. It was emphasized, nevertheless, in the defence plan, "that these strong points were to be the main centres of resistance (*feste Punkte*) of the new defence system and that they were to be held at all costs, even though surrounded by the enemy, to make easier the counter-attack by the troops from the back of the battle-zone (*aus der Tiefe*)."[8] The reconstruction of the artillery positions was equally backward. The batteries were still grouped in lines, easy to see from the air and easy to gas, instead of being spread out in depth according to the new instructions.

During the preparatory bombardment the British and Canadian artillery fired 2,687,000 shells on to the German position on a frontage of eleven miles. On the Vimy Ridge sector alone nearly a million shells were hurled across no-man's-land on a frontage of four miles, compared with the one and a half million on a fourteen-mile frontage to prepare the Somme assault on the 1st of July, 1916. The casualties of the German garrison

---

6 On the 13th of February Crown Prince Rupprecht informed Sixth Army headquarters that the British would probably attack the left wing of the Sixth Army (from the Scarpe to Croisilles) and attempt to capture the Vimy Ridge as soon as the German withdrawal to the Hindenburg Line began.

7 The Canadian Corps and the First Army bombardment began on the 21st of March, that of the Third Army on the 4th of April.

8 *Osterschlacht bei Arras, 1917*, Vol. 1, p. 96 (Reichsarchiv monograph).

during this week of suffering (*Leidenswoche*), as they aptly name it, were not heavy but from all accounts the men became exhausted both by the endless task of keeping open the dug-out entrances and by the difficulty of obtaining food owing to the condition of the ways of communication and to the shelling of the ration-carrying parties; numbers of men had no meal at all for two or three consecutive days. In such conditions no further progress was made in the reconstruction programme. Although the six-day inter-battalion reliefs were maintained throughout, with great difficulty, the resting battalions in the villages several miles behind the position were so constantly shelled by the British heavy batteries that they had to move out into the open and had little sleep during this period. By the eve of the infantry assault the front trench system had become lines of mud-filled shell-holes and the wire entanglement had been blown into shreds. One regimental history (2nd Bavarian Reserve, south of Thelus) describes the position as "consisting no longer of lines of trenches but of advanced nests of men scattered about where formerly lay the first and second trenches (front trench system), with a line of island positions along the site of the third trench (about 500 yards behind the first)." Another (262nd Reserve) describes its front trench system as "lost in a crater field," and, taking the battle-front as a whole, the three companies which normally garrisoned the front-trench system along the 1,000 yards of each regimental sector consisted of a number of isolated defence groups, with sentry posts in shell holes in front.

Striking an average, about one-third of the front divisions were within 600 yards of the British assault trenches and at the mercy of the full weight of the bombardment. The organization of the German Arras–Vimy defences on the morning of assault was, in fact, remarkably similar to that at Verdun on the morning of the 15th of December, 1916 (see Diagram).

3

The British and Canadian infantry assaulted at 5.30 a.m. on the 9th of April. The assault was preceded by a five-minute hurricane bombardment after a comparatively quiet night. This unusual bombardment procedure came as a surprise to the German garrison[9] and the majority of those in the deep dug-outs of the first and second trenches, cramped 25–40 men in each, had not time to clamber up the twenty or more steep steps to daylight before the entrances were in the enemy's hands. Many, when taken prisoners, were still half-dressed, and of those who tried to escape back a great number were without boots or else stuck in the knee-deep mud of the communication trenches and were subsequently captured.

At the moment of assault it was still dark. A westerly wind was blowing a squall of sleet and snow into the faces of the Germans, and the dawn light was delayed by the heavy clouds. These weather conditions favoured the assault, for it affected the aim of a number of machine gunners in the front trench system and in the fortified localities thereabouts. It was these few men who caused most of the casualties in the opening stage of the assault, but thanks to the darkness they were in most cases quickly outflanked, surrounded, and bombed. In places a stronger resistance was offered, especially in the Hindenburg Line sector, south of the Scarpe. Here, as also immediately north of the river,

---

9   Several of the German sentries had heard the arrival of infantry in the assault assembly trenches a couple of hours previously, but messengers were the only remaining means of communication and their reports reached battalion headquarters too late for artillery action to be taken (rocket signals were only to be used where an attack had actually begun).

where the battlefield had been less churned up by the shorter artillery bombardment, tanks, according to the German evidence, greatly assisted the British success both in the earlier and later stages of the attack; but the few in the Vimy Ridge sector were unable to master the mud of the German front trench system and stuck thereabouts.

Simultaneously with the start of the assault, the British and Canadian counter-batteries had shelled and gassed all the German battery positions between Givenchy and Wancourt, putting out of action a large proportion of the guns, exploding shell dumps, completely disorganizing the ammunition supply, and gassing the horses of the batteries and supply columns. In addition the artillery observation posts, chiefly along the crest of the Vimy Ridge and in the Monchy Riegel, were mostly either destroyed by shell or smothered by a smoke-screen. Seldom during the War can counter-battery work have been so effective. At best, the Germans had in position less than a third of the artillery opposed to them, and there was, as a result of this crippling counter-battery bombardment, only a feeble answer when the coloured rocket signals went up from the German front garrison asking for artillery support.

On wide frontages the assaulting infantry was able to press on without delay, or as fast as the mud allowed. Ankle deep in it the men dripped with perspiration, in spite of the temperature and snow falling, as they plodded across the puddled wilderness towards their first objective, about 600 yards beyond the front trench system. There was now a glimmer of daylight, but so dim that the isolated nests of Germans in the third trench, with sleet still blowing in their faces, were unable to see, till close upon them, whether the mass of men approaching were their own front garrison retiring elastically, as was to be expected, or the enemy. At the start the proportion of assaulting troops to the defending garrison was about four to one, excluding the reserve battalions of the front regiments, which were resting in villages four to six miles behind the battle-zone. As the front battalions had been eliminated in wide sectors, the scattered companies of the support battalions were now faced by nearly double that proportion of attackers. Some of them were surrounded before they could appreciate the situation, but a great proportion were able to take advantage of the new text-book's permission to yield, and fell back hurriedly to the intermediate and second lines. It was their wisest course in the circumstances. Within an hour, or less, the forward part of the battle-zone had been overrun on the greater part of the assault frontage, and consequently nearly a third of the front divisions captured or killed. The assault, pressing through these great gaps, caused the resistance in intervening sectors to collapse. By about 8 a.m. with few exceptions, such as on Hill 145 at the northern extremity of the battlefront, there remained in the battle-zone only the surviving companies of the support battalions, with a few remnants of the front battalions. The reserve battalions, the remaining third of the front divisions, though alarmed about 6.15 a.m., were still far from the scene of action.

Generally speaking the support battalion commanders, rather than watch their companies being eaten up piecemeal, discarded the new 'elastic' system and its 'group' organization. They spread out their companies along some defined line which made a rallying position for men and machine-gunners streaming back from the front. There was to be no more "yielding by detachments" except at their orders, and the force at their disposal was too weak to make local counter-attacks. There were exceptions, but this course seems to have been taken instinctively by most of the battalion commanders concerned. In the Vimy Ridge sector, where the intermediate line had been overrun on both sides of Thelus, the Ridge itself was abandoned and the companies were rallied along the Second Line or along the railway embankment at the foot of the escarpment. Farther south, however, to the Scarpe, the intermediate line was held and the corresponding, artillery protective, line south of the river.[10]

To these rallying positions withdrew also a number of survivors with machine guns from the fortified localities, for the course of the battle showed that, in a long prepared assault such as this, only in rare cases will a small, isolated garrison "hold on at all costs" for any length of time with an overwhelming attack passing both its flanks. Of the seventy or eighty fortified localities on the Arras battle-front the number that long resisted can be counted on one hand.[11] Although these, and a few less notable, hampered considerably the advance before they were overcome, it seems that those garrisons of the forward fortified localities, in this case the majority, who adopted a mobile attitude and assisted in forming a line of defence were more effective in temporarily stemming the assault and had a better chance of survival.

After a pause for nearly an hour fresh British and Canadian battalions began to advance on their next objective, 600 yards or more ahead. The sleet had turned to a heavy fall of snow which covered their approach. On the Vimy Ridge the Canadian Corps reached the objective, the intermediate line, but elsewhere, although the majority of the fortified localities in the intervening ground were forced either to surrender or fall back, the scattered companies in the rallying positions along the intermediate line or artillery protective line south of the Scarpe held fast; in a few places where forced back they retook the line by local counter-attacks. Crown Prince Rupprecht in his diary gives his opinion that these companies would have delivered counter-attacks all along the line at this period of the battle, as they had been trained, if local commanders had believed that strong reserves were behind them. But there was no sign or news of reinforcements and, in addition, there was a shortage of machine-gun ammunition and no artillery support, which made it impossible to demoralize by fire the advancing masses of British infantry, an essential preliminary to the immediate counter-attack.[12] These surviving companies of the front divisions therefore remained for the most part on the defensive and continued to resist for some hours, waiting expectantly for the promised reinforcements.

About 10.30 a.m. the day suddenly changed its colouring. The browns and greys of mud, smoke and sleet were gradually transformed as the sun broke through on the battlefield from a blue sky. To quote the history of the 1st Bavarian Reserve Regiment, "the squalls of sleet and snow which till now had hidden the landscape, ceased and the air suddenly became clean and clear, filled with spring sunshine." The survivors of the German front divisions in the battle-zone, looking back over the open country behind, still could

10 In greater detail, these rallying lines lay roughly, from right to left, along the second line at the foot of or on the escarpment of the Vimy Ridge (79th Reserve Division); along the intermediate line between the Farbus—Arras and Bailleul—Roclincourt roads (1st Bavarian Reserve Division), in the Railway Position (intermediate line) south of Maison Blanche Wood (14th Bavarian Division), along the railway embankment astride the Scarpe (11th Division) and in the 3rd trench of the Hindenburg Line (about 600 yards behind the first trench), south of Tilloy (17th Reserve Division).

11 For example, the most gallant defence put up in the strong point on Hill 145 (261st Res. Regt.) on Vimy Ridge, that in the strong point known as "Prinz Franz Hütte" (2nd Bav. Res. Regt.) on the Arras—Farbus road, and in the Chalk Pit (162nd Regt.) north of Wancourt, all of which held out till well on into the morning, and, on Hill 145, till the afternoon.

12 A full train-load of machine-gun ammunition belts destined for the Arras front had in fact gone astray a few days before and was held up till too late.

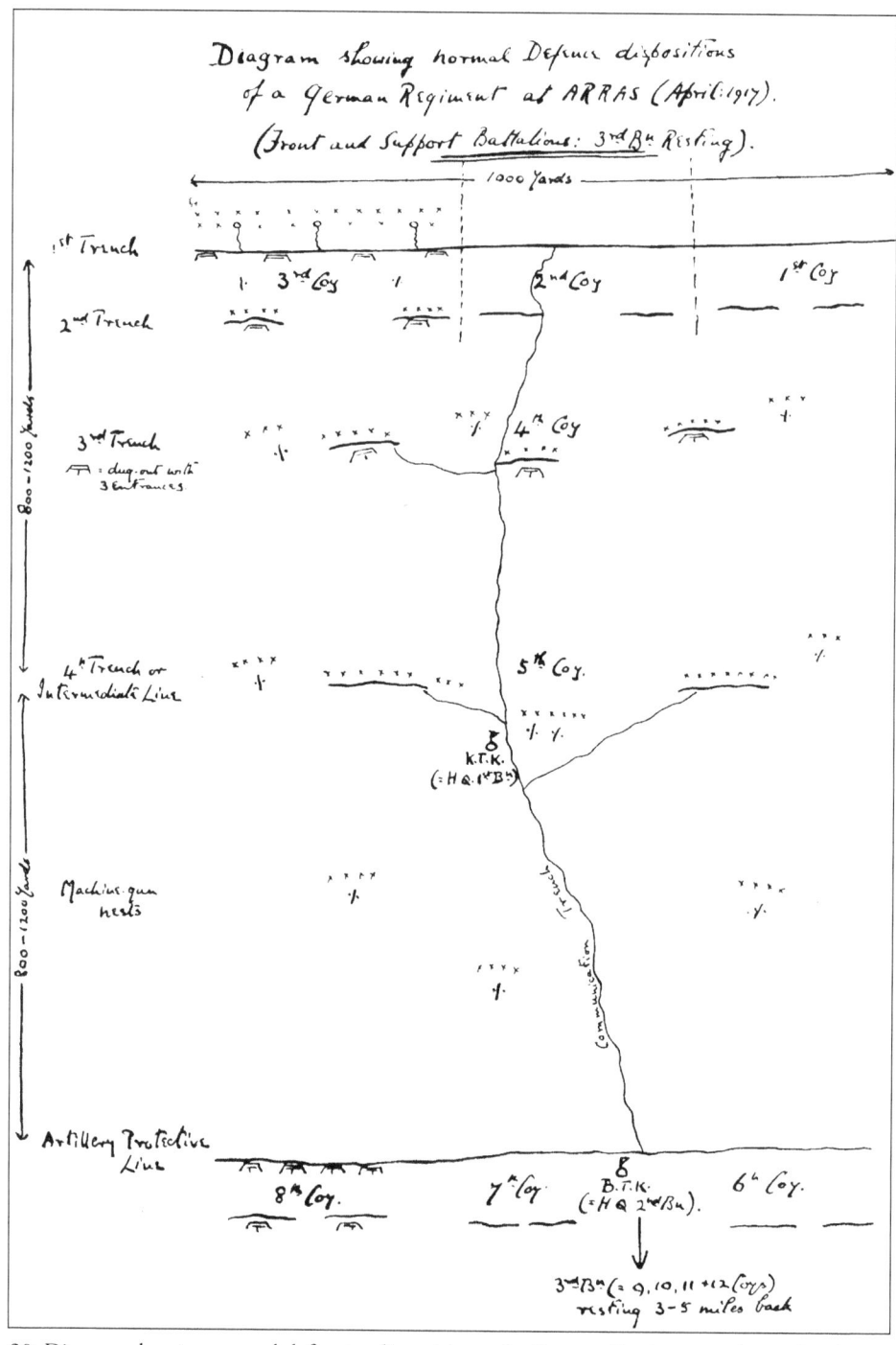

20. Diagram showing normal defensive dispositions of a German Regiment at Arras, April 1917

see no sign of reinforcements, and their supporting artillery was practically silent. By 11 a.m., and in places sooner, the British infantry began to penetrate unopposed the large gaps between the isolated rallying positions. There were but few previously sited machine-gun nests in the rearward part of the battle-zone to cover these intervening stretches of ground, and, as the attack passed on behind the flanks, the last lines of resistance broke. Facing the Vimy Ridge escarpment to which the advance of the Canadian Corps was limited, the Germans continued to hold the Second Line on a frontage of about four miles, but on the remainder of the battle-front the battalions fell back during the early afternoon across the open towards the Third Line and its equivalent; the Monchy Riegel, 3,000 to 5,000 yards behind.

The defending infantry had been defeated in detail. The front battalions had mostly been overrun in their deep dug-outs, and the support battalions, ordered not to reinforce the front battalions but to wait to deliver local counter-attacks, had therefore found themselves faced by an overwhelming superiority. Being without artillery support they had generally decided to hold a line until reinforced, but the reserve battalions arrived too late to assist and the support battalions were meanwhile either surrounded or forced to retire.

4

The absence of any German reserves immediately behind the Arias—Vimy battlefront on the 9th of April, 1917) is one of the dramatic tactical failures of the war. In addition to local reserves, which were the resting battalions of the front divisions, a first line of five reserve (*Eingreif*) divisions had been placed at the disposal of the Sixth Army headquarters, another 4 had been earmarked in O.H.L. reserve as a second line of reserve for the Sixth Army. The court of inquiry ordered by O.H.L. into what General Hindenburg calls the "*Debakel*" of Arras found, however, that although there had been no lack of warning from many sources,[13] "Sixth Army headquarters did not consider the offensive to be imminent." It also found that, in consequence, the five counter-attack divisions had not been brought forward near enough to the front, to assembly positions (near the Second Line, according to the new text-book) from which they could answer the enemy's breakthrough by an immediate counter-attack." Their absence ignored the wishes both of General Ludendorff and of Crown Prince Rupprecht of Bavaria. The former, in his "War Memories" (II, p. 419), says, "I begged (on the 6th of April) Group headquarters (Crown Prince Rupprecht) to bring its reserves nearer to the line in the area of the Sixth Army. The last attacks at Verdun, in October and December, 1916, had confirmed the old maxim that the right place for the reserves is close to the battle-front." The Crown Prince Rupprecht writes in his diary (II, p. 135) on the evening of the battle day "We now have to suffer for the fact that the Sixth Army headquarters, despite my expressed wishes (on the evening of the 6th), did not send its reserves up closer to the front line divisions. I cannot but feel myself to blame for not having ordered Sixth Army headquarters to move its reserves up nearer the front."

The inquiry also found that "the available artillery had not been put in either in sufficient time or quantity to fight the enemy's preparations." A great number of batteries, heavy and field, still lay parked in village squares and in Douai when the offensive opened, and the inquiry also criticized the ammunition supply arrangements, which became rapidly

---

13 As one example, the 11th Division headquarters astride of the Scarpe reported, on the afternoon of the 8th of April, that the British offensive was expected at any moment ("scheint unmittelbar bevorzustehen").

disorganized owing to lack of preliminary preparation. The Crown Prince Rupprecht in his diary, accused Sixth Army headquarters of being "careless (*sorglos*)" in these matters, and writes that the opening of the offensive came as surprise to that headquarters which "expected the British assault to be preceded by a continuous drum-fire bombardment lasting several days" and was saving its ammunition to reply to it. He adds that, not only the five counter-attack divisions but also the local reserves, the resting battalions of the front regiments, were consequently everywhere either held too far back or put in too late. For example, the reserve battalions of the 14th Bavarian Division, north of the Scarpe, were still back resting in Douai on the morning of the 9th and did not reach the battle-front until the early afternoon. Of the resting battalions of the other front divisions few were able to reach the rallying lines of the support battalions before the withdrawal of the latter had begun, and of those of the 17th Reserve Division, south of the Scarpe, two were held back, by orders of the division, all day behind Monchy, 6,000 yards away, as no other reserves were in rear. Like the counter-attack divisions, the resting battalions, which formed a third part of the front divisions, were too far away to give timely assistance.

It may be accepted that much of this neglect was due to a misjudgement by General von Falkenhausen, the Sixth Army commander, and his Chief of Staff, Colonel von Nagel, of the date of the offensive.[14] But that in itself does not suffice to explain away the complete breakdown of the machinery of the new defensive battle on this occasion. All the evidence points to the fact that an equal, or greater, contributory cause was the intention of Sixth Army to fight the battle on the Falkenhayn method of rigid defence,[15] regardless of General Ludendorff's instructions, and that he believed that the battle would follow a course similar to the previous defensive battles, that is, protracted fighting in and about the battle-zone which might last for days or weeks as in previous British offensives. The chief evidence for this point of view lies in the story of the five reserve, or counter-attack divisions. When placed at General von Falkenhausen's disposal on the 3rd of April they were on a line Tournai—Derain—Solesmes, 25 to 30 miles from the battlefront. For several weeks beforehand they had been trained, according to O.H.L. instructions, in open warfare on the assumption that the task immediately ahead of them was to deliver a counter-attack from behind the Arras—Vimy battle-front, as laid down in the new defensive battle text-book. And yet the Sixth Army order of the 3rd of April said that they were to be "ready to relieve the front divisions during the course of a long-drawn-out defensive battle" and made no mention of a possible counter-attack. It is evident that General von Falkenhausen regarded them simply as reserve divisions with which to relieve the front divisions after the latter had struggled for a few days on top of Vimy Ridge and along the Arras battle-line. He did not begin to move them forward, marching by road, until the afternoon of the 8th, in spite of the requests to do so earlier, and he gave as a reason for the delay that he "wished to avoid overcrowding the villages near the front." At dawn on the 9th, when the British offensive was launched, they were still east of the line Douai—Cambrai, twelve to fifteen miles from the battlefield,[16] and

---

14 Prisoners' statements gave the opinion that the offensive was not expected till about a week later, to conform with the French offensive in the Champagne, expected for the 15th or 16th of April.

15 General Falkenhayn had the direction of German Supreme Command (O.H.L.) from September 1914 to August 1916, and throughout the period organized the German defence on rigid principles, that is, fighting for every foot of ground irrespective of its tactical value.

16 One or two regiments of these divisions had previously gone forward to work on the new Wotan Line. As an example of how the British offensive took the German Sixth Army headquarters by surprise (in

his immediate action was not to rush them forward by rail and motor lorry, but, on the contrary, with the exception of a few battalions, their orders remained unchanged. To meet the offensive he ordered all available resting battalions from flank divisions, as well as 3 battalions of his Sixth Army reserve from Lille, to block the flanks of a possible breakthrough, and thereby to force the assault into a narrowing pocket. In this way he retained his reserve divisions intact for the eventual relief of the front divisions. It was the system on which the previous defensive battles against British offensives had been fought, i.e. Neuve Chapelle, Festubert, Loos and Somme, and successfully; and it seems clear that he intended to fight the Arras battle in a similar manner. Unlike General Ludendorff, he had not read the writing on the wall at Verdun.[17]

Although no mention is made in the German official monograph of this wide difference in outlook, it is referred to in the divisional history of one of the counter-attack divisions (4th Guard Division) "The British preparations for the Arras offensive were noticed long beforehand, but Sixth Army headquarters had not yet taken sufficiently into consideration the lessons learnt by experience in the Somme battles, which had been summarized by O.H.L. in its new text-book."[18]

To sum up the German evidence, the defeat in the battle of Arras was due to a failure to apply the principles of the new defensive battle text-book, both in the organization of the front divisions and their artillery, and in the disposition of the reserves. The story of the defeat at Verdun on the 15th of December, 1916, had been repeated. The Vimy Ridge and the Arras battle-front had been lost and, with it, a great part of the garrison of seven divisions, the losses of which during the day's battle (9th of April) are given as 474 officers and 15,174 other ranks and 230 guns.[19]

5

On hearing the result of the Arras battle General Ludendorff was, he writes in his Memoirs (vol. II, p. 421), "very depressed. Had our principles of defensive tactics proved false, and if so, what was to be done?" Actually the defeat had confirmed the main features of his

---

spite of warnings from most of its divisions in the line and from statements by captured British prisoners) one of these regiments (89th) of the counter-attack divisions marched out for the usual digging work in the early hours of the 9th and was not recalled to march to the battle-front till 7.50 a.m.

17 General von Falkenhausen was seventy-three years of age, which might account for a disinclination to accept a new doctrine, but in his defence it must be said that his immediate superior, the Crown Prince Rupprecht of Bavaria, a man twenty years younger, seems to have been equally surprised at the course of events. "No one," he wrote in his diary the following day (10th of April), "could have foreseen that the expected offensive would gain ground so quickly." On the other hand the Crown Prince Rupprecht's Chief of Staff, General von Kuhl who, with General Ludendorff and Colonel von Lossberg, had inquired into the German defeat at Verdun (15th of December, 1916), states in his *Weltkrieg* (Vol. II, pp. 84–5), "the elastic defence in depth (*bewegliche Verteidegung aus der Tiefe*) was not practicable on the Vimy Ridge, which lent itself to be captured in one blow (*schlagartig*)," and adds "that he would have preferred to abandon many sectors of the Arras front before the battle as being unsuitable for defence." If this was his belief, he had failed to convince either his own Chief or Sixth Army headquarters.

18 *Die 4. Garde Infanterie Division*, Kurt Gabriel, p. 85.

19 *Mein Kriegstagebuch. Kronprinz Rupprecht von Bayern*, Vol. III, p. 161 (entry for 19th of April, 1917). The British casualties on the Arras—Vimy battle-front during the period 9th –11th of April were about 14,000 all ranks, but that figure should not be taken as a comparison with the German. The British total includes every wounded man who attended a dressing station, whereas the German casualties were reckoned from divisional returns every ten days, and the figure given above for one battle-day is probably very approximate and would not include the lightly wounded who had returned to duty.

new text-book, the urgent need for a departure from rigid defence methods. The Crown Prince Rupprecht of Bavaria gives in his diary (entry 13th of April), his conclusions as to the lessons of Arras; briefly they were that if the enemy has time to build up an artillery organization with light railways to supply sufficient ammunition to a serried mass of guns, and with observation by air photography, he will be able to destroy the forward part of a position no matter how it is sited or how efficiently it is organized, and that any attempt to hold it can only result in a heavy loss of manpower, such as Germany could ill afford. He therefore saw no alternative but to give up that forward part, the front divisions only to fight delaying actions back through it to break up the infantry assault. Further, since the enemy now had sufficient munitions to take under fire several lines of trench simultaneously, he considered that local counter-attacks in the forward part of the position could have little hope of success in recapturing the front trench system, as the text-book demanded. He thought that its instructions should be altered or modified in the sense that the statement that the defensive battle should be fought "not *in* but *for* the foremost line" did not apply in such circumstances. On the contrary, he considered that the forward part of the position should be abandoned, and the defensive battle fought for the artillery protective line, or some line 1,000–2,000 yards in rear of the foremost line. He would have liked to meet the pursuing attackers by a counter-attack from a rearward position, about 8,000 yards distant, and it should not be expected to advance further than about that (artillery protective) line, as it would probably have inadequate artillery support to approach nearer the enemy's fixed battery positions. The great lesson of Arras, he adds, is that the enemy's artillery strength enables him to overrun the forward part of a position more speedily, so that the reserves of the defence must be kept nearer the battle-area and must be trained in open warfare. "In future the defensive battle must be fought offensively again and, in the training of infantry, trench warfare must take second place, more time being given to the attack in open warfare. For the same reason the artillery must be exercised in greater mobility for the encounter battle."

The Crown Prince Rupprecht's conclusions differ from General Ludendorff's text-book in two respects. For the defence of an established position against a long-prepared offensive supported by a superiority of artillery, he seems to have wished to abolish local counter-attacks and fortified localities within the battle-zone, the front line regiments fighting a delaying action back through it to the artillery protective line. Here the attack would be met by an immediate counter-attack by one or more *Eingreif* divisions from behind it or, if that failed, by a deliberate counter-attack before the enemy's artillery had moved forward and he would limit the objective of that counter-attack to the artillery protective line or thereabouts whereas the text-book insisted that it was to recapture the whole of the original position, battle and outpost zones. This belief that the front garrison of a position after enduring the great nervous strain of a prolonged and efficient bombardment would be incapable of fighting a battle was shared by others; for example, General Balck lecturing at a staff exercise of the German Third Army in 1917, said that experience had shown that the garrison of a position would have to be sacrificed in such circumstances and that "these men will have done their duty so long as they compelled the enemy to use up his supports, delayed his entry into the position and disorganized his line of attack," and he added that "the decision will be with the forces held in readiness behind the position." These conclusions, however, took no account of offensives with a limited objective, and for that reason alone the text-book organization had advantages.

The details of the new defensive battle were still in a fluid state, but the Arras battle firmly established the need for "defence-in depth" and the "immediate counter-attack from behind the battle-zone" as its two main pillars.[20]

6

Twice the new German defensive battle doctrine had failed because it had not been properly applied. General Nivelle, who had succeeded Marshal Joffre as French commander-in-chief at the end of 1916, gambled on a third repetition against his great offensive in the Champagne, a week after Arras. Doubtless he did not appreciate the reckless demand he was making on the laws of chance, although the capture by the French on the 16th of February, 1917, of the German document "Experience of the fighting at Verdun" might have warned him. That document, which disclosed the new defence-in-depth and the fact that the Verdun defeat was chiefly due to a failure to apply it, did not, however, alter his opinion, nor did the known capture by the Germans in a raid at Sapigneul (4th of April) of the plans for his offensive, twelve days before it was to be launched. The author of *Kritik des Weltkrieges* comments that there is "a borderline between determination in a commander, following undeterred a pre-arranged plan, and obstinacy, in the sense of refusal to bow before the obvious. General Nivelle had reached and crossed that borderline." He still clung to his belief that the method of attack which he had employed at Verdun was the key to the German fortress on the Western Front.

General Ludendorff had, however, made certain that the experience of Verdun and of Arras should not recur. To quote General von Kuhl's *Weltkrieg* (Vol. II, p. 88) on the preparations for the battle, "the correct application of the principles laid down in the new text-book for the conduct of the defensive battle were ensured by frequent discussions and exercised by the troops in training schools and practice areas." There was no element of surprise; and in the sector to be assaulted, known from the captured French documents, "the foremost lines were to be held thinly, and as many divisions taken out of the line as possible to act as *Eingreif*-divisions; these, too, were carefully trained in their special task." Behind 21 front divisions were 10 *Eingreif*-divisions, and in addition a second line of *Eingreif*-divisions was prepared ten miles behind again, in case the first line should prove inadequate. In all the Germans assembled on a frontage of forty-five miles and to a depth of twenty miles, about 300,000 infantry for the defensive battle.

The main French assault was made on the 16th of April on a front of twenty-five miles against the German position along the Chemin des Dames, a battleground not unlike a large-scale Vimy Ridge. It was to be delivered by 18 infantry divisions, approximately 400,000 men, against half the German concentration, about 150,000 infantry dispersed in great depth. It was to be "*brutal et continu*," capturing in one bound (*un seul élan*) the enemy's organized position and his battery positions. This first bound was to carry the assault through the entire German battle-zone, to cross the Chemin des Dames Ridge and to reach the north bank of the Ailette beyond the steep northern slope of the ridge, an average advance of 3,000 yards. Three hours were allotted for this movement and for

---

20 It is interesting to notice that from published accounts the new (1938) Siegfried Line of fortifications along Germany's Western frontier appears to conform to the German experience of the defence of zones of great depth, such as the Hindenburg Position in 1917, whereas the present French Maginot Line of fortifications, with a large permanent garrison, appears to be based on the principles of the rigid defence of a line employed in 1915 and 1916.

consolidation, when the second bound was to begin to objectives 3,000 yards beyond again, for which another three hours were allotted. It was to be followed by a third bound of about 2,000 yards, so that within about eight hours the infantry were to break through to a depth of 8,000 yards and open the way for the cavalry to exploit the victory.

The French, however, had not prepared the German position for assault so carefully as had the Canadian Corps the Vimy Ridge position. The preparatory artillery bombardment by 5,350 guns and howitzers, lasting ten days, was neither so accurate nor so intense.[21] In any case, the neutralization by artillery fire of the German battle-zone, which lay, like that at Vimy, mostly on the forward slope of the Ridge, was not the solution to the problem presented by the new defence-in-depth. The infantry assault, "*brutal et continu*," on a wide front deep into the German rearward battle-zone suited exactly the German dispositions. The result of the battle was that the German front divisions which had strengthened the back of the battle-zone along or just behind the crest line of the Chemin des Dames Ridge with a network of machine-gun nests, held that line till the end of the battle, with the help of the *Eingreif*-divisions, ready in the wooded valley of the Ailette behind the Ridge.[22]

The entire French offensive was defeated with a loss of 117,000 casualties (including 32,000 killed) in a few days, but the moral effect on the French Army and nation was more important than the casualty list. They had been promised a victory which would drive the Germans out of France and end the war, and, instead, not even the Chermin des Dames Ridge had been captured. Mutinies broke out, and a defeatism and weakness set in throughout the French Army which lasted for several months. Fortunately the Russians continued to hold nearly half the German Army on the Eastern Front, and the British Army by fighting the battles of the Scarpe, Messines and the Passchendaele campaign kept German attention away from the French sector during that critical period.

The defeat of the French offensive on the 16th of April finally allayed General Ludendorff's doubts as to the efficiency of his new defence doctrine.

7

The German success on the Chemin des Dames gives an added interest to the probable course of the Arras battle if those five counter-attack (*Eingreif*) divisions had been "close behind the battle-zone" on the morning of the 9th, ready to make that smashing counter-attack, which General Ludendorff intended and which the Crown Prince Rupprecht realized, too late, should be delivered.

Four of those *Eingreif*-divisions were to be put in north of the Scarpe, which was considered the most probable and most threatening direction for the exploitation of a possible victory. Covered by the low clouds, which prevented air reconnaissance throughout the first half of the morning, their leading regiments could have reached the crest-line of the Vimy Ridge about three hours after alarm.

The British and Canadian infantry, advancing by a deliberate timetable, did not reach the greater, southern, part of the crest-line until six hours after the opening of the assault,[23] and the inflexibility of this timetable method did not allow advantage to be taken

---

21 The French Official History (Vol. V) calculates that the Fifth and Sixth Armies which attacked this sector (twenty-five miles) had roughly six million shells for the whole of April; for the Vimy Ridge (four miles) one million shells were used for the bombardment alone.
22 A good account of the German defence is given in *Chemin des Dames*, Gustav Goes, Hamburg, 1938.
23 This compares with the three hours allotted by the French for their first bound, *brutal et continu*, over a similar distance against the Chemin des Dames position.

of the collapse of the German defence which had occurred. It gave time for the support battalions of the front-line regiments to rally along intermediate lines, and, behind that screen, the leading regiments of the *Eingreif*-divisions would have had two or three hours in which to consolidate a new line of defence.

The battle would have been joined about the steep wooded slopes on the eastern face of the Ridge, about the Bois de la Folie, Bois de Bonval, Bois Farbus and Bois de Maison Blanche. Those woods would have become famous in military history, but happily they have avoided that distinction and still grow in quiet obscurity with their wild daffodils and blue periwinkles. That final act of the battle of Arras was never played; the tale stopped short of its intended end, and only the white beacon of the Canadian Vimy Memorial remains as a reminder of it as well as being the symbol of a great victory.

14

The Battle of Vimy Ridge

9 April 1917[1]

The battle of Vimy Ridge is one to which the original title of this series of articles particularly applies – 'The Other Side of the Hill' – for it must be admitted that, without disparaging in any way the brilliant victory gained by the British First and Third Armies on the Arras—Vimy battlefield, an error of judgment by one of the opposing generals was largely responsible for the collapse of the German defence.

It is necessary, in order to appreciate the strange situation that existed on the morning of the 9th of April, 1917, on the Arras-Vimy front, to understand the opposing systems of attack and defence. The British system of attack was still on the French pattern, adopted after the disaster of Aubers Ridge in May 1915. It was based on shells and more shells, to the partial exclusion of the first principle of offensive warfare, surprise. The ideal to be attained was an enemy's position riddled with shells and, if possible, blown up from beneath; the infantry, preceded by a curtain of still more shells, would walk over the shambles of the front defence zone, "*cigarette à la bouche*" as the French described their intended progress, and then on beyond into the open country with a mass of cavalry to pursue any surviving enemy. The Germans regarded the decision to adopt this system of attack as a victory of matter over intelligence named it accordingly the "*Materialschlacht.*" The battles of Festubert and Loos in 1915 and those of the Somme in 1916 were a gradual striving towards this ideal; but it was not until 1917 that sufficient guns and ammunition were available to give it full expression. There was also ample time. The battle was planned and ordered in January, 1917, and the following months were available for the colossal preparations. Every yard of the enemy's trench zone was photographed from the air and mapped, and the infantry practised over mimic battlefields in every detail. For the day of the assault every battery had its allotted task from zero hour (5.30 a.m.) till the Vimy Ridge was finally captured, timed for 1.30 p.m., and the course to be followed by the barrage of shell for every five minutes during that period was drawn on a model map; each battalion, each company, knew its allotted position throughout that period. The scheme resembled the preparation for a modern Aldershot Tattoo in its disregard of anything the enemy might do.

Both the system and the disregard of the enemy's intentions were justified by the fact that from Aubers Ridge in May, 1915, to the end of the Somme battles in the autumn of 1916, the Germans had relied on a rigid system of defence. It answered its purpose up to a point but, as the Somme campaign dragged to its conclusion, it was clear that that point

---

1   References for this article: *Mein Kriegstagebuch*, Vol. II, Rupprecht von Bayern. *Der Weltkrieg, 1914–1918*, von Kuhl. *My War Memories*, Ludendorff. *Out of My Life*, Hindenburg. *Das K. B. Inf. Regt. No. 2*, Bayern Kriegsarchiv. *Das Gren. Regt. No. 119*, Stuttgart. *Die 4 Garde Infanterie Division*, Gabriel. *Die militarischen Lehren des grossen Krieges*, Schwartz. *Die Oesterschlacht bei Arras, 1917*, Reichsarchiv, Berlin.

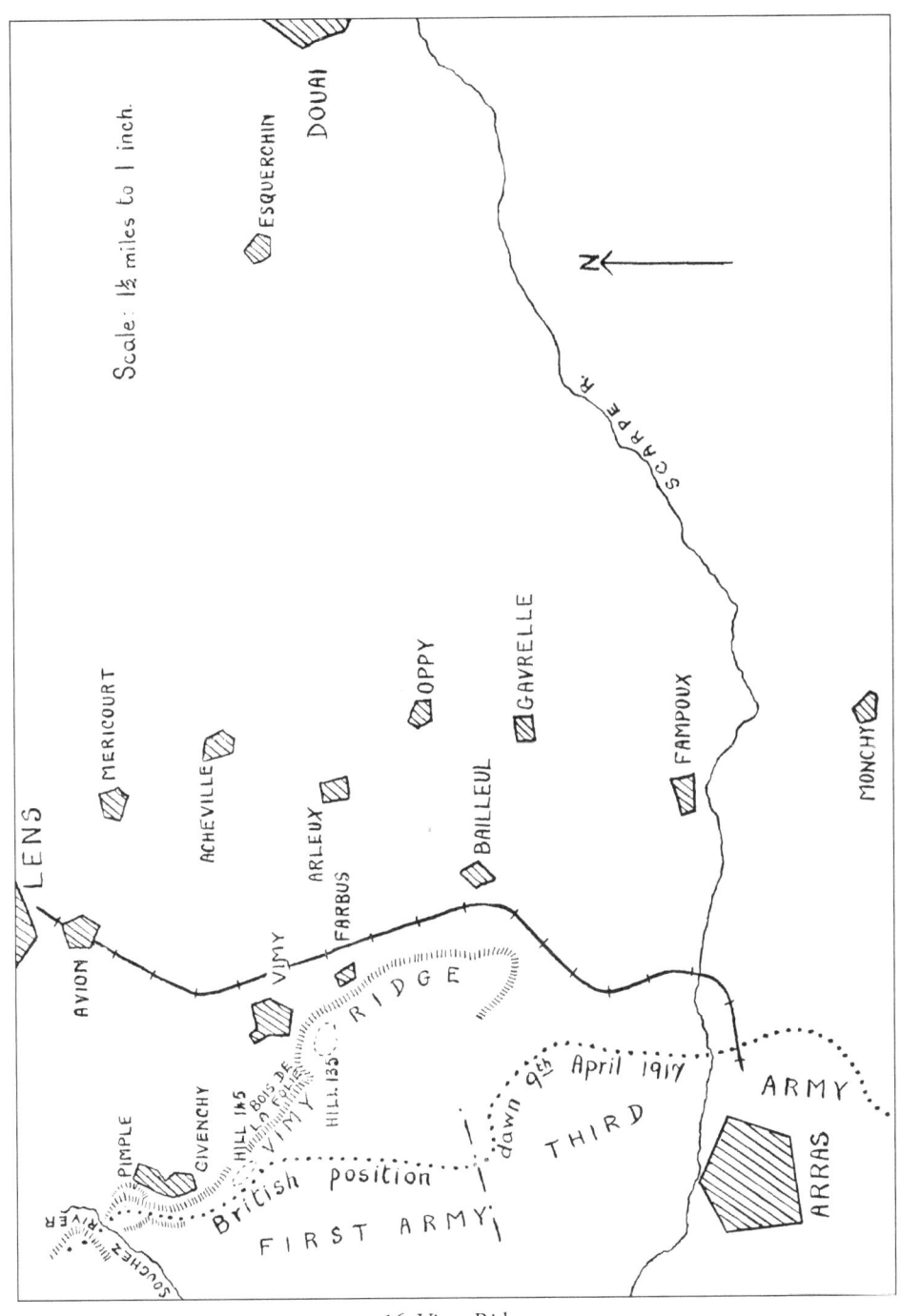

16. Vimy Ridge

had been reached and passed. The enormous losses incurred in the front defence zone, both in the artillery preparation and in the infantry assault, had led to a rapid deterioration of the fighting spirit of the finest German divisions and made some alternative system of defence imperative. One of the first gifts of General Ludendorff to his forces after the Hindenburg—Ludendorff combination took over the reins of the Higher Command in the autumn of 1916 was a new manual called "Conduct of the Defensive Battle" upon which, from January, 1917, onwards, the training of every battalion in the German Armies was based.[2] Instead of continuous lines of trenches, front, support and reserve, every yard of which had to be contested, the new method demanded a network of machine-gun posts and strong points, wired-in redoubts, scattered over the front defence zone. They would extend back about 1,000 yards and be closer together at the back than near the front. No attempt was to be made to hold the old trench system, but the net was to dislocate and to catch up in its meshes the assault as much as possible, inflicting damage on it and gaining time for the mainstay of the defence, namely the counter-attack (*Eingreif*) divisions, to come forward from their positions of readiness, four or five miles in rear, to the battlefield. These would deliver the counterstroke, either locally or combined as the situation demanded, drive back the exhausted troops of the assault and regain the lost ground. The front defence zone was to be held by fewer troops, *i.e.* one front-line division supported by one counter-attack division was to be spread out over 5,000 yards instead of the usual 3,000 yards, Casualties would be minimized and the offensive spirit would be introduced into what had become almost a passive defence, This system, which the Germans, not without reason, regard as the one pearl of wisdom that emerged from the ghastly slaughter on the Somme uplands in 1916, General Ludendorff ordered to be put into practice against the British and French offensives known to be imminent in the spring of 1917. A mobile, or, to use its German name, *elastische*, defence was the German reply to the British and French *materialschlacht*.

The German regiments that took over the Vimy Ridge front at the end of February 1917, when the first evidences of a British offensive were noticed, began at once to rebuild the defences on the new method, but found it no simple task. The deep dug-outs were principally in the first and second trenches, about fifty yards apart, and there were few in the third trench and back lines. Great efforts were made to correct this, but the terrible weather of that spring hindered progress and in mid-March, when the bombardment of the Ridge began, only a few of the intended redoubts and machine-gun emplacements had been constructed. From that time onwards so thorough was the British reconnaissance work and photography that no fresh work seen on the chalk surface of the Ridge escaped notice and subsequent destruction by artillery. On the morning of the assault there was still no network. The front line divisions were holding the 3,000 yards frontage as before, and most of the garrison of the front defence zone were, for want of any other shelter, still in the deep dug-outs of the first, second and third trenches. The situation of the front-line regiments on the Arras front on either side of the Scarpe was very similar.

---

2 It was issued to the German regiments on the 1st of December, 1916. In a foreword General Ludendorff wrote: "In strong contrast to the former system of defined lines of defence near together there will now be a zone of defence of considerable depth, within which will be room to manoeuvre. … The infantryman will no longer have to say to himself: "Here I stay and here I die." He will have the right to give ground to a certain extent in the defence zone if hard pressed. The lost trench lines will be retaken by local counter-attacks or by the counter-attack (*Eingreif*) divisions."

Dawn on the 9th of April was miserable for the time of the year, a cold west wind blowing sleet and snow into the enemy's faces, and the Germans were taken unawares. The assembly of the Canadian divisions had been admirably done, the bombardment had slackened down during the early hours, and then suddenly at 5.30 a.m. every gun opened on the German position and the infantry assault began almost simultaneously. Most of the Germans in the first and second trenches were captured before they could dress and scramble up out of the deep dug-outs. Here and there a German machine gun or groups of infantry opened fire in the half-light on the advancing lines, but the Canadian battalions, clogged and slowed down as they were by the mud and puddled shell-holes, were in a determined humour, and these centres of resistance were silenced one after another by many gallant acts of individuals and groups of men. The advance proceeded exactly to timetable. The intended network was smashed to pieces. Only on Hill 145, the highest point, where a sector of about 100 yards of the first trench and the wire in front had escaped destruction, did the Germans offer a more stubborn and, to the Canadian 11th Brigade, most costly opposition. By 11 a.m., with that exception, the entire crest of the Ridge was in Canadian possession. The heavy clouds were then dispersing and warm spring sunshine added glamour to this hour of triumph. The leading battalions, as they continued on down the wooded slopes on the eastern face, overlooked the great plain of Douai reaching away to the eastern horizon and could see only a few Germans, some running back and some moving about in the villages, but no force of sufficient strength to challenge them by a counterstroke. By 1.30 p.m. the entire Ridge, with the exception of Hill 145, was in their possession as planned by the timetable. Looking to the right the Canadians could see General Allenby's Third Army still pressing on deep into the German position towards Gavrelle and Fampoux and towards Monchy beyond the Scarpe. By capturing the Ridge the Canadians had made secure the northern flank of this advance eastward. The victory seemed and was complete. The British system of attack, the ideal worked for since May, 1915, had finally materialized, and to all appearances had justified itself.

Not till dusk, when the sky had again clouded over, were Germans seen in any strength. At that time, between 4 p.m. and 6 p.m. extended lines of infantry appeared moving towards the Ridge from Avion, Acheville and Arleux, and they reached the railway line at its foot under a heavy fire as night fell. Throughout the hours of darkness the Canadian outposts expected the counter-stroke but, though much noise was heard, no attack developed. By morning the crisis had passed. The more distant British batteries had moved forward within supporting distance and a new main line of resistance had been constructed along the crest of the Ridge. The chance of its recapture was now remote.

The network of the German front defences had utterly failed, if it can be said to have existed at all, and the counter-attack divisions, which might have turned the scales of the battle had they reached the foot of the Ridge at any time before mid-day on the 9th, had been absent. The betrayal of the German front-line regiments—over 2,000 men were taken prisoners on the Ridge alone by the Canadian Corps in the first hours of the assault—was felt by them more especially because it had been impressed upon every man before the battle that they were to hold on at all costs to the various strong points, even if surrounded, as they would be rescued by the counter-attack divisions, and they therefore trusted that these would be in a position of readiness behind them (Reichsarchiv monograph, p. 961). Of the cause of their absence there can be little doubt. On the 6th of April General Ludendorff had begged the Bavarian Crown Prince Rupprecht, commanding the northern

Group of Armies, to bring up his reserves nearer the line in the Sixth Army area, where the British offensive was known to be imminent. That evening five divisions (1st Guard Reserve, 4th Guard, 17th, 18th and 26th) were placed at the disposal of the Sixth Army (General von Falkenhausen), four more divisions being kept back as a second line of reserve. At the same time, and again on the evening of the 7th, the Bavarian Crown Prince asked General von Falkenhausen to move the five divisions forward to a position of readiness. The latter, however, did not consider the British assault would be delivered until the 15th, simultaneously with that of the French at Rheims which was expected on that date. The diary of the Bavarian Crown Prince shows evidence—such as statements by captured British prisoners, many of whom, according to a German regimental history (2nd Bav. Res. Regt.), talked freely about the preparations that the date of the assault was to be the 8th (it was postponed from the 8th to the 9th on the 5th of April) to confirm the report on the 7th from the 1st Bav. Res. Corps commander (facing the Arras—Vimy front north of the Scarpe) that the offensive might be expected at any moment; nevertheless General von Falkenhausen kept to his opinion, and in reply to the Bavarian Crown Prince said he did not wish to fill the villages near the battle-front too thickly with troops. So it was that the five counter-attack divisions remained in the Tournai—Douai district, twenty miles from the battle zone, instead of five as laid down in the new manual. They were still there when the battle opened at dawn on the 9th. Though ordered forward at once, they did not reach the battlefield till the following morning.

In the absence of the counter-attack divisions a number of resting battalions from regiments farther north had been hurried by train and motor-lorry to the battlefield. Two from the unengaged sector of the 16th Bav. Division, three from the 80th Res. Divisions and two from the 56th Division, all these from the Lens district, went to the assistance of the 79th Reserve Division between Vimy and Givenchy, while three more (one each from the 5th and 6th Bav. Divisions and one from the 49th Reserve Division) from the Lille district reinforced the right of the 1st Bav. Res. Division about Farbus. It was these battalions that the Canadians saw advancing towards the Ridge at dusk on the 9th.

Local counter-attacks had been ordered to recapture Hill 135 and the northern slope of Hill 145 during the night. The three and the Lille battalions were to attack through Farbus and capture the southern side of Hill 135, but found that their full strength was needed to hold the new line along the foot of the Ridge defensively. Three of the Lens battalions that were to attack Hill 135 from Vimy along the Arras road were given contrary orders by a local commander who did not know of the intended counter-attack, and they had reinforced the line along the Bois de la Folie before the movement could be counter-ordered. The northern slope of Hill 145 was to be attacked concentrically from Givenchy and the Pimple; the Givenchy attack lost its guides and never developed, while the Pimple attack became bogged in the mud of the depression west of Givenchy village. The failure of these attacks emphasizes once again the great hazard of asking troops to attack by night over unknown country. None of them reached even the Canadian outposts.

During the early morning (10th) the leading battalions of the five counter-attack divisions arrived on the scene, and also those of a sixth (the 111th) moving northward that had been diverted Douai to the battle-zone. But their artillery was quite unprepared to support a counterstroke. The Reichsarchiv monograph (p. 166) on the battle states that "at Douai a number of artillery formations still stood in the Place d'Armes on the morning of the 9th and the castle square at Esquerchin was filled with 15cm. howitzers and heavy guns," also the ammunition supply preparations were quite inadequate. In the circumstances the Bavarian Crown Prince decided to abandon all idea of a counter-stroke and ordered a withdrawal to the Third Line, four or five miles from the Ridge, to be begun. In his diary he blames himself for not having "ordered" the counter-attack divisions to be moved forward on the 7th, but the greater share of the blame was given to General von Falkenhausen who, with his chief of staff, was removed from command shortly after the battle.

General Ludendorff writes in his *Memoirs* that on receiving the news on the evening of the 9th of April he was deeply depressed. He had looked forward to the expected offensive with confidence, but the result seemed to show that the new principles of defensive tactics had proved false. Nevertheless, the lesson had been learnt, and when the French attacked on both sides of Rheims a week later the network of the front defence zone was prepared and the counter-attack divisions ready. The defeat of that French offensive was one of the major catastrophes of the war. The same system of defence was applied to meet the opening of the Flanders campaign three months later; the great British offensive on the 31st of July, 1917, planned on similar lines to that of Arras—Vimy, still ignoring the new German system of defence, likewise fell into the trap, with consequences disastrous for the remainder of that ill-fated series of battles.

It was fortunate that the system failed on the 9th of April, 1917, fortunate for the Canadian Corps on Vimy Ridge and far more fortunate for General Allenby's Third Army advancing deep into the German position on both sides of the Scarpe. No preparations had been made to meet a sudden onslaught of five, actually six (with the 111th), counter-attack divisions beyond the German front defence zone, and the course of the resulting battle may be left to the imagination.

15

The Fight for Inverness Copse

22–24 August 1917[1]

The result of the second battle of Third Ypres, the great push for the Passchendaele ridge on the 16th of August, 1917, was a most bitter disappointment. Even the southern part of the attack, intended to gain the central part of the ridge astride the Menin Road and the importance of which had been so especially stressed, had failed to progress. The Nonne Bosschen and Glencorse woods and Inverness Copse on this part of the ridge were still in German hands.

In spite of the heavy losses and the small chance of now obtaining his original objective, the German submarine bases along the Belgian Coast, Sir Douglas Haig decided to carry on his plan and capture at least the Passchendaele ridge before the winter. He intended to make another big push before the end of the month, and, in the meantime, to facilitate it, he ordered that the woods astride the Menin Road were to be occupied and a firm footing on the central part of the ridge immediately beyond them established. Accordingly the 56th Division, which had lost nearly 3,000 casualties in a few days in this sector, was relieved by the 14th Light Division, and, on the 22nd of August, the battle for the woods started afresh, the first objective being the capture of Inverness Copse, and Herenthage Park, which lay south of it.

The amenities of Herenthage Park had long since ceased to exist. Its lawns, gardens and shrubberies were now a desolation indistinguishable from the vast, muddy crater-field around, and the only trace of Inverness Copse, which bordered its northern side, was a mass of shattered tree stumps. The German front troops lay in shell holes along the western edge of the Copse astride the Ypres-Menin Road which continued through the Copse behind them.

Their orders were to hold this edge at all costs, as from the back of the copse the ridge began to fall away, so that its capture would have given the enemy excellent observation posts for a further advance. Although the German front position was the *Albrecht* line, which lay along the eastern edge, the first line of defence was the western edge about 600 yards in front.

From the Nonne Bosschen Wood southward past Inverness Copse to the swamps of Dumbarton Lakes at the southern end of Herenthage Park the line was held by the German 34th Division, each of its three regiments, the 30th, 67th and 145th, being responsible for a 600-yards' sector of the defence, but the brunt of the British attack on the 22nd of August was to come up against the 67th in the centre, holding Inverness Copse. This regiment had its front battalion, the 2nd, in the *Albrecht* line with two companies, the 5th and 6th, and a number of machine guns in concrete pill-boxes along the western edge of the copse and its other two companies in support in the main position. Its first

---

1 *Das Magd. Inf. Regt. 67.* Simon: Oldenburg, 1927. *Das Sächs. Inf. Regt. 177.* Krupse: Dresden, 1924.

THE FIGHT FOR INVERNESS COPSE

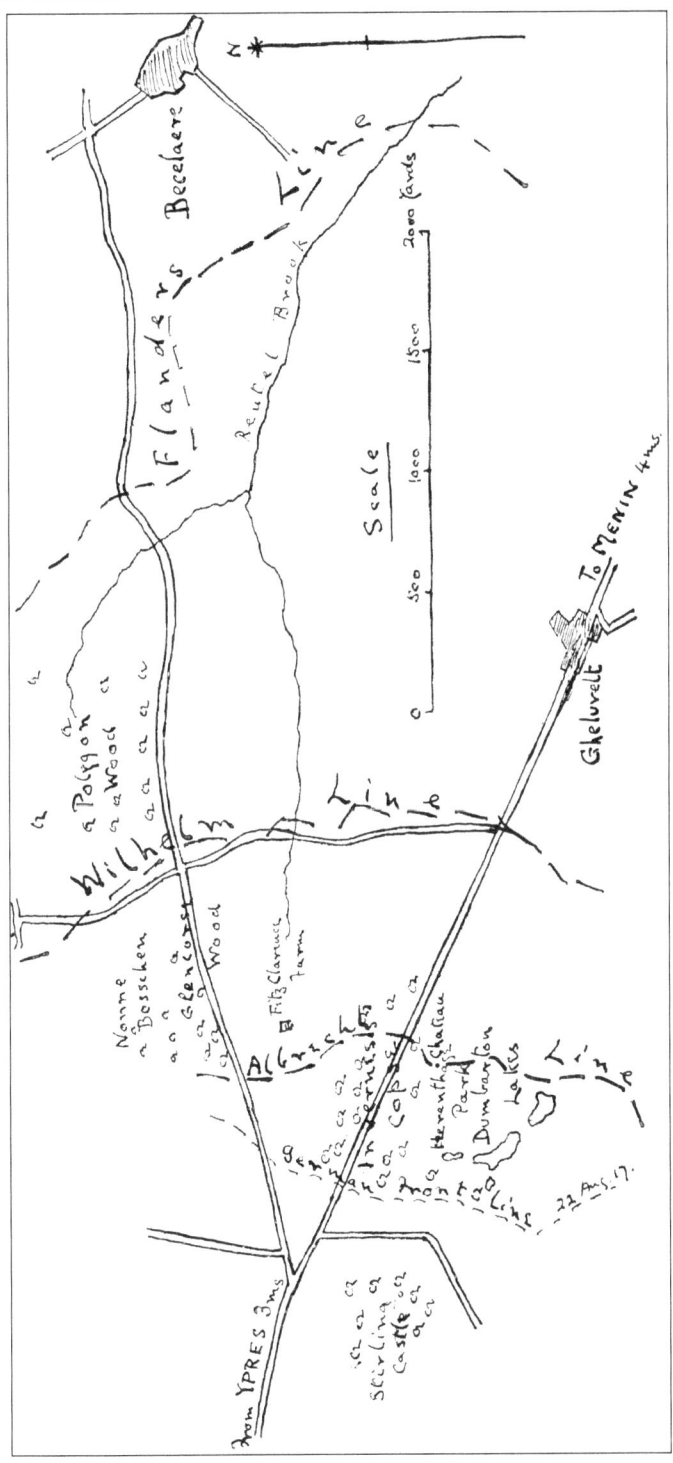

17. Inverness Copse and surrounding area

battalion was in the *Wilhelm* line about 1,000 yards in rear and its third was in reserve in the *Flanders* line, 2,000 yards behind again.

Throughout the night of the 21st Inverness Copse and its neighbourhood had been under a constant bombardment. The shells crashed among the tree-stumps and churned up once more those tortured wastes. At 6 a.m. the bombardment was so violent that the Germans stood to expecting an attack at any moment. As the minutes passed without the appearance of the enemy, and knowing the British fondness for the first light of dawn as the hour of attack, the tension among the Germans relaxed. Shortly before 7 a.m., however, the bombardment suddenly became terrific. A few minutes later the German sentries saw khaki figures moving forward through the cloud of smoke and mist, and then events moved rapidly.

The British Assault

The assault was carried out by the 43rd Brigade with two battalions in front, the 6th Somerset L.I. and the 6th Duke of Cornwall's L.I. Their objective was the *Albrecht* position from Fitzclarence Farm southward past Inverness Copse to Herenthage Château and thence forming a defensive flank back to the old line, this flank being additionally protected by the swamps of the Dumbarton Lakes. To cover the left of the advance the 42nd Brigade was to capture various strong points in Glencorse Wood and maintain touch with the forward movement.

Before the Cornwalls had gone fifty yards their leading waves were swept by machine-gun fire from Inverness Copse and checked. The Somersets on the right, however, entered the Copse with little loss and in a bitter struggle at close quarters with bayonets and hand-grenades gradually forced back the German 5th Company: The two German support companies, 7th and 8th, from the *Albrecht* line at once hurried up to reinforce, but the 7th on the left became entangled in the running fight with the Somersets and was unable to hold them. Soon after 8 a.m. the Somersets had reached Herenthage Château in the *Albrecht* line, an advance of over 600 yards, and after a short fight the ruins were captured and with it 60 prisoners. Although the two German companies, 5th and 7th, had been practically annihilated, the Somersets had also lost very heavily. They had reached their objective, but only a very thin line of some 90 men were there to hold it.

The retreat of the 5th Company had exposed the left flank of the 6th Company north of the Menin Road, and the company commander had at once strengthened his flank with light machine-guns. In consequence the Cornwalls, who as a result of their first check had lost touch with the barrage, that had moved forward a hundred yards every four minutes, were now completely held up. Their attack remained at a standstill until a tank—the only one of the four detailed to participate which succeeded in getting up the Menin Road—turned north at Inverness Copse and successfully attacked the strong points holding them up. It then proceeded along a sector of trench north of the Copse, driving the Germans out of it with machine-gun fire. The right supporting company, the 8th, from the *Albrecht* line, now arrived to reinforce, but was helpless against the fire from the tank. A number of men rushed at it hurling a mass of bombs at its side, but these were only as pin-pricks on the hide of a crocodile, and the Germans, losing heavily, had to fall back until an anti-tank gun which had been hurried up to the southern end of Polygon Wood opened fire and forced it to retire. The Cornwalls, following up the success of the tank, had been able to advance over 200 yards, but were still a long way from the *Albrecht* line, their objective, thereby leaving the Somersets in a dangerous position.

The First German Counter-Attack

The German 67th Regiment's headquarters in the *Flanders* line received its first definite news of the progress of the attack by pigeon post at 9.15 a.m. and, by 10 a.m., the support battalion (the 1st) in the *Wilhelm* trench was moving forward to reinforce the front line, with instructions to attack the enemy where met and to retake the front line position. Two companies of the 3rd Battalion in the *Flanders* line were ordered forward to take its place in support in the *Wilhelm* line. The 1st Battalion found the remnants of the 2nd Battalion in the *Albrecht* trench and taking them forward began to attack the Somersets. The latter were now too weak and scattered to offer any serious resistance and had to fall back towards the western part of the Copse. The 10th Durham L.I. was sent forward as reinforcement and together with the Somersets were able to hold a line about 250 yards from the western edge, southward from the Menin Road. Here they gained touch with the Cornwalls on their left and this line was successfully held. The Germans did not press their attack and frequent attempts by small parties to break through were stopped by machine-gun fire.

By the afternoon the German front line commander sent back to say that the line could no longer be held unless reinforcements quickly arrived. The two companies of the 3rd Battalion in the *Wilhelm* line were therefore sent up and arrived in the copse about 5 p.m. The remainder of the 3rd Battalion took their place in the *Wilhelm* line, its position in reserve in the *Flanders* line being taken by a battalion of the 177th Regiment.[2]

The Second German Counter-Attack

An order from the German 34th Division to retake the western edge of the copse arrived too late in the evening to carry out, and the attack was postponed until the following morning. During the night, starting at 2 a.m., the remainder of the 3rd Battalion was advanced up to the front line in the copse, the battalion of the 177th Regiment moved up from the *Flanders* line to the *Wilhelm* line in support, and its place in the *Flanders* line was taken by a battalion of the 103rd Regiment. The attack was to be launched at 5.5 a.m. preceded by a five-minute hurricane bombardment.

Five a.m. arrived. The companies lay ready to storm forward, but no artillery bombardment developed. It was discovered later that the guns were awaiting the usual rocket signal to show the front line was ready, whereas the front line thought that the bombardment was to start automatically at 5 a.m. At 5.5 a.m. the infantry therefore attacked without any artillery preparation. In the close fighting which followed the Germans claim to have advanced 200 yards and reached the western edge in places. Their attack, however, coincided with a proposed British tank attack. Five tanks were to have crossed No Man's Land at 4.30 a.m. to attack the various strong points that were holding us up and the infantry were to follow up their success. Only two tanks reached the front line and these, at about 6 a.m., turned north and south from the Menin Road along the German position. The latter fell an easy prey to them and with much bitterness of spirit the Germans were compelled to withdraw in face of the machine-gun fire from the tanks

---

2   As in so many cases during the war, this movement of reinforcements was reported back by us as a counter-attack which had been repulsed. The German histories frequently show the same error.

to their starting-off positions. Within half an hour the German artillery had located the tanks and opened fire on them. One was blown up by a direct hit, the Germans giving a loud hurrah as a dense cloud of smoke belched from it, and the other developed engine trouble, its crew of seven all being shot down as they attempted to escape.

The Somersets had been relieved overnight by the 6th K.O.Y.L.I. and the Cornwalls by the 10th Durham L.I. No further attempt was made to get forward during the morning, but, throughout the afternoon, the British artillery continued to bombard the copse. To make good their losses the remainder of the German 67th Regiment was sent up from the *Wilhelm* line to reinforce the battle position, and, by dark, all three battalions of the 67th Regiment were in the front line.

At 10.45 p.m. orders were sent from the German 34th Division for another effort to take the western edge of the copse and park the following morning. At 1 a.m., under cover of darkness, three companies of the battalion of the 277th Regiment from the *Flanders* line, a company of the 30th Regiment and the 4th Storm Detachment (7 platoons each of about 10 men with hand-grenades, revolvers and slung rifles specially trained for assault) with a contingent of flame-throwers, moved up into the line of the 67th Regiment. The whole of the 34th Divisional Artillery, supported by batteries of the adjacent division, were to carry out the preparatory bombardment. At 6 a.m. the troops in the front line were to advance, joining in with the storm troops as they came forward, leaving only two companies, each with four machine-guns, in position as rallying points, one north and one south of the Menin Road. The artillery barrage was to lift 300 yards after an interval of five minutes and to be maintained for an hour to prevent the arrival of British reinforcements. Airmen were to fly along the British front line and rake it with machine-gun fire to assist the attack. The regiments to right and left, the 30th and 145th, were to cooperate on the flanks.

The Third German Counter-Attack

At 5.30 a.m. a hurricane bombardment of great intensity opened on the British positions along the western edge of the copse, but it was short and the great mass of shell fell upon and behind the German position in the copse itself. It was too late to protest, and, at 6 a.m., the Germans, much discouraged, began to advance. Even the 300-yard lift did not carry the barrage as far as the British front line so that as the Germans approached they met a heavy fire and a stubborn resistance. In spite of this they were able to gain the western edge in a number of places, particularly south of the Menin Road. At 7.30 a.m. the British counter-attacked, but they were checked by the arrival of a further company of the 177th Regiment, which had come up to reinforce. As the shelling continued to fall short the German casualties rapidly increased. At 10.15 a.m. a message was sent back imploring the artillery to correct their range. "Our artillery is firing short in the most incredible manner. If this bad shooting continues, we shall have to retire. No sign of aeroplanes to help our attack."

In spite of these remonstrances the German troops were still shelled by their own artillery and began to fall back from the western edge of the copse. The situation seemed critical.

The troops of the British 43rd Brigade holding the front line were now very mixed up, and, in addition, had been reinforced by the 9th Rifle Brigade lent by the 42nd Brigade to assist. The Brigadier wished to deliver a counter-attack through the copse, as he considered that the enemy would be in a most disorganised state after the failure of their attack, but, at mid-day, the commanding officers in the front line replied that they had not sufficient troops both to counter-attack and to hold their present position in the event of a set-back.

At this same hour the Germans were themselves preparing another attack. The 2nd Battalion 177th Regiment had been sent forward to the *Wilhelm* line to take the place of the 1st and it moved up about mid-day to the *Albrecht* line. Passing through this it was in time to hold up the troops retreating through the copse. Soon afterwards, in spite of the terrific hail of shrapnel and high explosive, the whole line advanced once more through the copse, and, by 12.50 p.m., the British troops were falling back to and beyond the western edge. The German success seemed for a time so considerable that the situation was reported by 43rd Brigade headquarters to be "very grave," and further reinforcements were asked for from the neighbouring brigade. By 3 p.m. the news was more reassuring and it was found that the Germans had been definitely held up along the western edge of the park and copse and that our line was intact. An intention to counter-attack with two fresh battalions from the supporting brigade did not materialize owing to the uncertainty of our dispositions in the front line, so that Inverness Copse remained in German possession that night.

During the night hours the German 177th Regiment took over the line from the 67th, the remnants of which found their way back as best they could through the terrible shambles of the copse, leaving behind them over 650 casualties. The losses of the 177th Regiment did not exceed 250 at the outside according to its own statements, whereas the casualties of the British 43rd Brigade in these three days of fighting are given as over 1,400.

The great effort to capture Inverness Copse and with it the observation posts that would have assisted so vitally the advance on to the ridge further north planned for the following day, the 27th, had failed. Sir Douglas Haig's plan had to be modified and finally, owing to bad weather, postponed. It was not until the 20th of September, nearly a month later, that the British again attacked Inverness Copse, and then with success.

16

The Fight for Zonnebeke

26 September 1917[1]

Eight weeks had passed since the opening of the Flanders offensive on the 31st of July 1917. The capture of the ridge of hills, which lies west of Ypres and forms for miles round the great landmark of the Flanders plain, was to be the first step in Haig's plan both for clearing the German submarine bases from the Flanders coast and pushing the Germans from Northern Belgium. He had hoped to be in possession of the ridge within two weeks, but the incessant rain of the wettest August for many years had clogged the whole machinery of attack in the churned-up mud of that low-lying, water-logged district and the German defence had been more skilfully and obstinately conducted than he had anticipated, so that by the closing days of September the battle was still raging on the eastern slopes. Haig, although it was too late now to hope to attain the objectives with which he had started, decided to continue his efforts to capture the ridge before winter set in, preparatory to further operations the following spring.

The offensive on the 26th of September had a limited objective and was delivered on a frontage of six miles between the Menin road and St. Julien. The intention was to advance an average of about 2,000 yards to a position from which a direct attack could be made on the Passchendaele—Becelaere ridge. The village of Zonnebeke, nestling immediately below the ridge between two of the eastern spurs, the Klein Molen to the north and the Groote Molen to the south, lay in the centre of the front of attack. A mass of shell-craters and a few ruined walls were all that remained of it. The British front line here was 1,800 yards to the east of the village along the German Wilhelm position which had been captured six days previously, the Germans occupying a rough defensive line among the shell-holes about 300 yards away.

The German System of Defence

During the opening series of battles in August each German front-line division had two of its regiments (each of three battalions) in the front position and the third held back in divisional reserve. This organization had led to a great confusion of units in the frequent reliefs of the front battalions which soon became essential, and also the regiment in reserve was found to be too far back to influence the first phase of the battle, so that the front battalions were left unsupported until the arrival of the counter-attack divisions several hours after the first assault.

By the 26th of September a new system was fully established by which the front division had all its three regiments in the front line, each with a frontage of about 1,000 yards, and distributed in depth to over 3,000 yards with one battalion in front, one in

---

1 *Das Fusilier Regt. 34.* Hessenland. Stettin, 1931. *Das. Res. Inf. Regt. 102.* Baensch-Stiftung. Dresden, 1929. *Das Inf. Regt. 409.* Stalling. Oldenburg, 1929. *Das Bav. Inf. Regt. 9.* Becker. Würzburg, 1927.

THE FIGHT FOR ZONNEBEKE 169

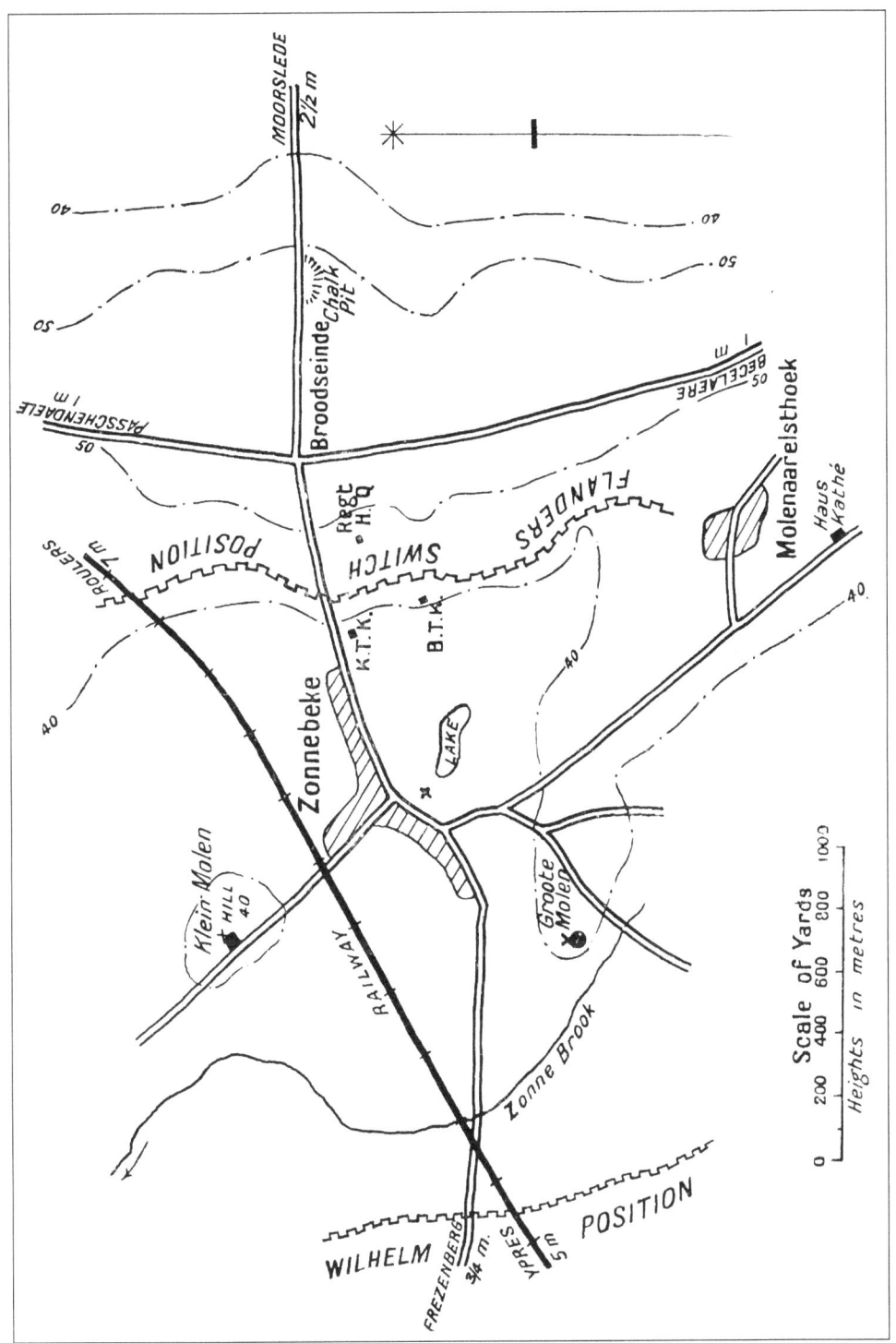

18. Zonnebeke, 26 September 1917

support and one in reserve. The general idea of the defence was for these battalions to advance successively to meet the fresh attacking battalions as they advanced through the troops who had carried out the first assault. The counter-attack divisions would be employed later in the day to deliver a staged attack supported by an artillery bombardment against the enemy's new line before he had time to consolidate it.

In the fight for Zonnebeke it will be seen how this theory worked out in practice.

The Defence against the First Assault

On the Zonnebeke sector the assault was to be delivered by British 3rd Division, the 8th and 9th Brigades of which were to attack north and south respectively of the Ypres—Roulers railway, each on a frontage of 800 yards. Each brigade had two battalions in front to make the first assault, that is, to carry the German first position and reach a line about 700 yards beyond. They were allotted an hour in which to reach this line, at which time the remaining two battalions of the brigade, preceded by the artillery barrage, were to advance through them to the final objectives, the Klein Molen ridge and Hill 40, Zonnebeke village and the Groote Molen ridge as far as the Haus Bathe road that runs along the top of it.

For the defence the German 34th Fusilier Regiment took over the Zonnebeke sector on the night of the 24th of September, its 3rd Battalion in the front line, its 2nd in support behind Zonnebeke village and its 1st in reserve behind the Broodseinde ridge, about 400 yards east of Broodseinde itself. Of the 3rd Battalion all four companies were in the front line, each holding a frontage of 250 yards. Each company had two platoons lying out in shell-craters, with listening posts a short distance in front and the other two platoons in support about 50 yards in rear: the latter occupied a series of concrete pill-boxes, all that remained to mark a former German artillery position there. The battalion commander's headquarters was 2,000 yards in rear at the eastern end of Zonnebeke village, for under the new system of defence he was an important person, and with the title of K.T.K. (*Kampftruppenkommandeur*) his word was law in the front battle zone. As fresh troops came up, whether of his own regiment or of the counter-attacking divisions, all in his sector came automatically under his orders.

By the early hours of the 25th, the three battalions were in their allotted positions and that day passed without incident except for a continuation of the British bombardment against the Broodseinde ridge and the artillery positions beyond it, assisted by aeroplane observation. At dusk the British were seen to be moving up troops into their front line and massing them behind. The German artillery were unable to take advantage of this owing to the excellent and accurate counter-battery work of the British guns. The general impression in the German front line of the imminence of an attack was confirmed by a message sent up during the evening that a big offensive would take place the next morning.

"The night passed fairly quietly," writes one of the officers of the 3rd Battalion. "The food-carriers were able to get up from Zonnebeke and I was able to visit the sentries and front platoons several times, the last about 3.30 a.m. About 4 a.m, shortly after I had returned to the pill-box which sheltered thirty-six men of the supporting platoon, the enemy suddenly opened a terrific artillery bombardment on our position. About 6 a.m. [the British infantry zero hour was 5.50 a.m.] a sergeant near the entrance shouted out that he thought the English were coming. I hurried out. The air was filled with smoke and this together with a ground-mist made it difficult to see more than 20 yards or so. I could see no sign of the enemy. Then the shelling slackened only to move on and become stronger than ever behind us. Suddenly I heard shouts of '*Engländer*' from in front. I called the men out and we took up a position in the mass of shell-holes on either side. Almost at once figures appeared moving towards us through the fog. They were coming on at a steady pace bunched together in groups between the water-logged shell holes. We opened fire and threw hand-grenades into the midst of them and they at once took cover in the shell-holes, I could see two of them fixing up a light machine gun which opened on us hitting several of my men before we could silence it. For a moment the attack here was held, but looking round I could see more English advancing past us to right and left, and realized that our only hope was to run for it. With the few men near me I started back towards Zonnebeke, but, after a few yards, saw it was hopeless as the enemy had already closed in ahead of us in their advance. The noise of machine-gun fire from the village made us hope that a counter-attack would soon be made to regain the position and four of us ran back to the pill-box, a last and almost desperate refuge. We had scarcely time to slam the door of thick oak planks behind us when it was ripped asunder by a hand-grenade followed by others that burst inside among us. Two splinters from them hit me, one near the spine that made movement impossible for me. Seven or eight Englishmen came in and carried me out, laying me in a shell-hole among three dead English and one of my sergeants, also dead."

The three heavy machine-gun sections of the battalion now came into action: one was at the Klein Molen, one at the level-crossing near the one-time railway station, with two guns in front at the culvert by which the railway crosses the Zonne brook, and the third at the south-eastern end of Zonnebeke lake. From all these points they had a good field of fire to meet an enemy advancing across the Zonne brook, once the front infantry position had been overrun. The two guns at the culvert were the first to come into action and had a busy time. Shouting, screams, the rattle of rifle-fire in front, heard even above the noise of the shelling, were the first signal that the enemy was approaching. Soon afterwards men came running back saying that the front line had been broken.

"I tried to stop these men," writes the machine-gun commander of this post, "and make them face front again alongside me. Others retiring on my left were rallied by a subaltern and led forward again through the mist. Soon afterwards the enemy appeared twenty yards or so in front. They came on leisurely in groups as if they had the place to themselves, believing perhaps that the artillery barrage had killed us all. We opened a burst of fire into them and they quickly dropped to cover. Others now appeared behind and on both flanks. We raked the front with fire, but soon they concentrated their Lewis guns on us. I got up to rush to better cover close by but a mass of bullets swept past at that moment and I was hit in three places, soon losing consciousness."

Before long both the machine guns were put out of action by direct hits and only one man of the crew got back to Zonnebeke.

In this manner the first assault pushed forward all along the line, little was left of the 3rd Battalion and the four British battalions passed on over it to the line of the Zonne brook. Here they halted and the four battalions in rear passed through them and continued towards the final objectives.

On the right the 2nd Suffolks took the Groote Molen spur and crossed the Haus Kathe road whilst on the left the 7th K.S.L.I. worked forward through Klein Molen on to the rising ground and Hill 40 beyond it. Both these Battalions had now gained their objective. In the centre, however, the 10th R. Welch Fusiliers and the 1st R. Scots Fusiliers, to south and north of the railway respectively, were held up 600 yards from their objective, the eastern side of the village. The main stumbling-block was the machine-gun post at the level-crossing near the station, which had been reinforced by a rifle-grenade section, and a number of men of the 3rd Battalion who had got back rallied round this post and extended out along the road. One of the latter writes that—

> …no sooner had they got into position than groups of the enemy appeared through the mist in front. The machine guns raked them with a hail of bullets and from then on fired almost continuously. To this day I still have a thrill of admiration whenever I think of one of those gunners in particular who fired incessantly, his every movement utterly unruffled in spite of a stream of bullets sweeping past him.

Nearby the rifle-grenade section also had hard work.

> The English advanced against us with flame throwers, but the rifle grenades formed a deadly defence against them before they could get in range of us. As the smoke and mist began to clear away the machine-gun fire was devastating, the advancing lines of the enemy were mown down and the survivors, retired into the dead ground of the Zonne brook.

This roughly marks the conclusion of the first phase of the attack.

The Local Counter-Attack

Shortly after 6 a.m. the first messenger from the front line arrived at the K.T.K's. (battalion commander's) post at the eastern end of the village. The shelling here had been exceptionally heavy and with high explosive bursting all round it the concrete pill-box shelter had rocked about like a ship and finally lay over at such an angle that the staff had to leave it and lie in the shell-holes outside. It was here the messenger found them and gave information that the right flank of the Battalion had been forced back, the rest of the position overrun and that the English were pushing forward rapidly on Zonnebeke. The K.T.K. at once sent a message to the 2nd Battalion, east of the village, to reinforce the 3rd wherever met and assist it to regain its former position, also a message to the regimental commander by telephone, the cable to him being miraculously as yet intact. The latter at once sent an order to the 1st Battalion in reserve, which reached it at 6.46 a.m., to move forward and to cooperate in the counter-attack by the 2nd Battalion. It was to advance on a frontage of two companies, the railway dividing them and giving the direction.

The move of the 2nd Battalion was disjointed. The 5th and 7th Companies, received their orders almost at once. No. 7 in its efforts to drive the English from the Groote Molen spur was, however, overwhelmed, the majority being taken prisoners. No. 5 advanced as far as the lake, but met the English coming round the eastern end of it. Their further progress was also held up by an English machine-gun post already established near the church and which they were unable to dislodge. There was a delay in getting the order to the right companies north of the railway, so much so that these did not begin to move until the right companies of the 1st Battalion had come up level with them.

The companies of the 1st Battalion, extended in lines of platoons, crossed the Broodseinde ridge and moved down the slope towards Zonnebeke. The mist and smoke still lay dense over the battle zone and protected them as they moved down the open hillside, but it also made direction difficult to keep and some of the leading platoons lost their way. On the left the company commander of No. 2 with the rear platoon nevertheless pressed on, keeping his right on the railway.

"On approaching the village," he writes, "we came into the English artillery barrage, which was very violent. The ground was in a terrible state, the craters made by the high-explosives were joining up with the older rain-filled shell-holes forming together small ponds with islands here and there formed by the crater edges which we had to use as stepping-stones. No one was allowed to halt or take cover otherwise they lost touch and would never regain it. By 7.30 a.m. we had reached the station road on the further side of the village and here near the level-crossing I came upon a machine-gun post of the 3rd Battalion. Its two guns had been knocked out of action and the leader was lying dead. The rifle-grenade section was nearby with its commander severely wounded. A number of men, many dead or wounded, lined the road on both sides. This gallant band had held up the advance and paid the price, but we had arrived only just in time for the English were already beginning to move forward again up the slope from the Zonne brook to attack the position. We lay down along the road, my line extending half-way to the church, and opened fire as fast as we could pull the triggers. Almost at once two of my other platoons, which had lost direction farther back, arrived together with a part of No. 6 Company (2nd Battalion), and these reinforced my weakly held position, extending it to the village square. The English artillery barrage had now gone on behind us and the infantry could not face our fire. After losing heavily a number retired to the dead ground by the Zonne brook, leaving a firing line about 200 yards from us. The firefight continued throughout the morning, but the enemy made no attempt to advance. An English machine-gun post located 200 yards west of the church caused much trouble and loss to us, but could not be silenced."

No. 4 Company had also moved up south of the railway and now took up a position about 200 yards behind in support of No. 2 Company.

On the right, north of the railway, No. 1 Company had come up into line with No. 8 Company, the right company of the 2nd Battalion, soon after 7 a.m. and the two went forward together. They came almost at once into the artillery barrage, the two companies being rapidly reduced to a strength of about 3 officers and 100 men. These continued to advance and met the English infantry coming over Hill 40. Seeing them the Germans ran forward cheering and the English, not realizing the weakness of the counter-attack, fell back beyond the Klein Molen road, abandoning the hill though retaining their hold on the Klein Molen itself and that part of the ridge north of it. Finding no German troops on either flank, they did not press the pursuit, but eventually took up position 150 yards east of the Klein Molen road, between the mill ruins and the railway. No. 3 Company, which arrived later in the morning with orders to capture Klein Molen, suffered exceptionally in passing through the artillery barrage and the survivors took up a position in support behind Hill 40.

The dispersal of the mist and smoke soon after 9 a.m. enabled the regimental commander, from his position on the Broodseinde ridge overlooking the battlefield, to see the progress of the fight. Lines of the enemy could be seen lying about shoulder to shoulder on the Groote Molen spur 600 yards away and southward as far as Molenaarelsthoek, while more lines could be seen in the distance in front of Frezenberg deploying and advancing on either side of the Zonnebeke road. The machine-gun section of No. 2 Battalion, which was near at hand, was ordered to open at once at the enemy's lines on the spur while messengers in their shirt-sleeves, the day now becoming hot under a full sun, were sent back with the information both to the field batteries behind the ridges and to the heavy batteries behind the Keilberg ridge, 2,000 yards in rear. The effect of the artillery and machine-gun fire, which resulted from this information, was so devastating that the further attack contemplated by the British on Zonnebeke about 10 a.m. never materialized.

The Main Counter-Attack

The three counter-attack divisions of the Group Ypres were assembled behind the Passchendaele ridge, and the orders for the movement to begin were issued at 11.30 a.m. The objective was to drive the English from the Klein Molen and Groote Molen spurs and recapture the German Wilhelm position. The 4th Bavarian Division was to attack on a frontage of 2,000 yards north of the Roulers-Ypres railway and the 236th Division south of the railway, the 234th Division moving in support. Each Division was accompanied by its special counter-attack field batteries and a dozen aeroplane-fighters.

The advance was at once seen and reported by the British aeroplanes, so that when, at 2.30 p.m., the leading battalions began to cross the Broodseinde ridge a terrific artillery fire assailed them. Some of the German artillery teams were hit, blocking the roads for the rest of the batteries and the infantry suffered very heavily as they moved down the open slope of the ridge. The advance of the Bavarian Division was further complicated by the swampy and flooded valley of the Paddebach behind the Klein Molen spur, which they found could only be crossed in two places. With greatly diminished numbers, the Bavarians alone losing 40 officers and 1,300 men in the movement, the attack nevertheless pushed on and eventually about 6 p.m. came up into the battle-line, reinforcing the original front line regiments of the 23rd Reserve and 3rd Reserve Divisions[2] in the Zonnebeke sector.

North of the railway the leading Bavarians, though in hopeless confusion, arrived at a most critical moment. Throughout the afternoon the Germans on Hill 40 had watched a succession of lines of the enemy's infantry crossing the rise in front and descending into the dead ground of the Zonne brook.[3] At 3 p.m. a fresh bombardment of Zonnebeke, especially the Hill 40 Line, began. At 4 p.m. heavy batteries with high explosive joined in the bombardment and the defenders on Hill 40 were now certain that an infantry attack was imminent.

"I shouted to all to be ready," writes a subaltern of No. 1 Company 34th Regiment, which had retaken the hill in the morning. "Machine guns were oiled, bayonets fixed and hand-grenades got ready. Shortly after 6 p.m. the English artillery bombardment increased to drum-fire intensity; then suddenly a pause followed by shouts all along the line, 'They're coming.' The first waves of the English infantry came up to within 20 yards of us when our 4 machine guns and every rifle opened on them. They at once took cover

---

2   The 23rd Reserve Division held from St. Julien—Klein Molen, and the 3rd Reserve Division from the latter place to the Polygon wood.

3   The advance of the reserve Brigade of the 3rd Division with orders to reach the objective given to the Division for the morning attack.

in the shell-holes and began to throw smoke bombs in our direction to cover the advance of the waves in rear of them."

It was at this moment that the remnants of the 5th and 9th Bavarian Regiments, of the 4th Bavarian Division, came over the crest of Hill 40 and the Klein Molen spur, bringing with them the supporting troops awaiting behind it. They were greeted with a mighty cheer, and in their enthusiasm those in the front line got up and ran forward taking the new arrivals with them, with continued cheering and blowing of bugles. In actual numbers the combined force of Germans that stumbled forward down the hill over all obstacles was not strong, and it seemed, to quote the same writer,

> ...a spontaneous act of madness, but it was the last thing the enemy expected. His front lines got up and rushed back taking the lines behind with them. We carried on as fast as we could over the broken ground and then as we got through the smoke an amazing sight greeted us. Great numbers of the enemy were fleeing panic-stricken down to and across the Zonne brook. Our light machine guns were hurriedly placed in position and swept the retreating mass with bullets. As we watched this scene, I can only say we literally wept for joy at such a success. Klein Molen was now ours again, but it was clearly hopeless to pursue with our small disorganized force and with our flanks unsupported, added to which English machine-gun fire was now enfilading our line from the direction of the church. So we took up a position east of the brook between Klein Molen and the railway, sent back a number of prisoners and supplied ourselves with captured rifles and ammunition, being short of the latter for our own.

South of the railway the 236th Division had been so severely handled during its advance down the open slope of the Broodseinde ridge by artillery fire and also by machine-gun fire from the Groote Molen spur, that at 5 p.m. when the survivors of its two leading battalions reached the battle-line the impetus of the attack was already spent. They forced back some advanced troops out of Molenaarelsthoek, but the British maintained their hold on the Groote Molen spur on a line immediately east of the Zonnebeke—Haus, Kathé road.

During the night the terrible confusion of units in the German front line was disentangled, but owing to the losses incurred by the British 3rd Division and the employment of its reserve brigade in the effort to capture Zonnebeke that day, a renewal of the British attack planned for the following morning was postponed.

17

Cambrai

The Action of the German 107th Division 19–24 November 1917

There is a legend that a German division arrived at Cambrai by train on the very morning of the British tank attack of the 20th of November, 1917, and that its opportune appearance as a reinforcement on a thinly held and previously quiet front changed the fortunes of the day. A division did arrive most opportunely, but on the 19th, not the 20th of November. This division was the 107th, a fighting formation brought from Russia in view of the March 1918, offensive, to be exchanged for a *Landwehr* division good enough to hold the line, but not equal to important active operations. Arriving on the eve of the battle, part of it was in position and most of it standing ready on the night before the battle, in view of the expected attack.

The 107th Division whilst on the Eastern Front had been in a corps commanded by General von Bernhardi, and in his recently published reminiscences[1] the General prints a letter which he received from the General Staff officer of the division, Captain Glokke. This provides an unexpurgated account of its action at Cambrai, its success being naturally attributed to the excellent training which it had received at Bernhardi's hands. From this letter, supplemented by the Official Monograph, *Die Tankschlacht bei Cambrai, 1917*, the following narrative has been extracted.

Immediately on the arrival of the staff of the Division at Cambrai in the morning of the 19th of November, the G.O.C., Major-General Havenstein, reported to General von Waster, the Corps commander, and General von der Marwitz, the Army commander. At both headquarters there was some talk of an impending British attack—an Irish deserter had spoken of one, so General Havenstein was told—but no one imagined how imminent it was or how powerful it would be.

On the 16th of November, the Army commander had reported to the headquarters of Crown Prince Rupprecht's Army Group: "Hostile attacks on a large scale against the Army front are not to be expected in the near future." On the 18th of November a strong raiding party on Gillemont Farm (fourteen miles south of Cambrai) captured forty prisoners of the 55th Division, and another sent in north of Trescault had brought back a sergeant and five men of the 1st Royal Irish Fusiliers (36th Division). From the men of the 55th Division nothing was extracted, but the six prisoners of the 36th are said to have stated during an examination that at the beginning of the next week a big attack was

---

1 *Denkwürdigkeiten aus meinem Leben* (Berlin, Mittler).

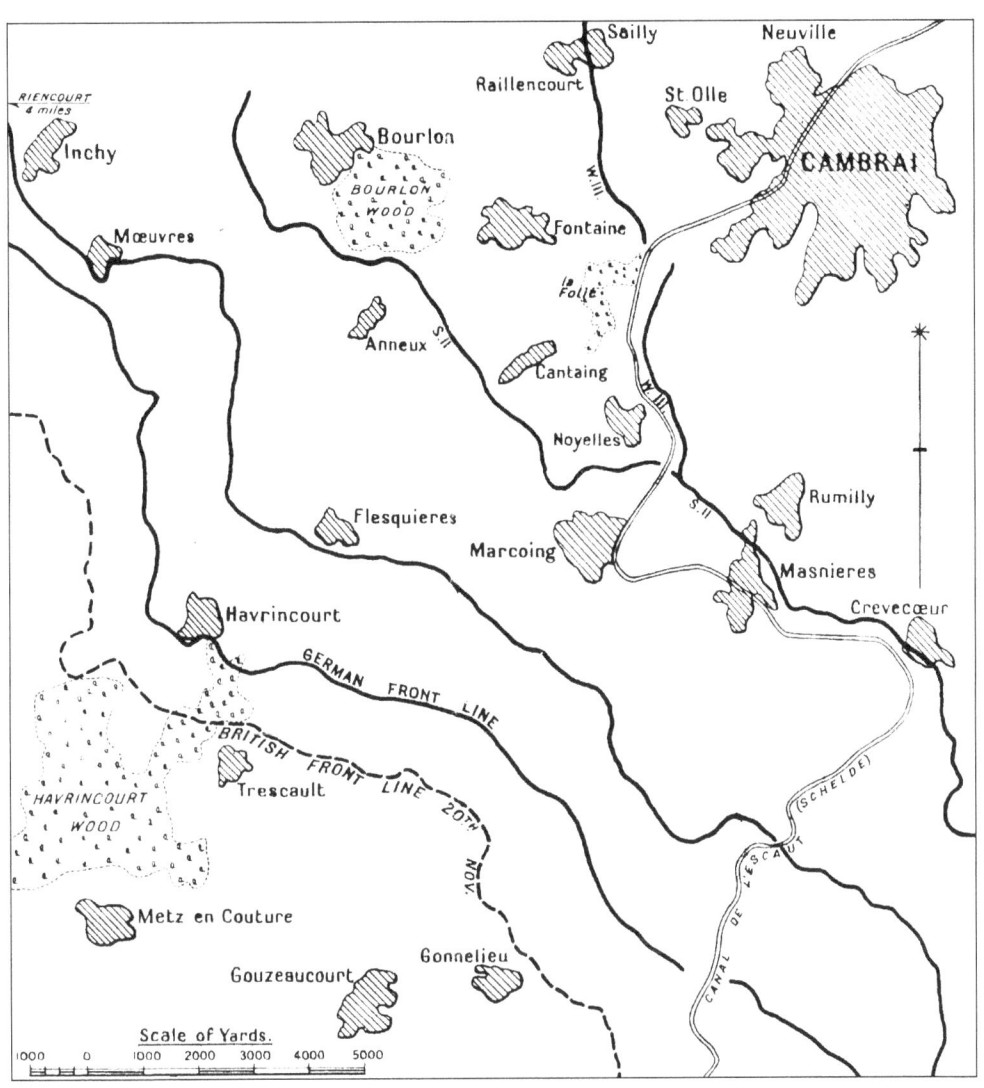

19. Cambrai, 1917

planned against Havrincourt; officers of various arms had been seen in the front trenches reconnoitring. One of the prisoners said that he had seen a tank hidden in the village of Metz-en-Couture; another said there were two tanks in Havrincourt Wood. A third prisoner said that he had heard from an artilleryman that the attack would be preceded by a bombardment of many hours. The interrogating officer reported, "The inference that the attack will take place on Tuesday [20th of November] as the majority assert, is doubtful, but there seem to be all the signs of preparations for a big attack on this front."

On the 19th some prisoners of the 6th Shropshire L.I. (20th Division) were taken, but no information was obtained from them. The British artillery fire was intermittent and scattered, and no deduction could be drawn from it; but numerous aeroplanes flew low over the German trenches. Aeroplane reconnaissance had not been possible for ten days owing to bad weather, but both infantry and artillery ground observers reported much activity in the British lines. Finally the fragment of a telephone message, "Tuesday Flanders," was picked up by the overhearing station in Riencourt (nine miles north-west of Havrincourt). Some small reinforcements—an infantry regiment and ten batteries—were sent up as reserve to Watter's Corps, "increased readiness" was ordered, and "Case Havrincourt," which provided for an attack against that village, put into force. Sufficient counter-measures against a local enterprise seemed to have been taken; an attack without heavy bombardment was considered out of the question, as the position was so strong.

The orders of Watter's Group (Corps) began:

> According to statements of prisoners taken on the 18th south of Havrincourt, an attack at an early date against Havrincourt is not unlikely.

An addition, that tanks might participate, was sent out at midnight.

The orders of Moser's Group, holding the line from Inchy northward, issued at 10.25 p.m. on the 19th, began:

> 1. According to prisoners' statements, a British attack on Havrincourt will take place on Tuesday. Tanks may take part. The four or five hours' artillery bombardment will probably begin between 3 and 4 a.m. [German time].
> 2. Fragments of a British telephone message overheard near Bullecourt (nine miles north-west of Havrincourt) make it appear that an attack may also take place against this Corps on Tuesday.

The first echelon, Regiment No. 222, parts of Regiment No. 52, and Field Artillery Regiment No. 213 of the 107th Division, had detrained on the 19th, and were billeted in and east of Cambrai. The relief of the 20th *Landwehr* Division, holding the front from Havrincourt (exclusive) to just beyond Moeuvres, was to be begun on the 25th, so the troops of the 107th hoped to get a few days' rest. But they were mistaken. As a temporary measure, in view of the possible attack, they were put under the 54th Division, south of the 20th *Landwehr* Division, in the Havrincourt sector. General Havenstein proposed on the 20th of November to visit the sector of the 20th *Landwehr* Division with his General Staff officer. The commander of the divisional artillery, Colonel Borchert, however, had taken a look at the 54th Division sector during the day; he had told off his brigades, and his batteries had been got into position during the night, but they naturally knew

nothing about the ground. It was proposed during the 20th to disturb the supposed British assembly near Havrincourt by bursts of fire and harassing fire, which should at the same time serve as registration.
On the morning of the 20th there was thick fog. Suddenly at 7 a.m. (German time), there was very heavy gun fire. The divisional staff congratulated themselves how promptly and well the bursts of fire ordered had begun; but "information trickled back that it was quite the other way round and things were already pretty unpleasant." At 9.40 a.m. an order was received:

> The 107th Division will occupy the S. II. Line from Bourlon Wood (exclusive) to Rumilly (inclusive). One battalion of No. 227 will be sent to Crèvecoeur.

In explanation, it was added that the British had broken through on a wide front between Moeuvres and Gonnelieu, and "the 107th must hold the position without fail and retake Flesquières." Regiments Nos. 52 and 227 were moving up. Part of Regiment No. 232 was still in the train. By battalions and smaller groups, as they became available, the infantry was led up to the sound of the battle through the fog into completely unknown country. The main British attack was directed exactly against the sector assigned to the Division. This was open, without a wood in it, with only a very small part covered by the Schelde and the Canal. The British infantry was advancing, protected by tanks, but supported by very little artillery fire.

As the German infantry reached the "very moderate protection" of S II. Line, Anneux—
Rumilly, the men saw in front of them, emerging from the fog, a long line of tanks. They fired at them, but the ammunition was not armour-piercing, and the bullets only rattled on the armoured monsters. These broke through the position uninjured, wheeled and circled about, till they were caught up by a second line. The latter continued on against the villages of Anneux and Cantaing, formed a continuous ring round them, and sent some tanks inside them. The infantry of the 107th Division was helpless and completely puzzled what to do: ammunition was useless and failing quickly as a result of rapid fire; the light trench mortars could not be used as the ammunition for them had been left behind in Russia according to orders, and had not been replaced; there was no artillery support, as the greater part of the batteries had already been overrun, and what remained could not see a target, and did not dare to shoot on account of the fog. The troops fell back slowly, therefore, to the line Fontaine—La Folie. Regiment No. 232, however, actually made an offensive return against Noyelles and retook it, but had to evacuate it again in the afternoon. In the midst of the turmoil Canadian cavalrymen appeared. Regiment No. 227 was successfully used to block the gap which was open between Noyelles and Masnières, and the cavalry was very soon dealt with, but the wildest rumours as to the situation began to spread. Now came the real catastrophe. From all sides there were cries for ammunition, if possible K (armour-piercing) ammunition, as so much had been fired away. According to report, there were only 600,000 rounds in the depôt at Iwuy (five miles north-east of Cambrai), a mere trifle. But the 54th Division also had a lien on this, and had taken the whole lot. The same thing had happened to the gun ammunition. The already overworked railway was bringing up what ammunition it could, and all available motor cars, lorries, artillery wagons, and even limbers were laid hold of to fetch it. The British were still coming on, and preceding them flew bad news of every kind: Bourlon

Wood lost and, in consequence, the already hard-pressed garrison of Fontaine had to withdraw in order to avoid being surrounded by tanks. La Folie had to be abandoned because ten or twelve tanks were making for it, and the men of Regiment No. 232 had expended all their ammunition. In the last line immediately in front of Cambrai, the so-called W III. Line, the infantry halted and fronted.

The ammunition supply now improved, and some artillerymen going back, armed with carbines, recovered all the guns except two of five batteries, so badly were they guarded by the British. There was now some artillery support, although the divisional commander ordered a large percentage of the guns to be scattered in the firing line to deal with tanks. The first reinforcements, Regiment No. 58 of the 119th Division, also began to appear, and henceforward they continued to trickle in unceasingly. The question was, where should the reinforcements be put in? In consequence of the abandonment of Fontaine and the entry of the British into the southern part of Bourlon Wood, there was a wide three-mile gap west of Cambrai between Watter's and Moser's Corps. It must be closed, and Cambrai must be held. An attempt was made to retake Fontaine by surprise during the night, but it failed, as the village simply spitted machine-gun fire. Better, therefore, to go back and to reinforce and hold W III.; to send the reinforcements as they appear to the right, northward towards Raillencourt; to close the gap gradually and to get into touch with the division on the right; to send patrols towards Fontaine to reconnoitre the village thoroughly, for it must at all costs be taken next day.

The British gave the Germans time for all this. They remained perfectly inactive during the night and the following forenoon. Two regiments of the 119th Division, Regiment No. 46 and Reserve Regiment No. 46, succeeded in reaching Raillencourt and St. Olle, the north-west suburb of Cambrai, respectively, and filled the gap, but it had remained open most of the night. The divisional and other artillery which arrived were distributed mainly between Neuville and Sailly. Unfortunately very little use could be got out of the "other" artillery for several hours, as it came without ammunition. Field Artillery Regiment No. 61, which fired special ammunition, was not available for forty-eight hours.

By midday on the 22nd, the 107th and 119th Divisions felt secure. Regiment No. 46 reported "Fontaine only lightly held. We are going to attack. Artillery support requested." This was very desirable, but premature and not ordered. However, "not to leave the brave fellows in the soup," the Division ordered, "General attack on Fontaine—Folie. Artillery cooperates at once." At 3.40 p.m. the Germans had reached the line named. The thing was done. They had air and space. The British were beaten and badly damaged. Fontaine had been strongly held: a thousand men and sixteen machine guns[2] between the 107th Division and Moser's Group. The gap was bolted and barred, connection and touch established with the division on the right in Bourlon Wood, and a strong position occupied. Again the wagons came up, this time bearing wire, hand-grenades and flares.

On the 23rd and 24th of November the 107th Division repelled all counter-attacks, and then appears to have been relieved.

---

2   Fontaine was held by 400 men of the 4th Seaforth Highlanders. See *History of the 51st (Highland) Division*, pp. 253–256.

Annotated Bibliography

See the Introduction for modern studies concerning tactics and the operational level of the war. Amongst the reference works, the *Ehrenbücher* are valuable – if relating to an arm of service, they invariably include detailed essays concerning organisation, tactics and combat experience unavailable elsewhere. They also include much data relating to units and their organisational and combat histories. The latter is also true of those *Ehrenbücher* devoted to states or regions, although there is also an emphasis on the heroic deeds of the participants, naturally.

Bibliographies

Deutschen Heeresbücherei in Berlin (hrsg.), *Heer und Wehr im Buche der Gegenwart Band 1. Verzeichnis der Neuerwerbungen der Deutschen Heeresbücherei vom Oktober 1919 bis September 1927* (Berlin: Mittler, 1929). This and its two subsequent volumes are very important for their coverage of the great mass of interwar publications in all European languages, but particularly German.

Deutschen Heeresbücherei in Berlin (hrsg.), *Heer und Wehr im Buche der Gegenwart Band 2. Verzeichnis der Neuerwerbungen der Deutschen Heeresbücherei vom Oktober 1927 bis September 1933* (Berlin: Mittler, 1934)

Deutschen Heeresbücherei in Berlin (hrsg.), *Heer und Wehr im Buche der Gegenwart Band 3. Verzeichnis der Neuerwerbungen der Deutschen Heeresbücherei vom Oktober 1933 bis September 1938* (Berlin: Mittler, 1939).

Gunzenhäuser, Max, *Die Bibliographien zur Geschichte des Ersten Weltkrieges: Literaturbericht und Bibliographie* (Frankfurt am Main: Bernard & Graefe, 1964. *Schriften der Bibliothek für Zeitgeschichte Weltkriegsbücherei* Heft 3, 1964). Invaluable.

Hardt, F.B. (hrsg.), *Die deutschen Schützengraben- und Soldatenzeitungen* (München: Piper, 1917)

Hellmann, Richard & Kurt Palm, *Die deutschen Feldzeitungen* (Freiburg i. Br.: Verlag der Fr. Wagner'schen Universitätsbuchhandlung, 1918/19, 2 Bände)

Higham, Robin with Dennis E. Showalter (eds.), *Researching World War I: A Handbook* (Westport CT: Greenwood Press, 2003). Wide-ranging, sometimes frustratingly so – the older bibliographies remain more useful for operational-level military history.

Kurth, Dr K., *Der deutschen Feld- und Schützengrabenzeitungen des Weltkrieges* (Leipzig: Noske, 1937)

Mohr, Eike, *Heeres- und Truppengeschichte des Deutschen Reiches und seiner Länder 1806 bis 1918* (Osnabrück: Biblio Verlag, 1989). A later, revised and expanded, two-volume edition was published in 2004. Utterly indispensable for any serious study of the armies of Germany and the German States during this period.

Philippe, Paul, Luc Sieben, Carinne van Tuijcom & Eric Meuwissen, *La Belgique et la Première Guerre mondiale Bibliographie* (Bruxelles: Musée Royal de l'Armée, 1987). Very much broader than its title suggests, and thus invaluable when researching any Western Front-related topic. Includes material in German besides English, French, Dutch.

Rohwer, J., *Neue Forschungen zum Ersten Weltkrieg: Literaturberichte und Bibliographien* (Koblenz: Bernard & Graefe, 1985. *Schriften der Bibliothek für Zeitgeschichte* Band 25)

Schramm, Prof. Dr (hrsg.)., *Deutsche Kriegszeitungen* (N.p.: n.p., 1917. Sonderheft des Archiv für Buchgewerbe, Heft 1/2, 1917, Band 54)

Showalter, Dennis E., *German Military History 1648-1982: A Critical Bibliography* (New York: Garland, 1984)

Wilkinson, Mary, Angela Wootton & Sarah Paterson (eds.), *Catalogue of Holdings on the Special Collection of First World War German Unit Histories* (London: Imperial War Museum Department of Printed Books, 2002). Very useful but exceedingly difficult to find.

Reference Works

American Expeditionary Forces. General Headquarters, France, *Histories of two hundred and fifty-one divisions of the German Army which participated in the war (1914-1918)* (Washington, D.C.: GPO, 1920)

Anon., *Ehrenmal des Unsterblichen Deutschen Soldaten* (München: Moser, 1936, 2 Bände)

Anon., *Ruhmeshalle unsere Alten Armee* (Fürstenwalde/Spree: Verlag für Militärgeschichte, c.1934. 5. umbearbeitete Auflage in 2 Bände is best edition).

Anon., *Thüringen im Weltkrieg. Vaterländisches Kriegsgedenkmal in Wort und Bild* (Leipzig: Lippold, 1921, 2 Bände)

Bayerisches Kriegsarchiv (hrsg.), *Die Bayern im Großen Kriege 1914-1918* (München: Verlag des Bayerischen Kriegsarchivs, 1923)

Benary, A. (hrsg.), *Das Ehrenbuch der Deutschen Feldartillerie* (Berlin: Kolk, 1930)

Büching, M. (hrsg.), *Die Braunschweiger im Weltkrieg 1914-1918* (Braunschweig: Appelhaus, 1920)

Busche, Hartwig, *Formationsgeschichte der deutschen Infanterie 1914-18* (Owschlag: privately published, 1998/99, 2 Bände). Important.

Cron, Hermann, *Geschichte des deutschen Heeres im Weltkriege 1914-1918* (Berlin: Siegismund, 1937. Band 5 of *Geschichte der kgl. Preussischen Armee und des Deutschen Reichsheeres*). An essential tool for the organisation of the Army. An English translation is:

Cron, Hermann, *Imperial German Army 1914-18: Organisation, Structure, Orders of Battle* (Solihull: Helion, 2000)

von Egan-Krieger, Major a.D. (hrsg.), *Die Deutsche Kavallerie in Krieg und Frieden* (Karlsruhe: Schille, n.d. [1928])

Deiss, F.W., *Die Hessen im Weltkrieg 1914-1918* (Berlin: Glaß, 1930)

Deutschen Offiziers-Bund (hrsg.), *Ehrenrangliste des Ehemaligen Deutschen Heeres auf Grund der Ranglisten von 1914 mit dem inzwischen Eingetretenen veränderungen* (Berlin: Mittler, 1926-29 including *Nachträge*. Reprinted Osnabrück: Biblio Verlag, 1987, 2 Bände)

Eisenhart Rothe, Ernst von, *Ehrendenkmal der Deutschen Armee und Marine 1871-1918* (Berlin: Deutscher National-Verlag, 1928)

Eisenhart Rothe, Ernst von, Erich von Tschischwitz & Walther Beckmann (hrsg.), *Deutsche Infanterie: Das Ehrenmal der vordersten Front* (Zeulenroda: Sporn, 1933)

Fellenhavel, H. von & W. Müller-Loebnitz, *Das Ehrenbuch der Rheinländer* (Stuttgart: Hinderer, 1931)

Grossen Generalstab, *Die Schlachten und Gefechte des Grossen Krieges 1914-1918: Quellenwerk* (Berlin: Hermann Sack, 1919). Essential tabular listings of engagements and units involved. An indispensable reference tool, and more reliable for tracing orders-of-battle and unit histories than the wartime British War Office publications or the US summary of divisional combat records.

Gruss, Hellmuth, *Die Deutschen Sturmbataillone im Weltkrieg. Aufbau und Verwendung* (Berlin: Juncker & Dünnhaupt, 1939). Draws fully on the now-destroyed archives in Berlin – remains a very important source.

Heiden, H., *Gewehre Frei! Weg und Ruhm der Maschinengewehrwaffe* (Berlin: Verlag "Der Wehrmacht", 1938)

Heinrich, Paul (hrsg.), *Das Ehrenbuch der Deutschen Pioniere* (Berlin: Tradition Verlag, n.d. [1931]

Heubes, M. & R. v. Scheda (hrsg.), *Ehrenbuch der Feldeisenbahner* (Berlin: Kolk, 1931)

Heye, W., *Die Geschichte des Landwehrkorps im Weltkriege 1914/1918* (Breslau: Korn, 1935/37, 2 Bände)

Hottenroth, E. & A. Baumgarten-Crusius, *Sachsen in Großer Zeit. Geschichte der Sachsen im Weltkrieg* (Leipzig: Lippold, 1919/20/21, 3 Bände)

Kaiser, F.N. (hrsg.), *Das Ehrenbuch der Deutschen Schweren Artillerie* (Berlin: Kolk, 1931/34, 2 Bände)

Kardel, H., *Schleswig-Holsteiner im Weltkrieg* (Neumünster: Wachholtz, 1933)

Krafft v. Delmensingen, K. & F. Feeser, *Das Bayernbuch vom Weltkriege 1914-1918* (Stuttgart: Belser, 1930, 2 Bände)

Kramer, R. von & O. Freiherr von Waldenfels, *Virtuti pro Patria. Der königlich bayerische Militär-Max-Joseph-Orden. Kriegstaten und Ehrenbuch 1914-1918* (München: Selbstverlag des königlich bayerischen Militär-Max-Josephs-Ordens, 1966)

Kraus, J. & H. Busche, *Handbuch der Verbände und Truppen des deutschen Heeres 1914 – 1918* (Vienna: Verlag Militaria, 2007 to date, ongoing). This promises to be the most reliable and detailed guide to the organisation of the German Army during the Great War.

Montbé, A. von, *Die Märker im Weltkrieg* (Berlin: Glaß, 1929)

Möller, H., *Die Geschichte der Ritter des Ordens „pour le merite" im Weltkrieg 1914-1918* (Berlin: Bernard & Graefe, 1935, 2 Bände)

Möser, O. von, *Die Württemberger im Weltkrieg* (Stuttgart: Belser, 1928, 2nd ed.)

Müller-Loebnitz, W., *Die Badener im Weltkrieg 1914/1918* (Karlsruhe: Braun, 1937)

Müller-Loebnitz, W., *Das Ehrenbuch der Westfalen* (Stuttgart: Hinderer, 1931)

Nash, David, *Imperial German Army Handbook 1914-1918* (London: Ian Allan, 1980)

Rehbein, A. (hrsg.), *Ehrenbuch der Grünen Farbe* (Berlin: Schulz & Paschke, 1926). Guide to the *Jäger* units.

Reichsarchiv, Bayer. Kriegsarchiv, H. Cron, Immanuel, H. Knötel, G.K. Distler, M. Lezius (hrsg.), *Mein Regiment* (Fürstenwalde/Spree: Verlag für Militärgeschichte, 1938)

Reichskriegsministerium (hrsg.), *Gefechtskalender des Deutschen Heeres im Weltkrieg 1914/1918* (Berlin: Mittler, 1935). This hard-to-find but very useful resource provides a one or two-page summary for all major actions of the Army during the war, followed by a detailed order-of-battle.

Reichskriegsministerium, Heeressanitätsinspektion (bearb.), *Sanitätsbericht über das Deutsche Heer (Deutsches Feld- und Besatzungsheer) im Weltkrieg 1914-1918* (Berlin: Mittler, 1934-38, 3 Bände).

Reichswehrministerium (hrsg.), *Kriegsveterinärbericht des deutschen Heeres: 1914-1918* (Berlin: Reichswehrministerium, 1929)

Schracke, Karl, *Geschichte der deutschen Feldpost im Kriege 1914/18* (Berlin: Verlag der Reichsdruckerei, 1921)

Theiss, R. & O. Regele, *Die Radfahrtruppe* (Berlin: Eisenschmidt, 1925). The bicycle units.

Thiele, Oblt. (hrsg.), *Zur Geschichte der Nachrichten Truppe 1899-1924 Band 1* (Berlin: Selbstverlag, 1925). Only volume published.

War Office, General Staff, *The German Forces in the Field: 11th November 1918* (London: Imperial War Museum, Department of Printed Books, 1995, facsimile of 7th revised ed.)

War Office, General Staff, *Handbook of the German Army (Home and Colonial)* (London: Imperial War Museum, Department of Printed Books, 2002, facsimile ed. of 1914 edition)

War Office, General Staff, *Handbook of the German Army in War: April 1918* (London: Imperial War Museum, Department of Printed Books, 1996, facsimile edition of April 1918 edition)

War Office, General Staff, *Vocabulary of German Military Terms and Abbreviations* (London: Imperial War Museum, Department of Printed Books, 1995). Extremely useful.

Westecker, W., *Westfalen stand wie ein Fels. Die westfälischen Regimenter im Weltkrieg 1914 bis 1918* (Dortmund: Westfalen Verlag, 1939)

Wickert, P., *Das Ehrenbuch der Pommern* (Berlin: Weller, 1930)

Official Histories

Reichsarchiv (hrsg.), *Der Weltkrieg 1914 bis 1918. Die militärischen Operationen zu Lande* (Berlin: Mittler, 1925-44):

Band 1: *Die Grenzschlachten im Westen* (1925)

Band 2: *Die Befreiung Ostpreußens* (1925)

Band 3: *Der Marne-Feldzug. Von der Sambre zur Marne* (1926)

Band 4: *Der Marne-Feldzug. Die Schlacht* (1926)

Band 5: *Der Herbst-Feldzug 1914. Im Westen bis zum Stellungskrieg. Im Osten bis zum Rückzug* (1929)

Band 6: *Der Herbst-Feldzug 1914. Der Abschluß der Operationen im Westen und Osten* (1929)

Band 7: *Die Operationen des Jahres 1915. Die Ereignisse im Winter und Frühjahr* (1931)

Band 8: *Die Operationen des Jahres 1915. Die Ereignisse im Westen im Frühjahr und Sommer, im Osten vom Frühjahr bis zum Jahresschluß* (1932)

Band 9: *Die Operationen des Jahres 1915. Die Ereignisse im Westen und auf dem Balkan vom Sommer bis zum Jahresschluß* (1933)

Band 10: *Die Operationen des Jahres 1916 bis zum Wechsel in der Obersten Heeresleitung* (1936)

Band 11: *Die Kriegsführung im Herbst 1916 und im Winter 1916/17. Vom Wechsel in der Obersten Heeresleitung bis zum Entschluß zum Rückzug in die Siegfried-Stellung* (1938)

Band 12: *Die Kriegsführung im Frühjahr 1917* (1939)

Band 13: *Die Kriegführung im Sommer und Herbst 1917. Die Ereignisse ausserhalb der Westfront bis November 1918* (1942)
Band 14: *Die Kriegführung an der Westfront im Jahre 1918* (1944)
Sonderverbände (all Reichsarchiv (hrsg.), Berlin: Mittler):
Das deutsche Feldeisenbahnwesen:
Band 1: *Die Eisenbahnen zu Kriegsbeginn* (1928)
Kriegsrüstung und Kriegswirtschaft:
Band 1: *Die militärische, wirtschaftliche und finanzielle Rüstung Deutschlands von der Reichsgründung bis zum Ausbruch des Weltkrieges* (1930)
The above 'Sonderverbände' or volumes devoted to special subjects remained incomplete.

Reichsarchiv (hrsg.), *Schlachten des Weltkrieges* (Oldenburg/Berlin: Gerhard Stalling, 1925-30): this series provides a variable but generally excellent account of individual battles and operations, and is strongly recommended as a companion to the 'main' official histories listed above.
Band 1: Beumelburg, Werner, *Douaumont* (1925)
Band 2: Friedeburg, Friedrich von, *Karpathen- und Dnjester-Schlacht 1915* (1925)
Band 3: Tschischwitz, Erich von, *Antwerpen 1914* (1925)
Band 4: Steuber, Werner, *Jildirim, Deutsche Streiter auf heiligem Boden* (1926)
Band 5: Strutz, Georg, *Herbstschlacht in Macedonien, Cernabogen 1916* (1925)
Band 6: Gebsattel, Ludwig Freiherr von, *Von Nancy bis zum Cap des Romains 1914* (1925)
Band 7a: Heydemann, Kurt, *Die Schlacht bei St. Quentin 1914 Teil I: Der rechte Flugel der deutschen 2. Armee am 29. und 30. August* (1925)
Band 7b: Heydemann, Kurt, *Die Schlacht bei St. Quentin 1914 Teil II: Garde und Hannoveraner vom 28. bis 30. August* (1925)
Band 8: Bettag, Franz, *Die Eroberung von Nowo Georgiewsk* (1926)
Band 9: Vogel, Walter, *Die Kämpfe um Baranowitschi Sommer 1916* / Strutz, Georg, *Die Erstürmung des Brückenkopfes von Jakobstadt 21.-22. September 1917* (1927)
Band 10: Beumelburg, Werner, *Ypern 1914* (1926)
Band 11: Dieterich (bearb.), *Weltkriegsende an der mazedonischen Front* (1926)
Band 12a: Krafft von Dellmensingen, Konrad, *Der Durchbruch am Isonzo, Teil I: Schlacht von Tolmein und Flitsch (24. bis 27. Oktober 1917)* (1926)
Band 12b: Krafft von Dellmensingen, Konrad, *Der Durchbruch am Isonzo, Teil II: Die Verfolgung über Tagliamento bis zum Piave* (1926)
Band 13: Gold, Ludwig & Martin Reymann: *Die Tragödie von Verdun 1916 Teil I: Die deutsche Offensivschlacht* (1926)
Band 14: Gold, Ludwig & Martin Reymann: *Die Tragödie von Verdun 1916 Teil II: Das Ringen um Fort Vaux* (1928)
Band 15: Gold, Ludwig & Martin Reymann: *Die Tragödie von Verdun 1916 Teil III & IV: Die Zermurbungsschlacht. III: Toter Mann – Hohe 304. IV: Thiaumont-Fleury* (1929)
Band 16: Mühlmann, Carl, *Der Kampf um die Dardanellen 1915* (1927)
Band 17: Beumelburg, Walter (after Wolfgang Fürstner), *Loretto* (1927)
Band 18: Schmidt, Ernst, *Argonnen Herbst 1914* (1927)
Band 19: Schäfer, Theobald von, *Tannenberg* (1927)
Band 20: Stosch, Albrecht von, *Somme-Nord: Die Brennpunkte der Schlacht im Juli 1916 Theil I* (1927)

Band 21: Stosch, Albrecht von, *Somme-Nord: Die Brennpunkte der Schlacht im Juli 1916 Theil II* (1927)
Band 22: Bose, Thilo von & Alfred Stenger, *Das Marnedrama 1914 Teil I* (1928)
Band 23: Bose, Thilo von & Alfred Stenger, *Das Marnedrama 1914 Teil II* (1928)
Band 24: Bose, Thilo von & Alfred Stenger, *Das Marnedrama 1914 Teil III 1. Abschnitt: Die Kämpfe des Gardekorps und des rechten Flügels der 3. Armee vom 5. bis 8. September* (1928)
Band 25: Bose, Thilo von & Alfred Stenger, *Das Marnedrama 1914 Teil III 2. Abschnitt: Der Ausgang der Schlacht* (1928)
Band 26: Dahlmann, Reinhold & Alfred Stenger, *Das Marnedrama 1914 Teil IV: Die Schlacht von Paris* (1928)
Band 27: Beumelburg, Werner, *Flandern 1917* (1928)
Band 28: Behrmann, Franz & Walther Brandt, *Die Osterschlacht bei Arras 1917 Teil I: Zwischen Lens und Scarpe* (1929)
Band 29: Behrmann, Franz & Walther Brandt, *Die Osterschlacht bei Arras 1917 Teil II: Zwischen Scarpe und Bullecourt* (1929)
Band 30: Kalm, Oskar Tile von, *Gorlice* (1930)
Band 31: Strutz, Georg, *Tankschlacht bei Cambrai 20.-29. November 1917* (1929)
Band 32: Bose, Thilo von (partly after Ernst Otto), *Deutsche Siege 1918. Das Vordringen der 7. Armee über Ailette, Aisne, Vesle und Ourcq bis zur Marne (27. Mai bis 13. Juni)* (1929)
Band 33: Bose, Thilo von (partly after Ernst Otto), *Wachsende Schwierigkeiten 1918. Vergebliches Ringen von Compiègne, Villers-Cotterêts und Reims* (1930)
Band 34: Stenger, Alfred (after Konrad Herrmann), *Der letzte Deutsche Angriff, Reims 1918* (1930)
Band 35: Stenger, Alfred (after Ludwig Lange & Konrad Herrmann), *Schicksalswende. Von der Marne bis zur Vesle 1918* (1930)
Band 36: Bose, Thilo von (after Konrad Herrmann), *Die Katastrophe das 8. August 1918* (1930)

Regimental Histories

The interested reader is directed to the indispensable work by Mohr described in the Bibliographies section above. For ease of reference, this section has been organised by chapter, and provides full bibliographic details for all regimental histories detailed by the author.

1. The night attack at Landrecies, 25 August 1914

Fliess, Otto & Kurt Dittmar, *5. Hannoversches Infanterie-Regiment Nr. 165 im Weltkriege* (Oldenburg: Stalling, 1927. Erinnerungsblätter Preussen Band 189)

Rübesamen, Friedrich Wilhelm & Willi Bartels, *Feldartillerie-Regiment Prinz-Regent Luitpold von Bayern (Magdeburgisches) Nr. 4* (Magdeburg: Faber, n.d. [1927/28, 2 Bände. Erinnerungsblätter Preussen Band 237)

Werner, Bernhard, *Das Königlich Preussische Infanterie-Regiment Prinz Louis Ferdinand von Preussen (2. Magdeburgisches) Nr. 27 im Weltkriege 1914-1918* (Berlin: Bernard & Graefe, 1933, Deutsche Tat im Weltkrieg Band 5)

2. Neuve Chapelle, 10-12 March 1915

Anon., *Das Königlich Preussische Clevesche Feldartillerie-Regiment Nr. 43 1899-1919* (Oldenburg: Stalling, 1932. Erinnerungsblätter Preussen Band 351)

Braun, Julius, *Das Königlich Bayerische Reserve-Infanterie-Regiment Nr. 21* (München: Bayer. Kriegsarchiv, 1923. Erinnerungsblätter Bayern Band 18)
Castendyk, Hermann, *Das Infanterie-Regiment Herzog Ferdinand von Braunschweig (8. Westfälisches) Nr. 57 im Weltkrieg 1914-1918* (Oldenburg: Stalling, 1936. Erinnerungsblätter Preussen Band 364)
Groos, Karl & Werner von Rudloff, *Infanterie-Regiment Herwarth von Bittenfeld (1. Westfäl.) Nr. 13 im Weltkriege 1914-18* (Oldenburg: Stalling, 1927. Erinnerungsblätter Preussen Band 222)
Henke, Carl, *Das 1. Westfälische Feldartillerie-Regiment Nr. 7 1816-1919* (Berlin: Kolk, 1928. Erinnerungsblätter Preussen Band 244)
Leonhardt, Hans & Hans von Troilo, *Das 5. Westfälische Infanterie-Regiment Nr. 53 im Weltkrieg 1914-1919* (Oldenburg: Stalling, 1924. Erinnerungsblätter Preussen Band 109)
Otto, Adolf, *Kriegstagebuch des Kurhessischen Jäger-Bataillons Nr. 11* (Schmalkalden: Wilisch, 1931)
Rinck von Baldenstein, Werner et al, *Das Infanterie-Regiment Freiherr von Sparr (3. Westfälisches) Nr. 16 im Weltkriege 1914/1918* (Oldenburg: Stalling, 1927. Erinnerungsblätter Preussen Band 208)
Windthorst, Karl, *Das Mindensche Feldartillerie-Regiment Nr. 58 im Weltkriege 1914-1918* (Dortmund: Ruhfus, 1930)
Zunker, Hermann, Friedrich Martin Hüger & D. Vietor, *Das Königlich Preussische 2. Westfälische Feldartillerie-Regiment Nr. 22 und seine Tochterformationen im Weltkriege 1914-1918* (Münster: Privately published: 1924)

3. Aubers Ridge, 9 May 1915
Anon., *Das Königlich Preussische Clevesche Feldartillerie-Regiment Nr. 43 1899-1919* (Oldenburg: Stalling, 1932. Erinnerungsblätter Preussen Band 351)
Castendyk, Hermann, *Das Infanterie-Regiment Herzog Ferdinand von Braunschweig (8. Westfälisches) Nr. 57 im Weltkrieg 1914-1918* (Oldenburg: Stalling, 1936. Erinnerungsblätter Preussen Band 364)
Henke, Carl, *Das 1. Westfälische Feldartillerie-Regiment Nr. 7 1816-1919* (Berlin: Kolk, 1928. Erinnerungsblätter Preussen Band 244)
Schulz, Walter, *Infanterie-Regiment Graf Bülow von Dennewitz (6. Westfälisches) Nr. 55 im Weltkriege* (Detmold: Meyer, 1928)
Windthorst, Karl, *Das Mindensche Feldartillerie-Regiment Nr. 58 im Weltkriege 1914-1918* (Dortmund: Ruhfus, 1930)
Zunker, Hermann, Friedrich Martin Hüger & D. Vietor, *Das Königlich Preussische 2. Westfälische Feldartillerie-Regiment Nr. 22 und seine Tochterformationen im Weltkriege 1914-1918* (Münster: Privately published: 1924)

4. The fight for Hill 70, 25-26 September 1915
The author does not cite specific sources for this chapter, but the following references have been extrapolated from his writings:
Anon., *Das Königlich Sächsische 13. Infanterie-Regiment Nr. 178* (Dresden: Baensch-Stiftung, 1935. Erinnerungsblätter Sachsen Band 75)
Giesecke, Richard A. (hrsg.), *Erinnerungsblätter der 178er Weltkrieg* (Dresden: Giesecke, 1917 [Band 1]; Dresden: Verlag d. Schönheit, 1922 [Band 2])
(There appears to have been no history of the 22nd Reserve Infantry Regiment published).

5. The German attack at Vimy Ridge, May 1916

Karitzky, Erich, *Reserve-Jäger-Bataillon Nr. 9* (Stalling: Oldenburg, 1925. Erinnerungsblätter Preussen Band 148)

Klähn, Friedrich, *Geschichte des Reserve-Infanterie-Regiments Nr. 86 im Weltkriege* (Stalling: Oldenburg, 1925. Erinnerungsblätter Preussen Band 149)

Ritter, Holger, *Geschichte des Schleswig-Holsteinschen Infanterie-Regiments Nr. 163* (Hamburg: Leuchtfeuer-Verlag, 1926. Erinnerungsblätter Preussen Band 184)

6. The German defence during the Battle of the Somme July 1916

Bezzel, Oskar, *Das Königlich Bayerische Reserve-Infanterie-Regiment Nr. 6* (München: Schick, 1938. Erinnerungsblätter Bayern Band 88)

Brennfleck, Josef Karl, *Das Königlich Bayerische 16. Infanterie-Regiment Großherzog Ferdinand von Toskana im Weltkrieg 1914-1918* (München: Bayer. Kriegsarchiv, 1931. Erinnerungsblätter Bayern Band 71)

Gerster, Matthäus, *Das Württembergische Reserve-Infanterie-Regiment Nr. 119 im Weltkrieg 1914-1918* (Stuttgart: Belser, 1920. Die Württembergischen Regimenter im Weltkrieg Band 7)

vom Holtz, Georg, *Das Württembergische Reserve-Infanterie-Regiment Nr. 121 im Weltkrieg 1914-1918* (Stuttgart: Belser, 1922. Die Württembergischen Regimenter im Weltkrieg Band 20)

Nörr, Hermann, *Das Königlich Bayerische 19. Feldartillerie-Regiment* (München: Schick, 1930. Erinnerungsblätter Bayern Band 65)

Theysohn, Karl, *Das Königlich Bayerische 20. Feldartillerie-Regiment* (München: Schick, 1934. Erinnerungsblätter Bayern Band 84)

von Wurmb, Herbert, *Das Königlich Bayerische Reserve-Infanterie-Regiment Nr. 8* (München: Schick, 1929. Erinnerungsblätter Bayern Band 54)

7. The German defence of Bernafay and Trônes Woods, 2-14 July 1916

Bamberg, Georg, *Das Königliche Sächsische Reserve-Infanterie-Regiment Nr. 106* (Dresden: Baensch-Stiftung, 1925. Erinnerungsblätter Sachsen Band 25)

Braun, Kurt, *Das Reserve-Infanterie-Regiment Nr. 104 im Weltkriege* (Leipzig: Freter, 1921)

Giesecke, Richard A. (hrsg.), *Erinnerungsblätter der 178er Weltkrieg* (Dresden: Giesecke, 1917 [Band 1]; Dresden: Verlag d. Schönheit, 1922 [Band 2])

Heydenreich, Fritz, *Das Königlich Sächsische Feldartillerie-Regiment Nr. 245* (Dresden: Baensch-Stiftung, 1921. Erinnerungsblätter Sachsen Band 2)

Jancke, Herbert, *Das Königlich Preussische Feldartillerie-Regiment von Clausewitz (1. Oberschlesisches) Nr. 21* (Oldenburg: Stalling, 1923. Erinnerungsblätter Preussen Band 76)

Pache, Alexander, *Das Königlich Sächsische 16. Infanterie-Regiment Nr. 182* (Dresden: Baensch-Stiftung, 1924, 1926, 2 Bände. Erinnerungsblätter Sachsen Band 13)

Schmidt-Osswald, Ernst (hrsg.), *Das Altenburger Regiment (8. Thüringisches Infanterie-Regiment Nr. 153) im Weltkriege* (Oldenburg: Stalling, 1927. Erinnerungsblätter Preussen Band 183)

Uebe, Friedrich, *Das 2. Oberschlesisches Feldartillerie-Regiment Nr. 57* (Oldenburg: Stalling, 1923. Erinnerungsblätter Preussen Band 77)

8. Mametz Wood and Contalmaison, 9-10 July 1916

Hase, Armin, *Das Königlich Sächsische Infanterie-Regiment Nr. 183* (Dresden: Baensch-Stiftung, 1922. Erinnerungsblätter Sachsen Band 5)

Mügge, Ernst, *Das Württembergische Reserve-Infanterie-Regiment Nr. 122 im Weltkrieg 1914-1918* (Stuttgart: Belser, 1922. Die Württembergischen Regimenter im Weltkriege Band 21)

von Mühlmann, Mohs, *Geschichte des Lehr-Infanterie-Regiments und seiner Stammformationen* (Zeulenroda: Sporn, 1935. Aus Deutschlands grosser Zeit Band 74)

Soldan, Georg, *Das Infanterie-Regiment Nr. 184* (Oldenburg: Stalling, 1920. Erinnerungsblätter Preussen Band 1)

9. Delville Wood, 14-19 July 1916

Bloem, Walter, *Das Grenadier-Regiment Prinz Carl von Preussen (2. Brandenburgisches) Nr. 12 nach den Erinnerungsblättern des Majors v. Schönfeldt* (Berlin: Bernard & Graefe, 1940. Deutsche Tat im Weltkrieg Band 48)

Pache, Alexander, *Das Königlich Sächsische 16. Infanterie-Regiment Nr. 182* (Dresden: Baensch-Stiftung, 1924, 1926, 2 Bände. Erinnerungsblätter Sachsen Band 13)

Reymann, Martin, *Das Infanterie-Regiment von Alvensleben (6. Brandenburg.) Nr. 52 im Weltkriege 1914-1918* (Oldenburg: Stalling, 1923. Erinnerungsblätter Preussen Band 75)

von Rosenberg-Lipinsky, Alfred, *Das Feldartillerie-Regiment General-Feldzeugmeister (2. Brandenburgisches) Nr. 18 1914-1918* (Oldenburg: Stalling, 1922. Erinnerungsblätter Preussen Band 38)

Schmidt-Osswald, Ernst (hrsg.), *Das Altenburger Regiment (8. Thüringisches Infanterie-Regiment Nr. 153) im Weltkriege* (Oldenburg: Stalling, 1927. Erinnerungsblätter Preussen Band 183)

von Schönfeldt, Ernst, *Das Grenadier-Regiment Prinz Carl von Preussen (2. Brandenburgisches) Nr. 12 im Weltkriege* (Oldenburg: Stalling, 1924. Erinnerungsblätter Preussen Band 103)

Schöning, Hans, *Leib-Grenadier-Regiment König Friedrich Wilhelm III (1. Brandenburgisches) Nr. 8 im Weltkriege* (Oldenburg: Stalling, 1924. Erinnerungsblätter Preussen Band 128)

Uebe, Friedrich, *Das 2. Oberschlesisches Feldartillerie-Regiment Nr. 57* (Oldenburg: Stalling, 1923. Erinnerungsblätter Preussen Band 77)

10. The Somme, 15 September 1916

Anon., *Das Königlich Bayerische 10. Infanterie-Regiment Prinz Ludwig* (München: Bayer. Kriegsarchiv, 1925. Erinnerungsblätter Bayern Band 36)

Anon., *Das Königlich Bayerische 14. Infanterie-Regiment Hartmann* (München: Schick, 1931. Erinnerungsblätter Bayern Band 75)

Dunzinger, Albert, *Das Königlich Bayerische 11. Infanterie-Regiment von der Tann* (München: Bayer. Kriegsarchiv, 1921. Erinnerungsblätter Bayern Band 2)

Jäger, Hans, *Das Königlich Bayerische 19. Infanterie-Regiment König Viktor Emmanuel III. von Italien* (München: Schick, 1930. Erinnerungsblätter Bayern Band 68)

Lang, Georg, *Das 6. Königlich Bayerische Infanterie-Regiment im Weltkrieg* (Kallmünz: Oberpfälz. Landbuchh., 1919)

Reber, Karl, *Das Königlich Bayerische 21. Infanterie-Regiment Grossherzog Friedrich Franz IV. von Mecklenburg-Schwerin* (München: Schick, 1929. Erinnerungsblätter Bayern Band 57)

Schaidler, Otto, *Das K.B. 7. Infanterie-Regiment Prinz Leopold* (München: Bayer. Kriegsarchiv, 1922. Erinnerungsblätter Bayern Band 11)

Weiland, Ernst, *Hölle Ginchy. Mit dem Königlichen Bayerischen 7. Infanterie-Regiment Prinz Leopold in der Somme-Schlacht, Sept. 1916* (Eisleben: Winkler, 1929)

Weniger, Heinrich, Artur Zobel & Maximilian Fels, *Das Königlich Bayerische 5. Infanterie-Regiment Grossherzog Ernst Ludwig von Hessen* (München: Schick, 1929. Erinnerungsblätter Bayern Band 59)

11. The capture of Thiepval, 26 September 1916

Fliess, Otto & Kurt Dittmar, *5. Hannoversches Infanterie-Regiment Nr. 165 im Weltkriege* (Oldenburg: Stalling, 1927. Erinnerungsblätter Preussen Band 189)

Gruson, Ernst (hrsg.), *Das Königlich Preussische 4. Thüringische Infanterie-Regiment Nr. 72 im Weltkriege* (Oldenburg: Stalling, 1930. Erinnerungsblätter Preussen Band 303)

Korfes, Otto, *Das 3. Magdeburgisches Infanterie-Regiment Nr. 66 im Weltkriege* (Berlin: Kolk, 1930. Erinnerungsblätter Preussen Band 302)

Schmidt-Osswald, Ernst (hrsg.), *Das Altenburger Regiment (8. Thüringisches Infanterie-Regiment Nr. 153) im Weltkriege* (Oldenburg: Stalling, 1927. Erinnerungsblätter Preussen Band 183)

Vischer, Alfred, *Das 10. Württembergische Infanterie-Regiment Nr. 180 im Weltkrieg 1914-1918* (Stuttgart: Belser, 1921. Die Württembergischen Regimenter im Weltkrieg Band 9)

von Vormann, Wolfgang, *Infanterie-Regiment Fürst Leopold von Anhalt-Dessau (1. Magdeburgisches) Nr. 26 Band 3: Das Kriegsjahr 1916* (Oldenburg: Stalling, 1925-29. Erinnerungsblätter Preussen Band 143)

12. In front of Beaumont-Hamel, 13 November 1916

Reymann, H., *Das 3. Oberschlesische Infanterie-Regiment Nr. 62 im Kriege 1914-1918* (Zeulenroda: Sporn, 1930. Aus Deutschlands grosser Zeit Band 7)

13. The Battle of Arras, 9 April 1917

A large number of regiments were present at Arras, although the author only provides brief mentions of a small number of specific units, histories for which are noted below.

Dziobek, Otto, *Geschichte des Infanterie-Regiments Lübeck (3. Hanseatisches) Nr. 162* (Oldenburg: Stalling (Offizier-Verein), 1922)

Helbling, Max, Ernst von Brunner & Martin von Dittelberger, *Das Königlich Bayerische Reserve-Infanterie-Regiment Nr. 2* (München: Bayer. Kriegsarchiv, 1926. Erinnerungsblätter Bayern Band 41)

von Schacky, Siegmund, *Das Königlich Bayerische Reserve-Infanterie-Regiment Nr. 1* (München: Bayer. Kriegsarchiv, 1924. Erinnerungsblätter Bayern Band 26)

von Schwerin, Curt & Karl Schmidt, *Reserve-Infanterie-Regiment Nr. 261 in Ost und West* (Berlin: Selbstverlag ehemal. Angehöriger des RIR 261, 1932)

14. The Battle of Vimy Ridge, 9 April 1917

von Gemmingen-Guttenberg-Fürfeld, Max, *Das Grenadier-Regiment Königin Olga (1. Württembergisches) Nr. 119 im Weltkrieg 1914-1918* (Stuttgart: Belser, 1927. Die Württembergischen Regimenter im Weltkrieg Band 39)

Staubwasser, Otto, *Das Königlich Bayerische 2. Infanterie-Regiment Kronprinz* (München: Bayer. Kriegsarchiv, 1924. Erinnerungsblätter Bayern Band 24)

15. The fight for Inverness Copse, 22-24 August 1917

Anon., *Das Königlich Sächsische 12. Infanterie-Regiment Nr. 177* (Dresden: Baensch-Stiftung, 1924. Erinnerungsblätter Sachsen Band 18)

Simon, Eduard, *4. Magdeburgisches Infanterie-Regiment Nr. 67 Band 2: Von den Kämpfen um Verdun bis zum Ausgang der Weltkr.* (Oldenburg: Stalling, 1927. Erinnerungsblätter Preussen Band 156)

16. The fight for Zonnebeke, 26 September 1917
Etzel, Hans, *Das Königlich Bayerische 9. Infanterie-Regiment Wrede* (Würzburg: Becker, 1927. Erinnerungsblätter Bayern Band 51)
Geiseler, Erwin, *Das Infanterie-Regiment Nr. 409* (Oldenburg: Stalling, 1929. Erinnerungsblätter Preussen Band 278)
Kraehe, Konrad, *Das Füsilier-Regiment Königin Viktoria von Schweden (Pommersches) Nr. 34 im Weltkriege mit Überblick über die Zeit 1720-1914* (Stettin: Hessenland, 1931. Erinnerungsblätter Preussen Band 341)
Trümper-Bödemann, Erhard Max, *Das Königlich Sächsische Reserve-Infanterie-Regiment Nr. 102* (Dresden: Baensch-Stiftung, 1929. Erinnerungsblätter Sachsen Band 57)

17. Cambrai – the action of the German 107th Division, 19-24 November 1917
Although not utilised by the author for this chapter, these regimental histories pertain to the action. There are no histories for the 222nd, 227th and 232nd Infantry Regiments.
Anon., *Das 2. Grossherzogliche Hessische Feldartillerie-Regiment Nr. 61 im Weltkriege 1914/18* (Oldenburg: Stalling, 1927. Erinnerungsblätter Preussen Band 213)
Anon., *Das Feldartillerie-Regiment Nr. 213* (Zeulenroda: Sporn, 1930. Aus Deutschlands grosser Zeit Band 14)
von Puttkamer, Oscar-Jesco, *Das Königlich Preussische Reserve-Infanterie-Regiment Nr. 46 im Weltkriege* (Zeulenroda: Sporn, 1938. Aus Deutschlands grosser Zeit Band 102)
Reymann, Martin, *Das Infanterie-Regiment von Alvensleben (6. Brandenburg.) Nr. 52 im Weltkriege 1914-1918* (Oldenburg: Stalling, 1923. Erinnerungsblätter Preussen Band 75)
Schmidt, Walter, Otto Winkelmann & Martin Altermann, *Das Königlich Preussische 3. Posensche Infanterie-Regiment Nr. 58 im Weltkriege* (Zeulenroda: Sporn, 1934. Aus Deutschlands grosser Zeit Band 59)
Zunehmer, Max, *Infanterie-Regiment Graf Kirchbach (1. Niederschlesisches) Nr. 46 im Weltkrieg 1914/1918* (Berlin: Bernard & Graefe, 1935. Deutsche Tat im Weltkrieg Band 20)

Helion Studies in Military History

No 1 *Learning from Foreign Wars. Russian Military Thinking 1859-73* Gudrun Persson (ISBN 978-1-906033-61-3)
No 2 *A Military Government in Exile. The Polish Government-in-Exile 1939-45, a Study of Discontent* Evan McGilvray (ISBN 978-1-906033-58-3)
No 3 *From Landrecies to Cambrai. Case Studies of German Offensive and Defensive Operations on the Western Front 1914-17* Capt G.C. Wynne (ISBN 978-1-906033-76-7)
No 4 *Playing the Game. The British Junior Infantry Officer on the Western Front 1914-18* Christopher Moore-Bick (ISBN 978-1-906033-84-2)
No 5 *The History of the British Army Film & Photographic Unit in the Second World War* Dr Fred McGlade (ISBN 978-1-906033-94-1)
No 6 *Making Waves. Admiral Mountbatten's Radio SEAC 1945-49* Eric Hitchcock (ISBN 978-1-906033-95-8)
No 7 *Abolishing the Taboo. Dwight D. Eisenhower and American Nuclear Doctrine 1945-1961* Brian Madison Jones (ISBN 978-1-907677-31-1)
No 8 *The Turkish Brigade in the Korean War Volume 1. Kunu-Ri Heroes (November-December 1950)* Dr Ali Denizli (ISBN 978-1-907677-32-8)
No 9 *The Diaries of Ronnie Tritton, War Office Publicity Officer 1940-45* Edited by Dr Fred McGlade (ISBN 978-1-907677-44-1)
No 10 *The Thinking Man's Soldier. The Life and Career of General Sir Henry Brackenbury 1837-1914* Christopher Brice (ISBN 978-1-907677-69-4)
No 11 *War Surgery 1914-18* Edited by Thomas Scotland and Steven Heys (ISBN 978-1-907677-70-0)
No 12 *Counterinsurgency in Africa. The Portugese Way of War 1961-74* John P. Cann (ISBN 978-1-907677-73-1)
No 13 *The Armed Forces of Poland in the West 1939-46* Michael Alfred Peszke (ISBN 978-1-908916-54-9)
No 14 *The Role of the Soviet Union in the Second World War* Boris Sokolov (ISBN 978-1-908916-55-6)
No 15 *Generals of the Danish Army in the First and Second Schleswig-Holstein Wars, 1848-50 and 1864* Nick B. Svendsen (ISBN 978-1-908916-46-4)
No 16 *A Considerable Achievement. The Tactical Development of the 56th (London) Division on the Western Front, 1916-1918* Matt Brosnan (ISBN 978-1-908916-47-1)
No 17 *Brown Waters of Africa. Portugese Riverine Warfare 1961-1974* John P. Cann (ISBN 978-1-908916-56-3)
No 18 *Man of Steel and Honour. General Stanislaw Maczek. Soldier of Poland, Commander of the 1st Polish Armoured Division in North-West Europe 1944-45* Evan McGilvray (ISBN 978-1-908916-53-2)
No 19 *The Gaysh. A History of the Aden Protectorate Levies 1927-61 and the Federal Regular Army of South Arabia 1961-67* Frank Edwards (ISBN 978-1-908916-87-7)
No 20 *The Whole Armour of God. Anglican Army Chaplains in the Great War* Linda Parker (ISBN 978-1-908916-96-9)

No 21 *Wars, Pestilence and the Surgeon's Blade. The Evolution of British Military Medicine and Surgery during the Nineteenth Century*
Thomas Scotland & Steven Heys (eds.) (ISBN 978-1-909384-09-5)

No 22 *With Trumpet, Drum and Fife. A Short Treatise covering the Rise and Fall of Military Musical Instruments on the Battlefield*
Major Mike Hall (ISBN 978-1-909384-17-0)

No 23 *Battlefield Rations. The food given to the British soldier for marching and fighting 1900-2011* Anthony Clayton (ISBN 978-1-909384-18-7)

No 24 *Railroads and Rifles. Soldiers, Technology and the Unification of Germany* (new edition) Dennis E. Showalter (ISBN 978-1-909384-19-4)

Lightning Source UK Ltd.
Milton Keynes UK
UKHW020814260221
379332UK00003B/60